‘Each time someone buys a copy of this book, … cry wank.’

Catherine Deveny, writer and comedian

‘I first met Fiona when I was leader of the Opposition in the ACT Legislative Assembly and later as chief minister. It was her fault that as a Liberal leader, my photo was on the front page of the *Canberra Times* opening a brothel on World AIDS Day! Over the years Fiona has become a trusted friend. Her advocacy was fundamental to the ACT legalising X-rated videos and legalising brothels, as well as ensuring that sex workers operated in a safe and regulated environment. This book is a great read and unlike any other political memoir.’

Kate Carnell, Australian Small Business and Family Enterprise Ombudsman

‘Fiona Patten is not your usual calculating, synthetic politician. Her racy book about how she got to the top recounts many intriguing stories along the way. Against the odds she’s achieved real and meaningful changes to Australian drug policy. I think she’s a brave person to have written this.’

Alex Wodak AM, President, Australian Drug Law Reform Foundation

‘Fiona Patten is a true original. She saw a need and filled it: to create space, and a political party, that honours Eros as a fundamental human right and need.’

Nina Hartley (TM), RN, US porn star and author of *Nina Hartley’s Guide to Total Sex*

SEX, DRUGS AND THE ELECTORAL ROLL

My unlikely journey from sex worker to Member of Parliament

FIONA PATTEN

First published in 2018

Allen & Unwin
83 Alexander Street
Crows Nest NSW 2065
Australia
Phone: (61 2) 8425 0100
Email: info@allenandunwin.com
Web: www.allenandunwin.com

A catalogue record for this book is available from the National Library of Australia

ISBN 978 1 92557 513 2

Set in 12/19 pt Minion Pro by Midland Typesetters, Australia
Printed and bound in Australia by Griffin Press

10 9 8 7 6 5 4 3 2 1

The paper in this book is FSC® certified. FSC® promotes environmentally responsible, socially beneficial and economically viable management of the world's forests.

To Mum and Dad. Not sure what they would have thought of this, but they would have had something nice to say I know. And to Robbie, my soul.

CONTENTS

SEX, DRUGS AND THE ELECTORAL ROLL

1

THE NEW GIRL'S OPENING

Winning a seat in the Victorian parliament at the 2014 state election made me the first former sex worker to be elected to a parliament anywhere in Australia. But what is most important here is not me as a politician or me as a former sex worker; it's the journey from sex worker to politician that counts as something different. Some might see this as just another form of *Pygmalion* politics because there have been quite a few Eliza Doolittles elected to Australian parliaments in recent times. No need for a 'please explain' here. No Australian members of parliament, however, have ever come from our commercial sex industry, which for many people has been about as low on the political pecking order as you can get. It's just another sign that politics, like the rest of society, is experiencing what the US futurist Terry Patten calls 'the acceleration of crazy'. It's not actual mad politics but a long overdue shake-out of the various paths to political life where we're increasingly seeing real people who represent sections of the community who would never normally get a go in the major parties.

And here's another first. I am the only woman in Australia to have started her own political party and then been elected. I started the Sex Party because I was pissed off with what was on offer from the three major parties. It wasn't just their policies either—it was the way they 'did' politics. Over the years, they have become like corporations. Places where only the machinists and the technical workers rise up through the ranks into managerial and then executive positions. Nothing wrong with that, as long as they keep up with the rapidly changing world around them. But they haven't. Instead they've became inbred and the lack of new DNA in their ranks is obvious. Occasionally they see the need to introduce new blood into their body politic, but they generally try to achieve this by roping in a celebrity stallion or broodmare rather than trying to change the culture from within.

Labor's failed attempt to bring disaffected baby boomers back to the fold by offering 'Oiler' Peter Garrett a prize spot in the ministry did nothing to stop disenchantment within the party—they gave him the environment portfolio and then asked him to praise nuclear energy. The Liberals approached the former Human Rights Commissioner, Tim Wilson, to run for the Victorian seat of Goldstein in the hope that it would stop the drift of small-'l' Liberals away from the party. They would have been far better off addressing the wholesale takeover of some Victorian branches and executive positions by radical Christian groups and the remnants of Family First.

The proof is blindingly obvious. Marriage equality took two decades of lobbying to get over the line, even though it was clear that there was majority support for it in the community. Voluntary assisted dying (VAD), drug law reform, censorship reform, abortion law reform, stem cell research and other major progressive social issues have all had majority public support in opinion polls for a decade. And where are we up to with all of that?

Voluntary assisted dying failed to get up in the New South Wales parliament in late 2017 because the leaders of both major parties voted against it, yet all the polling showed majority support for it in the community. In Victoria, we finally got it through the upper house by two votes with social conservatives fighting it all the way. Like NSW, polling showed majority support in the community. Medical cannabis has been legislated in a number of state parliaments, but in Victoria, which is generally more progressive than other jurisdictions, locally grown product is still not available and only a handful of patients have successfully used the scheme to access imported products. It's over two years since the legislation was passed and is clear evidence that the major parties are so locked into machine politics that they just can't come at paradigm shifts anymore. In fact, marriage equality is the only progressive issue that has been legislated federally and look how long that took. The $120 million plebiscite that was forced on to everyone was the product of half-a-dozen religious extremists in the Coalition threatening to crack the shits with Prime Minister Malcolm Turnbull. In fact, the failure of government to deal with this issue has been due to these same Coalition MPs, along with a little help from the conservative Shop, Distributive and Allied Employees Association (SDA) on Labor's side. It's not a matter of progressive versus conservative forces anymore. It's a systemic failure of the major parties to understand the progressive trends in the electorate because of their moribund core values and long-term relationships with ultra conservative institutions.

How many young Liberals these days are taught the legacy of former party reformers like Don Chipp and John Gorton? None. They're saddled with role models like former policeman, Peter Dutton, the former actress, Bronwyn Bishop and the former boxer and trainee Jesuit priest, Tony Abbott—all caricatures of politicians from the turn of the last century. Even former Prime Minister, Malcolm Fraser, the man who brought down the Whitlam Labor government in 1975, had to flee his own party before he died because he couldn't take the stultifying social conservatism anymore.

Labor is no better. The party of the worker and social equality has been busy stripping pensioners and single mothers of benefits, denying marriage equality (then supporting it when it suits them politically), censoring adult entertainment and siding with the Coalition on asylum seekers. Their ties with conservative unions has seen them as hamstrung on progressive issues as the Coalition. The Greens can claim the higher moral ground on some of these issues, but therein lies their problem: the holier than thou ethic now pervades the party of doctors ever since former leader, Bob Brown, retired. If they can't get the emissions trading scheme they want, they won't allow one at all. And if you thought they would never stoop to the bully-boy tactics of Labor and Liberal, think again. The Greens have created some of the best online trolls of any party in Australia, pulling down candidates from other parties with a unique style of personal smear and innuendo that dodges defamation laws. On the eve of elections, the captains of the Green army now camp out in staff cars at major polling booths. They plaster all available fencing for hundreds of metres with plastic bunting and then monitor security cameras on their laptops in the back of their cars throughout the night. If someone from another party even goes near their signs to try and squeeze one of their own in, they are accosted by 'Green soldiers' telling the 'foreigners' to go back to where they came from. I've seen them doing it!

As a member of the Victorian upper house, I get along with most of my colleagues on both sides. As individuals, most of them are decent and well-meaning people who I like. I would claim many as new friends. But even they recognise the limitations of their party structures. Our parliaments need renewal from more politicians who have led genuinely independent lives before they were elected. There are way too many former union officials, former ministerial staffers and lifelong party workers as sitting members. And we don't need any more lawyers either, thank you. They already occupy 25 per cent of federal parliamentary seats. We're all sinking under the weight of thousands of new laws every year without any of the old ones being updated. In 100 years' time (if we haven't all expired from 50-degree summer temperatures), our lives will be so over-regulated that we'll need a permit to fart. Don't laugh—the President of Malawi proposed such a law only a few years ago!

Thankfully, Australia has a long tradition of leavening po-faced politics with humour and satire. My first day in the Victorian parliament engaged with that dishonourable tradition via the pomp and ceremony of the formal induction. On offer was the chance to swear in front of Almighty God and on her *Book of Kells* that I would prosecute the office of Member of the Legislative Council justly and honestly. Or I could take a secular affirmation. It was a no-brainer.

As I lined up with an unprecedented number of other heathens to take the latter, little did I know that the religious right was already busy in the bleachers above, heaping scorn on me for going down the secular path. A certain member's staffer was in the public gallery, texting his Christian boss on the floor of the parliament that I was about to go the ungodly route and affirm. 'I thought she'd swear on a vibrator,' the rather pompous upper house member texted back to his staffer.

After affirming, I sat down on the red velvet seat that had been reserved for me between the Shooters and the Greens. The staffer fired off another salvo: 'Yeah, I'll bet when she stands up it will look like she'd sat on an ice cream.' It wasn't so much that I was offended by the crude language but the fact that he hardly knew me. I don't mind that kind of language in the right place with the right person. The thought of swearing on a stack of vibrators was perversely appealing. But the fact that he thought that there was something in the swearing-in ceremony that could in any way have sexually excited me said way more about him—and maybe his membership at Salon Kitty's—than it did about me.

My deep throat on this occasion happened to be none other than 'The Preference Whisperer' himself, Glenn Druery. He was sitting quietly in the public gallery behind said staffer, watching his protégés from the Shooters being sworn in. Glenn could see everything coming up on the staffer's mobile phone. He took a few photos of the conversation and sent them to me. A couple of days later, *Crikey* ran a short burst on the event via their Tips and Rumours column. I stuck a copy under the door of the recalcitrant MP. At the time, I told *Crikey* that I was planning to work a few of the exact quotes from the texts into an adjournment speech at some later date, just to remind the MP of his folly. As yet that hasn't happened, but I still have the texts.

My second appearance on the floor of the Victorian upper house on the 12th February 2015 saw me delivering my maiden speech. These speeches keep on giving long after they are delivered, and upon the death of a member, his or her maiden speech is often quoted when memorialising their life. If you've ever been confused by a politician's apparent lurch to the left or the right, or if they are somehow behaving contrary to their party's core beliefs, just go back to their maiden speech. There will be a page towards the end that will sum up what they believe in. It won't say who they are and it won't say what their party believes in, but it will tell you how they will vote on core issues if it is left up to their own beliefs and ideals. This part of my maiden speech dealt with hypocrisy, slut-shaming and civil liberties.

Earlier in the day I had agonised over what to wear. Was the maiden speech a sombre affair or was it celebratory? Was my lemon-hued Scanlan Theodore two-piece the right thing or was the tailored pinstripe suit the way to go? In the end, I thought I would dress as if I had been subpoenaed to court rather than going to the races, so the pinstripe suit won out. I stood in my place, and after thanking my family I began on my core values.

'I may be the first former sex worker to be elected to a parliament anywhere in this country.'

The charitable silence granted to first-time speakers deepened across the chamber like a low-pressure trough. An attendant in a maroon blazer shifted uneasily in his seat. Another smoothed his goatee down on each side as if he were nervously applying product. These were seasoned parliamentary staff who'd seen it all. They'd ejected rabble rousers, called ambulances and watched tearful speeches. More so, it was their job to protect the two large wooden doors at the back of the Legislative Council from being assaulted by members who would come, as per the tradition, armed with a big Black Rod to try to bash the doors at the opening of each parliament. They were not to be trifled with. The clerk, looking erudite and earnest behind a stack of red leather rule books, craned his head up off the notice paper and worked his gaze around the room like an animal sensing the air.

'However,' I continued, 'I am sure that the clients of sex workers have been elected in far greater numbers before me.'

It was partly an acknowledgement and partly a declaration. An acknowledgement of the many women in Victoria who had been slut-shamed by men in positions of authority, but also a declaration to the parliament that the slut was now among them.

An uncertain silence rolled off on to the crimson Axminster carpet. It was my maiden speech; I knew I was safe from hecklers and interjectors. It had been decreed many years earlier that my parliamentary virginity would lie intact until I had finished.

Suddenly, however, the mood changed. The clerk lowered his head over his notes again and some of the women started smiling. The men just looked at their shoes. Someone later said it felt like a sibylline moment in Australian politics.

2

ROOTS

It's my experience that families flow like rivers. Some crash and roar over rocks and some meander quietly along. Some families consolidate wealth without even trying, some are broke no matter what they do. Some get on fabulously and some can't stand each other. Some are always on the move, while others live their whole lives in the same suburb. Often these tendencies waterfall through the generations. It's something I have noticed in my own ancestry, as well as of those around me. I was born Fiona Heather Margaret Patten in the old Canberra Hospital, Acton, on 6 May 1964. I parachuted into a family of seafarers and inveterate travellers. Up until the age of fifteen, I would replicate my mother's early experience by not living in the same place for more than two years at a time.

****

My late father, Colin Richard Lloyd 'Rick' Patten, was a navy commander from Adelaide, and my late mother, Hazel Ann Street, was an English immigrant. Both eschewed their first names and chose to live under their middle names, Rick and Ann. Although I've never ditched my Scottish Christian name, I did continue the family tradition in a way by taking my middle name (and, more importantly, my granny's) as my sex worker name. So, for a period of time in the 1980s, a small section of the male community knew me simply as 'Heather'.

Dad's father, Eric Patten, was a captain in the Australian army based at Duntroon in Canberra. He left the army in the 1930s to become a journalist for the *Adelaide Advertiser* and ended up as Keith Murdoch's man in the federal parliamentary press gallery. Dad and Grandpa had a fiery relationship from all accounts. They were both strong-willed, loved warfare and had deep voices. Given the early influences in his life as a young boy, it was not surprising that my father applied for a scholarship and was accepted into the navy as a cadet midshipmen at HMAS *Cerberus* near Melbourne in 1951. He was fifteen years old. After two years of officer training, he was packed off to the United Kingdom to do a long communications course.

On his second UK exchange trip with the Royal Navy in 1963, Dad met and married Mum in Scotland. It was a quick romance and a genuine case of love at first sight—for Dad, anyway. Initially my mother's parents were not that enthusiastic at the thought of their daughter marrying someone from the colonies, and with good reason. In the early days of their courtship, my father didn't ingratiate himself all that well with them. Late one night, he arrived unannounced at their Scottish home in Helensburgh, drunk and refusing to leave, until he was granted an audience with Mum's father. Once Grandpa got out of bed, Dad asked him for Mum's hand in marriage. I am not sure where Mum was, but the way I remember the story is she was yelling at him from an upstairs window to come back when he was sober.

Before the wedding, Dad wrote to his parents in a letter that now forms part of the Patten archives:

> I am getting married. Even after two years in Scotland I have been able to resist the blandishments of the sheep and got engaged to a woman. The woman is called Ann Street. She is 22 today, a virgin (through no fault of mine I am ashamed to say), brunette, short, attractive, intelligent, wears contact lenses which I didn't know for a year, efficient, strong character, good child bearing hips, wonderful personality, wonderful, beautiful, sweet, charming—and I am prepared to spend the rest of my life with her without a single regret. And I love her dearly.

Back in Australia, the year after they were married, Dad was posted to HMAS *Harman* near Canberra, working with the Director of Communications. I was born later that year, the same year as the fatal collision between the aircraft carrier HMAS *Melbourne* and the battleship HMAS *Voyager* off the coast of southern NSW. Dad had a good mate on board the *Voyager* who was killed in the accident. He was to have become my godfather when the exercise had finished. Bizarrely, in early 1965, Dad joined the crew of HMAS *Melbourne* as a lieutenant commander and was sent off to sea again. He relished navy life, while my mother was resigned to it. On this particular occasion, however, rather than join the rest of the navy wives in Woolloo-mooloo, my mother packed me up with a few belongings and we set sail for the comfort of her family home in Scotland. Six months later we flew back to Sydney where my sister Kirsty was eventually born. In 1966, Dad was posted to Australia House in London, meaning yet again we all got back on board an ocean liner. As the London posting was coming to an end, my brother Ian was born, and not long after we returned to Australia once more.

These are my earliest memories: being on a large ship in the middle of the ocean and feeling like I was going somewhere new and exciting. That feeling of moving effortlessly through water is a deeply satisfying one for most people. Anyone who has ever sat in a rubber tyre and drifted down a river or got on a surfboard and felt the thrill of moving across a wave will vouch for it. I loved it as a child and I still love it now. From those early days, being in and around water became my second life, and swimming developed as a lifelong passion.

* * * *

Later in Dad's career he was selected for pilot training but failed the course. He could take off fine, but he couldn't land. Over the years, he worked his way up to the rank of commander. It was a position that had considerable responsibility attached to it, but he never took himself too seriously and remained quite the party animal and the social butterfly—traits that he passed on to all his children in spades. A loving and caring man with family and friends, he was as forgiving of his children as any father could be, but he didn't suffer fools lightly. Often he didn't suffer smart people lightly, either. He had a sharp tongue and a volatile temper when pushed beyond his limits. The older he got, the more he disliked politicians and people in authority. Like his father, Dad began to exploit his considerable talents as a wordsmith after he left the navy. His letters to the editor in the *Canberra Times* were legendary for their wit and sarcasm; in later life, he became the ultimate curmudgeon.

My mother was born into an upper middle class English–Scottish family. Her early schooling was done as a boarder in a little convent in France and later in Sherborne, England. Her mother and father continued to travel the world and she was flown to Singapore and Malaysia in army planes for Christmas and school holidays. She lived all over Europe before settling back in Scotland and working for the legendary Blackie and Son publishing house, where she was an assistant to the publisher commissioning such children's series as the *Sooty* books. She then spent many years living outside the UK. As often happens with people living in diaspora communities, national traits sometimes tend to become rather amplified, and my mother tended to be very British outside Britain. Despite all that travel, the family were very close. Travelling made them all great collectors and Street houses were always full of antiques and craft objects—another trait that was handed on to their children.

My relationship with my mother was a close one, although she was the disciplinarian of the family. I don't recall her as overly affectionate and she was not one for public displays of emotion, but she was incredibly kind and could dissolve into tears at the drop of a hat. She was devoted to her family and would get up at five o'clock every morning, drive three kids to swimming training several times a week, and then to Saturday competitions that were many hours from home.

She always made sure that her children had plenty to do: swimming, soccer, water polo, rugby, Brownies, Girl Guides, pottery, gymnastics and hockey were all thrown at us. I think it was as much for her as for us because it enabled her to develop her own networks and to learn about the neighbourhood. They're skills that I use a lot today. I like being busy and I like being at work.

When my sister came out as gay at age nineteen, my mother found it hard to come to terms with at first. Kirsty had had a few average relationships with women in her early days and I think Mum was just worried that she would run the gauntlet of discrimination and have a miserable life. My father dealt with it much better and didn't really see it as a problem. When Kirsty would come to visit them with a girlfriend, Mum would make up two single beds. It was her way of saying she didn't approve, but she was also not going to make a fuss. When Kirsty met her current partner, Linda, everything changed, and the single beds were zipped together. Unfortunately, Mum died before they had their daughter, Bonnie, but she knew Linda was pregnant and was extremely happy for them.

* * * *

My maternal grandmother, Heather Street, was born in India and was brought up towards the end of the Victorian era with servants and plenty of privilege. Leaving India in the early 1900s, her mother, father and her sister Hazel moved to a sprawling colonial home set in tropical gardens on The Peak in Hong Kong, where they lived for many years. Granny was then sent to boarding school in Scotland at the age of seven. Before the advent of commercial air travel, her family had been around the world five times before her twelfth birthday.

Granny and I were polar opposites in our areas of endeavour and yet we were very close. I was lucky to travel a lot with her when I was younger, visiting her old homes in various countries. As an advocate for the sex industry in my later life, she was fond of telling me, 'I don't take much notice of what you say, dear, but you always look nice.' She eventually moved to Australia in the late 1980s and was as close as you'd get to a Scottish aristocrat living in the suburbs of Canberra where she worked for the National Gallery as a guide and for the Scottish Trust. Always up for a party and a bit of dry sherry, she had a strong influence on my developing personality. Although not always interested in the lives we led as her grandchildren, she loved doing things with us like shopping, travelling, castling and gallery visits. She gave me a great appreciation of the art of collecting. She had impeccable taste and introduced me to the designs of the great Charles Rennie Mackintosh. On one memorable trip to Scotland, she took me to the famous Hill House in Helensburgh which Mackintosh had designed for Blackie and Son publishers, where Mum had worked as a girl.

Before Granny passed away in the late 1990s, she gave me a small antique wax seal of a young women's profile and a slightly larger silhouette of a young man in navy uniform. The former was that of the famous Lady Emma Hamilton, mistress to Britain's most famous admiral, Horatio Nelson, and muse to one of Britain's great painters, George Romney. Emma Hamilton was the Paris Hilton of her day—except that she started life as the poor daughter of a London blacksmith. Her looks and charm took her through a series of relationships with men of wealth and standing, starting at the ripe old age of fifteen. She created dance and fashion trends along the way and was famous for being famous in the late 1700s. Her sexually provocative portraits and nude performances scandalised some parts of society, while in others they were legendary.

The wax seal had been given to my great-great-great-grandfather, Captain William Standway Parkinson, who was the subject of the silhouette that accompanied it. With his fine features, collar-length wavy brown hair and piercing brown eyes, he cut a very dashing figure indeed. The two antiques have been handed down through the family over many years, but whether Lady Emma or Nelson were the original owners is uncertain. Souvenirs of Lady Emma were quite the rage in their day and it was known that Nelson used to give them out to those he favoured. Parkinson was a midshipman on the Royal Navy ship HMS *Boreas*, which Nelson captained. Plying his way through the West Indies in 1784, Parkinson was said to be one of the first big supporters of Nelson and he quickly worked his way up through the ranks. He received his first commission in 1794 and served as junior lieutenant on the *Dido* in its historic battle with the French frigate, *La Minerve*, a year later. He went on to command the number three ship to Nelson's flagship after they defeated the French fleet in 1798.

I like to think that Lady Emma and Captain Parkinson were secret lovers, or at least soul mates who had a common love and admiration for Nelson. Maybe they had a threesome, although no record of this seems to exist. The spirit of the two of them attaches strongly to their little portraits as they sit proudly on my lounge room wall.

* * * *

My interest in sex, politics and feminism has strong roots in my mother's family. The celebrated Australian suffragette and feminist of the 1930s, Jessie Street, was my great-aunt by marriage and was one of the first relatives who my mother met when she came out to Australia in the 1960s. Jessie's daughter, Belinda, lived on a farm in Braidwood, NSW, and we were regular visitors there during the 1970s. Unfortunately I never got to meet Jessie there as she died in 1970. Jessie's granddaughter, Margo, is my godmother.

Jessie Street is probably best known for being the only female Australian delegate at the establishment of the United Nations. She oversaw the inclusion of gender, alongside race and religion, as non-discriminatory clauses in the United Nations Charter. Equally, she was well known for her major role in removing the constitutional discrimination against Aboriginal people through the 1967 referendum. Like my grandmother, Jessie Street was born in India and lived her early childhood in well-to-do circumstances with a lot of international travel.

As I developed a political career of my own, I've noticed how certain aspects of my life seem to have strangely mirrored some of Jessie's. As a young woman in 1914, Jessie worked in a London reception centre assisting other young women who had been arrested as sex workers, and in 1916 she started the Social Hygiene Association in Sydney to promote sex education. She renewed her interest in sexual health after the Korean War because of the high levels of STIs among the returning soldiers.

During the late 1980s and early 1990s, I spent two years as manager of the sex worker outreach group, Workers in Sex Employment (WISE), and as a member of the Australian Federation of AIDS Organisations (AFAO). Both positions involved looking out for the welfare of sex workers and promoting sex education to the broader community amid the growing number of HIV and AIDS infections.

In 1930, Jessie was elected president of one of the most influential feminist groups in Australia, the United Associations of Women (UA). This group ran major campaigns in support of divorce law reform, the appointment of women to public office and to jury service, and the election of women to parliament. My election as president of the Eros Foundation (now the Eros Association) in the early 1990s became basically about lobbying governments to stop prohibition around adult goods and services, and I'm sure many modern-day feminists would see that position as a far cry from Jessie's UA. Indeed, some would see it as anti-feminist. I strongly disagree: porn has often been the canary in the coal mine when it comes to censorship, and there are countless instances throughout history where the banning of porn was a precursor to the banning of feminist speech—generally by the same group of men. If you are prepared to defend the right of people to watch porn, you'll defend their right to most other forms of free speech.

In 1933, Jessie was involved in setting up the first contraceptive clinic in Sydney. In 2016, I moved a private member's bill that saw exclusion zones put in place around Victoria's abortion clinics to stop protestors harassing women attending the clinics.

Jessie was one of the first women to stand for federal parliament and she ran for public office three times without quite getting there. One of those tilts in 1943 was for Malcolm Turnbull's current seat of Wentworth, where she achieved a swing of 20 per cent against the incumbent Eric Harrison of United Australia Party (later to become the Liberal Party). This wanker then stood with his back to her while she made her concession speech and refused to shake her hand. Although I have run five times for public office, only three of them were serious attempts at getting elected. My third serious attempt, unlike Jessie's, was lucky for me, and I received similar hostility from my opponents.

I've often reflected on Jessie's life and her work, and I feel that my election to public office goes some way to building on her efforts in early feminism and maybe completing a chapter in the Street family story.

3

ADOLESCENCE

I tend to believe that childhood is often viewed in later life through a series of remembered incidents rather than as a cohesive narrative. Apart from my early memories of being on the ocean, the most enduring childhood ones are of two vivid and recurring dreams. I don't dream them anymore, but I think they infiltrated my subconscious and have probably affected me at various times in my life. Around the age of six or seven, I started dreaming that I was being followed by a man around the rocky coves of Sydney Harbour. I would be wandering alone around these still bays when this man caught me and pushed me into one of the rock pools. I instantly panicked until I realised I could breathe underwater and then the dream would sometimes transform into a wonderful underwater paradise where I swam fast, like a dolphin, without the need for air.

The second dream started at the age of fourteen and involved being in conversation with God. But it wasn't a happy dream. He was trying to sell me on the idea of becoming a nun. While it didn't sit well with me, I didn't want to upset him, either. So I kept saying that if I could just have fun for a while, then I would do it. Apart from Sally Field's flying nun and Julie Andrews' Maria, I had no idea what a nun did. I was not interested in religion, but in the dream I found myself resigned to my fate of becoming an obedient nun anyway. The debate with God was about how long I could have fun before taking to the cloisters. The dream came to me on and off for nearly two years.

* * * *

My early years were spent much like those of my mother and father—travelling. Before I was fifteen, I had lived in Canberra on three different occasions, in Sydney twice, and in London and Washington. My mother had trained her children well in the art of settling in. In her mind, there was never a doubt that we would not make friends when we arrived at a new school or neighbourhood. Because she had lived in so many places herself, she had strategies for meeting people that she passed on to us. I never felt that I wouldn't fit in to a new environment or work situation, and my mother's childhood strategies were particularly useful in my first few months of being elected to parliament.

When we left the rolling green landscapes of Maryland in the US in 1979, we were leaving the most stable home life that my mother and her children had ever had—four years in the one spot. In the US, swimming had become an important part of my life and I had been on track to qualify for the National Championships with an A ranking from the Amateur Athletic Union. Moving back to our family home nestled in the parched and crunchy bushland of Canberra's nature suburb of Aranda severely disrupted this momentum.

There had been a moment coming back from the States when we were all sitting in a quiet arcade in a San Francisco shopping centre, about to fly to Hawaii, when we came across an Australian family having an argument. Their accents seemed so strong and coarse that my mother and I broke into tears, saying we didn't want to go back to a country full of *that*. I was only fourteen, but even then Australia felt primitive compared to the US. How things have changed!

Like many people who went through their secondary education from the late 1970s to the 1980s, my academic years were pockmarked with rebellion, disappointment and some pretty riotous behaviour. If I had an academic dharma, I never found it. I was always uneasy with knowledge that filled my brain and left my arms and legs trailing loosely beside me. My early report cards all reflected this attitude: 'Very capable, but doesn't try . . . Very happy to contribute constructively in class but is disruptive . . .' I did advanced Maths, Physics and Chemistry and scored in the top percentile in the final exams, but I just couldn't find that sweet spot that would have allowed me to apply myself. I also studied Industrial Arts, Technical Drawing, Wilderness Studies and Landscape Design. My swimming coaches had more praise for my training and competition, but even then there was always something else more interesting for me to do.

Although my parents were happy with the paths they had chosen for themselves, they were not my choices. The shingle that read 'Patten, Street & Daughter' was never going to be hung over my door. My love of the ocean and water did mean I thought about joining the navy for a short time, and on the advice of my father I once attended a naval careers' day. It didn't go well. The navy spokesman tried to tell me that women would never be allowed to serve at sea, a disagreement ensued, and that was the end of my interest in fighting, or rather *not* fighting, for my country. I'm sure he remembered that discussion when only a couple of years later all women enrolled in the Royal Australian Navy were told they were finally eligible to serve at sea. And as much as I loved my mother and was in awe of her ability to organise her family, I did not want to become the suburban Goddess Durga with the eight flailing arms.

I finished my last two years of secondary education at Hawker College in Canberra. I enjoyed the social side of school, even though I was by now a pretty average student. Looking back on my study choices, I see they were mostly left-brain subjects. But at the time I was far too interested in enjoying myself and the rapidly expanding frontiers of adult social life. Friends, boyfriends, sport and paid work all took precedence. Because Mum and Dad were great library-goers and the house was always full of fiction, I was also surprisingly comfortable just curling up on the couch with a good book.

Like many teenagers, it was around this time that my mother caught me smoking. She was a great fan of reverse psychology, so rather than dock my pocket money or make me do extra chores, she simply locked me in my room with the windows closed and made me smoke a whole packet of Marlboro. These days the Department of Family and Community Services would probably have had her up before the courts for doing such a thing, but it certainly cured me of a big tobacco habit.

I lost my virginity at the age of fifteen—just a few months before it would have been legal. I remember it well. We had been back from America less than a year and my sister and I had started playing water polo. In those days, there were no women's teams, so we played against the boys. I'd met Brett at one of the games and we had been going out for a couple of months. He was eighteen, tanned and very fit. We had tried to have sex unsuccessfully a couple of times at the park behind Lake Ginninderra. For some reason it just wouldn't go in. However, one day in the rumpus room of our Aranda home with Mum and Dad at work, things were different, and after a few minutes my young suitor had arrived at the vinegar stroke. Unfortunately for him, my younger brother Ian arrived at the door at the same time and burst in as Brett was bursting out. The look on Ian's face was a mix of confusion and fascination. Never one to let embarrassment or shame get in the way of what he wanted to do, Ian only swung around on one heel when I yelled 'Get out', and, with a smile that stayed with him for days, he slowly exited my love bunker.

My second serious boyfriend was a Seventh-Day Adventist with a large penis. Neil's parents gave me my first taste of religious extremism when they locked him out of the house on some of Canberra's freezing cold nights and made him sleep in the outside verandah, all because he'd been out with me. They assumed we were drinking and having sex when often we had only gone to the movies. It was cruel. His house was close to school, so we did sometimes have sex there and go back to class on his motorbike. Strangely, his large penis was never a problem to get in.

All this took place during the time that Lindy and Michael Chamberlain were being done over in the courts and discriminated against because of their religion. Neil's parents sent a preacher over after school to talk to us about the 'wages of sin'. It was hilarious and we laughed at him. He left after about half an hour, obviously thinking we were lost causes, and we went off into the bedroom and had sex before Neil's parents came back home.

* * * *

When I was in Year 11, my mother found a bunch of used condoms in a waste paper basket in my room. She reckoned that it was time I had 'the talk'. I had already well and truly processed sex by the time I was thirteen or fourteen, but I heard her out. While the talk was a rite of passage of a kind, it did nothing to prepare me for being raped a year later.

The summer holidays between Year 11 and 12 were spent on the NSW south coast at Pretty Beach. My family had often stayed there and I had a lot of friends whose parents also camped there over the years. There were more boys than girls in our group, but it was a friendly bunch and not overly macho. We all liked hanging out together and had done so for quite a few years. In the balmy evenings when our parents were socialising we would light driftwood fires on the beach and break out a cheap goon bag of moselle.

On this particular day, I had been for a long walk on the beach and was starting to head home. A slightly older guy I had just met at the campfire the night before joined me. We walked and talked, and then he suggested that we go and smoke a cigarette in the dunes near the campsite. I was happy to do this as I certainly didn't want to be busted by my parents or their friends smoking around the camp.

Once in the dunes he started trying to grope and kiss me. I pushed him away in a casual manner so as not to look like a baby gazelle in the eye of the tiger. 'Sorry, mate, I'm just not interested,' I told him. What happened next saw a bilious mix of his home life, entertainment choices, lack of boundaries, sense of male entitlement and complete lack of empathy for other human beings spew forth from his pathetic little self. He was much bigger than me and I only had a T-shirt and swimmers on—so getting inside them was not difficult for him. Despite my strongest protestations, he started to rape me on my back in the sand. I told him to stop in no uncertain manner, but he was having none of it. When I realised that he was not going to stop, I decided to accept what was happening and began taunting him. I told him what a loser he was and that I didn't ask for this and didn't want it. I even tried to make fun of what he was doing. I couldn't push him off me, but fortunately he came within a few minutes and it was all over.

I jumped up and told him what an arsehole he was. I was shaken, and as I stumbled out from the dunes on to the beach I immediately ran into a group of my parents' friends. I thought about telling them what had just happened, but I felt like such a fool to have gone into the dunes with him that I just stared at the sand and put one foot in front of the other. He followed me home, apologising all the way. I was more angry than scared, and I told him I was going to tell all his friends about what he'd just done, which only served to increase his pathetic apologies.

I don't think I ever thought of going to the police. Maybe I should have, but there were no phones down there so I never thought of calling anyone. As most women would tend to, in these circumstances, I was feeling guilty and stupid. Who hadn't been told not to go into secluded places with men you didn't know? As so often happens, I took a lot of the blame on myself and for quite a while afterwards I didn't feel safe walking on the beach alone.

That night we had our regular campfire and after a little while I started taking his male friends to one side and telling them about what he had done. They were all genuinely shocked and upset and I have to say they acted honourably after it. In the morning, the rapist fled, as many of his friends had dumped him. One of his best mates told me, 'Don't worry, he won't be here tomorrow.' He never came back to Pretty Beach.

I didn't really talk again about what happened that day until I was asked to address the 2013 Brisbane Slutwalk. As the annual march of an international movement that calls for an end to rape culture—including victim blaming and slut-shaming—I figured it was the right time to speak about it.

* * * *

Drugs were as much a part of the final two years of secondary education as they are now, although the mix has changed these days. I had first enjoyed pot when I was in the US at a school camp for the 'gifted and talented' (because the teachers were impressed at how well I picked up the English language, being from Australia). I smoked a bit at high school parties and I got busted in Hawaii smoking with some army cadets. I can remember thinking that prohibition of marijuana made about as much sense as trying to prohibit sex, and I was going to have me a share of both.

I became well versed in the market place. I had no dreams of getting rich, but I did become quite blasé about my buying and selling. I remember being counselled by a friend after he watched me carving up a large block of Lebanese blonde hash on the Space Invaders machine at Captain Gregg's bar on a busy Friday night. This was the same year my omniscient mother found a small block of hash in my bedroom and $1500 that I was intending to use to pay for a holiday at South Molle Island. Most of the cash was for the dealer. Mum, in her infinite wisdom, flushed the hash down the toilet, gave me some of the cash to pay back the dealer, and immediately booked me in to see a drugs and alcohol counsellor who spent most of the time counselling Mum. Some months later, she gave all the money back to me for the holiday.

About a month after finding out that her eldest daughter was selling pot, the same daughter then fell pregnant. My mother knew it even before I did. I was pretty messy with my period in those days and Mum was constantly cleaning blood from my clothes around the same time each month. She would have missed seeing it and pounced like a hawk.

She waited until I was alone at the breakfast table one morning and asked me straight out if I was pregnant. I said I didn't know, but it had been long enough since my last period to make me worried. She drove me over to Family Planning for a pregnancy test. It was positive. Not long after that, she made a special dinner and asked the drug-dealing father-to-be to come on over. She gave him a hard time and accused both of us of being stupid and irresponsible. He didn't know which way to look, but by the end of the evening she had made peace with both of us.

Abortion was still illegal in the ACT in the 1980s, so the good folk at Family Planning gave us the number for a clinic in Sydney. Mum took control and made the appointment. My father had been very understanding and with good reason: Mum told me that before she'd met him he had got a girl pregnant in London (weirdly, her name was also Fiona) and she'd had an illegal abortion that had been dangerous. She was okay, but their relationship did not survive.

Dad booked the hotel for us and Mum and I drove to Sydney. The night before the abortion we had a great dinner together. Mum and I rarely did the mother and daughter thing on our own. I was even allowed to have a glass of wine. The next morning we headed off. The clinic was in the back streets of Surry Hills and as we approached I could tell that Mum was far more nervous about it all than I was. Her face had stiffened considerably and her mood clouded over, while I just wanted to get the whole thing over and done with. As we walked up to the front door we saw that someone had thrown red paint along the footpath and the wall leading to the clinic. Clearly done to intimidate young women, it visibly upset my mother. At the end of the river of blood were a couple of creepy old men with pamphlets and signs. They were chanting religious slogans. I didn't even hear what they said as I was far too intent on getting into the clinic, but they shook Mum up.

Once inside, the staff at the clinic apologised for the protestors and then proceeded to reassure Mum about the procedure. I remember it as a bright place, full of girls around my age and a few older women. They were mainly with girlfriends or boyfriends, but not too many with their mothers. The waiting room was divided in the middle by a low wall. On one side were those nervously waiting to be called, while on the other were those cheerfully drinking tea with biscuits and waiting to be discharged.

The abortion itself was quick and, with a local anaesthetic, not painful. I remember there was a lovely tree painted on the ceiling to look at and a nurse held my hand the whole time.

Once I was back in the recovery room, I was on a high and could have run a mile. I was a little too happy for my mother's liking: I guess she expected me to feel some sort of sorrow. I never did. We ran the gauntlet of the old men on the way out and Mum and I spent the afternoon shopping. We drove back to Canberra the next day.

Apart from those arseholes at the front of the clinic, and the red paint, we had a great time together. But I never forgot the effect that the pro-lifers had on my mother, and more than 30 years on, my private member's bill in the Victorian parliament would lead to the banishment of those ugly protestors from every abortion clinic in Victoria.

4

GETTING PAID

I've been gainfully employed since about the age of twelve. In those early days, most of my paid work involved teaching swimming, but I also delivered junk mail and worked in holiday camps. After leaving the navy, Dad had begun work with the weather tech company Delairco and I often helped at technology trade shows. At fourteen, I did a stint at a local McDonald's in Canberra as the official 'sauce girl', putting the tomato sauce, mustard, pickles and onion on the orders. I liked the job and had a good relationship with the young manager, but after a particularly messy sauce fight in the kitchen one evening, my shifts dried up and I quit.

After leaving secondary school, I sat the Commonwealth Bank trainee test and became a junior clerk. It was a miserable start. The assistant manager immediately informed me that my dresses were either too thin or too tight or somehow just inappropriate. I liked the other people who worked at the bank, but I didn't like him and he didn't like me. As punishment for my 'attitude', he would send me into the archives in the roof of the bank for days at a time to find errors in old teller ledgers. I thoroughly enjoyed this work. Better still, I was allowed to wear what I wanted up there.

I lasted three months before the area manager called me in one day and said, 'You're not enjoying this much, are you?' I told him I thought it was boring and I couldn't work with the assistant manager's attitude. To my great surprise, he agreed to pay me four weeks in advance in lieu of notice and I was free to leave. I could hardly contain my joy.

Two days later, I landed one of the best jobs I've ever had. I became a car wash chick. The Whale Car Wash floated on a sea of soapy water at the corner of Lonsdale and Elouera Streets in Canberra's commercial precinct of Braddon. The job required a 7.30 a.m. start and I only worked when it was busy. No cars, no work. I started getting roses from anonymous customers and even appeared in the car wash's TV commercial.

The ad agency had hired a glamour girl with a big bosom to get into a white bikini and sit on the bonnet of a car while it was being washed to prove how gentle the machines were. I was the far less glamorous size 8AA girl vacuuming the car and handing out tickets in the second scene, but the way they shot it made it look like it was me in both scenes. They ran that ad for over ten years on the local commercial stations and friends were amazed at my TV transformation.

I also liked the two blokes, Barry and Harry, who worked there with me. One had a cleft palate and one had an acquired brain injury. Barry ended up being sent to Goulburn jail for six weeks because of unpaid fines. I remember how unfair I thought that was, but he was quite happy about it. He'd never been on a train before, so the trip to Goulburn was exciting, and when he got there he would get regular meals and even snacks, he told me. He didn't have to work and he could play ping-pong and basketball all day with a bunch of new friends.

The car wash job offered irony as well as infamy. The bank manager who had paid me out at the Commonwealth Bank would walk past each morning on his way to work. Often he would see me there with the soapy sponges and vacs and just shake his head. I thought it was hilarious. I'm sure he thought I would end up living on the streets.

I saved a few thousand dollars at the car wash and when I turned eighteen I took a gap year and travelled alone to the UK where my Granny and Grandpa were still living in Scotland. I visited family as well as some of my Pretty Beach friends who were now living in the Jersey Isles. There was also the obligatory Contiki bus tour. Granny showed me some of Scotland's grand gardens. For the first time, I started to develop an appreciation of design using plants.

The following year I started a four-year course in Landscape Architecture at the University of Canberra, but quickly changed stride and moved to Industrial Design within a few months. I think I was attracted to the more functional aspects of this course than the static nature of architecture. It was a small class and I was the only female. That didn't bother me, but it did highlight my lack of practical woodwork and mechanical education. I fell in love with a final-year Industrial Design student called Pete and had a great and naughty time.

* * * *

Stone Day at the University of Canberra was held to mark that day in the late 1960s when then Prime Minister John Gorton laid the foundation stone for the institution. Of course, the large chunk of granite at the front of the building immediately took on the more colloquial meaning and getting stoned there became the order of the day. Well, it did for me and my friends, anyway. By then it had become Stone Week and the celebrations and special events were many and varied.

The Stone Week of my second year was a turning point in my academic career. A few of my friends had chopped an old white EH Holden station wagon so that it resembled a giant convertible. On the grassed areas outside the union building we crammed as many stoned students as we could into the car and drove up and down the concourse—much to the annoyance of the union organisers.

One night the university's Shakespeare company decided to hold a performance of *Much Ado About Nothing* in the Union Refectory. Still stoned, my new boyfriend Pete and I thought it would be totally in keeping with the theme of the event to judge the performance using the standards that the Bard's own audiences would have used. So we scoured the university halls of residence for eggs and fruit, and made our way to the balcony that skirted the performance area below.

At the point where Hero the heroine starts swooning at her wedding, we let fly, reigning eggs down onto the players. I think we even yelled some old English sayings like 'Hweat!', 'What Ho!' and 'Eow!' The outraged actors yelled back 'Fuck off!', but in accents more redolent of Dubbo than Dunsinane. It wasn't until the next day we realised how upset everyone was. Pete and I were called into the Vice Chancellor's office and ordered to pay hundreds of dollars in carpet and costume cleaning. We argued that it hadn't been ill-intentioned and had in fact been in keeping with Stone Day antics. But the Vice Chancellor would have none of it.

As punishment, we were barred from all union facilities. Not being able to go to the union bar was effectively like being banned from the campus. Pete finished his final year soon after, and the idea of coming back for another two years with the bans and without my boyfriend made uni a less attractive place to be.

Still of a mind to study design, I decided to quit university and do the popular three-year fashion course that was on offer at the local TAFE. It covered everything: tailoring, pattern-making, textile manufacture, industrial sewing, design drawing and even fashion parades. It was the learning experience that engaged both my limbs and my limbic system, and it was the first time I felt like I was on track to something tangible. It was also the first time I had sex for money.

* * * *

I was supporting myself by waitressing at the Parkroyal Hotel on Northbourne Avenue. After work one day, I joined some of the staff and a few regular guests who were having drinks at the bar. After a couple of wines, one of the guests quietly asked me if I'd like to spend the night with him. I liked him without being wildly attracted. He was quite a bit older, probably in his mid-thirties and had a well-worn feel about him.

I was in two minds, so I thought I'd let him take himself off the hook by putting an outrageous condition on his request. I smiled into my drink and said, 'Well, how about a hundred bucks to go with that?' I thought he'd feign outrage and, if anything, try and negotiate me down. But no. He just looked me through slightly narrowed eyes and said, 'Okay'.

I was stunned. He didn't even haggle over the price. I was thinking 'That didn't go to plan so I suppose I'd better go through with it!' He gave me the money while we were in the bar and then we went back to his room. He was the oldest guy I'd ever fucked. We drank a lot and I fell asleep with him, but I left at dawn. Unfortunately, I was sprung by the night manager who just happened to go past as I was doing the walk of shame down the hallway. It didn't go down well with management, they were very disapproving. They didn't sack me, though, because I was popular with the guests and a hard worker. I didn't think much more about it after that, though the $100 did stick in my mind. It was twice the amount that I had just been paid for five hours of waitressing!

I started work at a restaurant where waitresses were instructed to wear a badge that said, 'Don't Let Keating Stop You Eating'. It was a protest about the proposed fringe benefits tax that the Hawke government was about to introduce. When the tax came in, the restaurant changed its name to Fringe Benefits, but the damage had already been done. The long business lunches with the big tips suddenly stopped. The tax also affected revenue at many brothels: many businessmen would take their clients to a brothel to celebrate or seal a deal.

It seems like a century ago now that you could claim a sex worker on your business expense account, although many of the brothels changed the name on their credit card facilities to try to fool the tax office—and their customer's partners who might see the credit card statement. One that I remember was called 'ACT Plant Hire'. Another brothel used an Italian-sounding restaurant name for their credit card facility until the wife of a regular client rang the brothel looking to book a table. She wanted to surprise her husband for an anniversary and knew that he loved that restaurant because she'd seen from his credit card statement that he dined there frequently.

* * * *

About six months into the fashion course, I lost my licence for driving over the limit. Feeling hard done by and in need of a break, I absconded from lectures with a few friends and we went to the coast for a couple of days on a magic mushroom field trip. Harvesting gold tops and blue meanies in the cow paddocks at Nelligen is an ancient and honourable tradition dating back to the late 1960s when Canberra's hippy pioneers first invaded the south coast. Following the harvest, we drove to my parents' beach house at Bawley Point, though Mum and Dad didn't know about it.

After three days of psychedelic partying, we dragged ourselves back to Canberra, whereupon I was immediately summonsed to my mother's office in town. At that stage she was working for the Overseas Telecommunications Commission in Canberra's CBD. She was in a very dark mood, but still feeling the effects of the mushrooms I was finding it hard to understand why. As it turned out, she had just seen the court report of my drink-driving charge that she was never supposed to see. After a secret deal, my sister Kirsty had promised to get up early the day after court and remove the court reports section from the *Canberra Times* before my parents could see it, which she had. But as luck would have it, the report had my age as Fiona Patten, 31, of Aranda. A friend of my parents had seen it and thought it hilarious that the newspaper had aged me by ten years.

So she just had to fax it to them! At least my father saw the funny side of it. Not long after, he had the faxed court report framed and presented to me at my 21st birthday party.

I finished the fashion course, but I never graduated. One of my teachers had set us a ridiculously simple test about basic computing that I thought was an affront to my intelligence and I answered the questions in much the same way. I also resented his overbearing attitude. He failed me on this test, and the course, even though I managed to get 99 per cent on everything else. Angry and fed up with institutions, I was ready to move out into the world.

5

BODY POLITICS

With three incomplete university and TAFE courses behind me, I decided to give tertiary education the flick. Fashion design was still my passion, but I now took the skills that I had learned at TAFE and started my own business. I moved down to Bawley Point, this time with my parents' permission, and set up my own production studio.

Bawley is part of a 250-kilometre stretch of coastline that runs from Ulladulla to Eden and in my opinion is one of the most underrated areas in the world. Still largely undiscovered by Sydneysiders to the north, many of the beaches and headlands are equal to anything in Bali or the Greek Islands. Real estate is relatively cheap and there are four distinct seasons, even if the winters can get a bit nippy. With my passion for swimming, living near the ocean was what it was all about.

Every weekend I would pack up my silver Datsun Sunny with my new hats and dresses and head off up the Clyde Mountain back to Canberra. I had a regular stall at the Gorman House markets where

I sold my wares among the antique traders and foodies. I also sold a selection of my 'sea legs' to the local surf shops. These were aerobic tights that I had screen printed with shells, seaweed and fish images, and they were very popular. I also worked a few days a week waitressing at the Tabourie Lake Motor Inn, a few kilometres north of my coastal sweat shop. For a girl just starting out in her own business, I was doing all right.

Then luck, stupidity and responsibility all joined together to force a slight detour in my plans. A girlfriend who had been working with me at the motel was going overseas. She needed to get back to Bawley Point one night following a big pool party send-off. Normally we'd spend the night in the bunkhouse at the motel, but she didn't want to miss her flight the next day. Complicating matters was the fact that her car headlights weren't working. We decided that she could follow close behind me for the ten-minute drive and that not much could go wrong. It was pouring with rain and I was still in my bikini with a cheesecloth cape draped around me. About halfway, I missed a tight corner at low speed and rolled the car, hitting a tree. I wasn't wearing a seatbelt and I was thrown into the back seat.

When I finally extricated myself from the wreck, the roof line in the front of the car had been flattened below the level of the steering wheel while the back was relatively untouched. Thanking my lucky stars, we drove back to Bawley in my friend's car with no lights. I was battered and bruised and probably had mild concussion. We got home and decided the best thing to do was to have a joint. Then we fell asleep.

Next morning, I woke to the vision of my neighbours hovering above my bed and asking me if I was all right. They'd seen the car wrecked on the side of the road and there was no phone in the house for them to call me. They called my parents and then took me to Ulladulla to see the police and a doctor. The police were very suspicious. The doctor diagnosed slight concussion and a few cuts. The worst thing was that my parents were now rushing down from Canberra, which meant I had to clean their house, mow the lawns and change the sheets, all in two hours.

* * * *

Two months later, at the end of 1987, I had the opportunity to be part of large music and fashion festival in Canberra. The organisers slotted a fashion parade into the event and I was invited to show my latest range. I was doing a lot of pleated work and geometric hats. It was a slightly summer military style with the prerequisite 1980s shoulder pads. The show's coordinator, Tiffany, pulled me aside at the after-party and asked me if I would be interested in working with her. We did a couple more shows before deciding that maybe we should take it a step further and open a shop. We would showcase local designers and the new emerging young Australian designers, including Wayne Cooper, Morrissey Edmiston, Scanlan Theodore, and others. Not wanting to think small, we called it Empire and had grand visions of building it into a chain of stores. But a stuffy old public servant refused to allow us to register the name, perhaps because of the reference to monarchy or some other silly reason that at the time sailed over my head.

We needed to find a name that would bring in smart and affluent shoppers as well as stand for something we believed in. So one night we grabbed a few friends, some butcher's paper and a few Texta Colours and headed off to a bar in Manuka. One of my drinking buddies, a young lawyer named Mark Love, suggested 'The Body Politic' for our business name. Tiffany and her mother were into numerology and reckoned the numbers just didn't add up for a successful retail outlet. I wasn't big on the psychic sciences, but we all managed to agree on 'Body Politics' instead. We drank a toast to the new name and the next morning toddled off to the Companies Office and registered it. Little did I know that within a few years the name would grace the cheque book of my sex industry lobbying business and that Mark would become a very successful Canberra lawyer, representing the Canberra X-rated video moguls in the High Court.

We had a name and a business plan. Now we just needed some money. Tiffany and I started fundraising and between the NAB and a few friends, we managed to raise $30,000. The only catch was an interest rate of around 15 per cent. But we were starting a business empire and interest rates were in the same category as a bar tab—just something that went with business. Within a few weeks, we had found a small shop in the centre of Canberra's CBD and we were off and running.

Garema Place is the beating heart of the national capital's retail sector and it represents a weird and eclectic mix of culture. One hundred years ago, it was where the railway line from Sydney to Canberra terminated, but after the bridge over the Molonglo River was washed out in 1880 floods, the track was torn up and the lakeside suburb of Kingston became the end of the line. But the ghost of the railway line survived and Garema Place became a natural spot for businesses to aggregate.

It was also a place to demonstrate and parade. Over the years, it hosted a wide range of activities from anti-porn protests to multicultural festivals. A Christian bookshop traded profitably on the ground level, while underneath Jax nightclub had been the preferred hangout for dozens of dope dealers. Young skaters flew alongside suited businessmen and young mothers with prams. In the centre of it all was a bizarre nude fountain sculpture called *Father and Son*, which had been presented to the people of Canberra by Alexander Downer in memory of his father, Sir John Downer. Bandaids were frequently stuck on the older man's genitalia and the addition of bubble bath into the water often made it look like a gay sauna. This was the front yard of my first business and I loved it.

The shop flourished in its first few months. Most of the new designers in Canberra approached me to take their clothes because Body Politics was about all there was for indie fashion. I pitched a good portion of my range as alternative workwear to Canberra's public servants and was somewhat influenced by the two big Japanese designers of the day: Akira and Issey Miyake.

My clothes tended to have a very tailored look. I liked high-waisted dresses that incorporated asymmetric draping made from soft wools. I liked to contrast this with wire buttons. It looked vaguely Edwardian but was quite architectural. I also made quite a few square- and pyramid-shaped berets. Japanese fashion was emerging along with Madonna's 'underwear as outer wear'. The Buffalo collective's work was still strong, showing men in leather skirts and Doc Martens with lace. Part early goth, part punk, part Wild West. We only took items from other young designers if they were in their first five years of designing. The items also had to be well made and suit the ethos of the shop. When I bought what I liked, it generally sold. When I tried designs that I thought were good but didn't necessarily like, they didn't sell. I learned quickly that it's much easier to sell something that you like.

By the late 1980s, Canberra was starting to develop a strong identity. It wasn't the cultural backwater that Melburnians and Sydneysiders portrayed it to be. The city had just reached 300,000 inhabitants, the Canberra Raiders had won their first Rugby League premiership and the ACT had wrenched itself away from the Commonwealth with the creation of its first local parliament.

Owning a small retail outlet in the hub of the city's night life was a boon for my social life and for many of my friends'. It was a hangout spot during the day. People would spend hours in the arcade just outside the shop. We had a cryptic-crossword morning crew, a 'still-doing-the-crossword' lunchtime crew and then a 'cheap champagne after work' crew. That one often went late into the night and then we would all pile up to the new nightclub that had opened above my shop called Heaven.

Like my father, I was always up for a party, and I loved Canberra's night life. There was a private stairway to Heaven next to my front door and it became well worn over the next year. It was the first gay and lesbian friendly club in Canberra. I went there with friends a few nights a week, and soon I was running regular fashion parades up there as well, not to mention partaking of the liberal supply of drugs going around. There were times in the early hours of the morning, after the parades and the dancing, when I would have sex in the stairway leading down to my shop, or in the shop itself under the dress racks. It didn't seem that wild at the time, but on reflection I was certainly living life to the full.

My customers came from a broad cross-section of the community. Business women looking to add some style to their Fletcher Jones basics, art school students, TV presenters, and, of course, Canberra's many public servants. But I was also seeing the young gay guys from the AIDs Council where I had recently started volunteering. A growing number of sex workers fleshed out my clientele.

But as 'the recession we had to have' started to bite, my client base began shrinking. I still had business women, like the future ACT Chief Minister Kate Carnell. They were looking for smart, one-off corporate designs, and still had cash to spend. Kate would end up becoming a good friend in later years and a great ally in decriminalising sex work and licensing X-rated videos.

The other group that had ready cash with an eye for independent fashion were the sex workers. I made new friends in the shop and soon got to understand the issues they were dealing with. Surprisingly, they were mostly political, and the women often commented on the appropriateness of my shop's name, and soon I found myself slipping imperceptibly into the world of sexual politics alongside the fashion industry.

* * * *

The ACT's sex worker outreach program was called WISE: Workers in Sex Employment. One of my best friends, Judith Taylor, had recently taken over the running of the organisation and over champagne one day she told me she was looking for ways to engage with sex workers outside of the brothels. For many sex workers, socialising with non-sex workers was challenging as they did not necessarily want to 'come out' to others about what they did for a living. So we discussed how we might be able to incorporate Body Politics into an informal event exclusively for sex workers.

My aunt Evelyn had a well-known restaurant in an upstairs building at 41 Whyalla Street, Fyshwick. It was set among the brothels, adult shops and white-goods warehouses. It was a large open space with beautiful timber floors that she had managed to imbue with that New York-loft feel. I had waitressed there and knew it well.

I asked Evelyn if I could hold a fashion parade after her restaurant customers had left and, in the summer of 1989, I started inviting Canberra's sex workers to 3 a.m. parties once all the brothels had closed. The show generally kicked off with about twenty sex workers sipping champagne, smoking and occasionally doing a little speed around an improvised catwalk, while the models strutted their stuff up until about 5 a.m. As the first rays of sunlight kissed the flat roofs of the plumbing suppliers and the service station next door, I put croissants in the oven and brewed strong coffee. Then everyone would slowly head home at about the same time as the orange Toranas and tradies' vans started appearing in the street, and they were in bed by 8 a.m. The 'whored' of tipsy sex workers that would trip out of that building dressed in the latest indie fashions must have been a crazy sight for all those workers.

For all its excesses, the late 1980s were good for young women. Our expectations were suddenly mixed with a degree of entitlement. Our shoulder pads were big and our hair was bold. The Australian fashion industry was relatively new, but it was growing and Sydney's Oxford Street was taking off. The same applied to sex work. Brothels now started to see a stream of young women who were sick of getting paid $15 an hour to wait on fat, abusive businessmen in pizza parlours when they could fuck them for ten times that amount and get complimented on their job.

The only downside was the economy. I had opened my business at the very beginning of the recession and the interest rate that Tiffany and I had signed up to would eventually split the partnership and then snuff out my little rag trade. It was around this time that we also saw the phasing out of clothing protections. I could sense one of those career shifts coming on that I would experience a few more times in the years ahead.

At the end of my second year in business, a local nightclub promoter, Gavan Evans, introduced me to a guy called Mark Tolley, a softly spoken barman at a nearby watering hole called De Depot. The bar was owned by a local businessman, Geoff De Depot, who also owned the ACT's large aquarium and zoo on the edge of the Scrivener Dam. Mark was calmness personified. His clear blue eyes and velvety voice were incredibly attractive. He and another friend of mine had just set up a pizza and pasta takeaway business from the back of De Depot called Faster Pasta and the place was humming. After we had been introduced, he flirted with me, bought me drinks and asked me out on a date. I soon moved in with him at his Dickson home only to discover that he lived with five cats. The allergies were wild and I lived on antihistamines for most of the eighteen months we shacked up together.

About six months after meeting Mark, I made the first formal vow of my life and announced our engagement. The trouble was, I made it to a bunch of our friends at the bar one night while Mark was at home asleep. Geoff De Depot offered his aquarium for the ceremony. In the style of Botticelli's *Venus*, I would dress as a mermaid and come out of a shell in the tunnel that ran underneath the shark tank. The whole ceremony would play out to the strains of the B-52's' 'Rock Lobster'. Mark found out about the plan the next day when he turned up for work and his mates all congratulated him. He immediately went out and bought me an engagement ring.

My mother, however, was appalled at these latest shenanigans and hatched a plan to disrupt this oceanic orgy. Using reverse psychology (again), she ran an ad in the betrothed section of the *Canberra Times*, the *Sydney Morning Herald* and *The Australian*, welcoming the engagement. I gagged badly when I saw it. To add insult to injury, Mum bought me a pair of ugly 'his & hers' bedside lamps from Fantastic Furniture as a present. I gagged again. The more she beat it up, the less enthusiastic I became. But I was in love with Mark and loved our relationship. A kick-arse party with all my friends would be fabulous. But the reality, which my mother could see, was that neither of us were really ready.

We called off the engagement, but stayed together. Several months later, I think we were both beginning to have serious doubts. Then I met an old boyfriend at the bar one night and ended up having sex with him in the toilets. After that, Mark and I both agreed to call it quits.

Just when my life was looking tired and cramped, my granny stepped in with an offer that would take me away from it all for a month, and we flew to Europe for a four-week holiday. It was just what I needed. I had a girlfriend step in and run the shop while I was away and I entered a completely different headspace for a month.

Coming back to Canberra, however, it was obvious that Body Politics was not making enough to cover rent, wages and the extortionate interest on the establishment loan. Rather than haggling with Tiffany over the increasing loan repayments, I asked my mother and father if they would guarantee a second loan to buy her out. I knew Tiffany wanted out and my thinking was that with just me at the helm I could turn things around. But after another few months it became clear that this wasn't going to happen, either. Still unable to let go of my baby, I took a job as the manager of women's wear at Country Road's Canberra Centre store. It was the first time I had worked for a corporate fashion house, and while I enjoyed the responsibility and challenges, I liked the regular and regulated pay even more, and I always managed to get good bonuses for my monthly sales. Little did the management at Country Road know that I was putting much of my salary back into keeping Body Politics afloat. It was a pattern of behaviour that I would adopt again and again with businesses and political ventures in the future, but after a couple of months even this became untenable. I succumbed to the inevitable, closed the shop, and went to my parents and the bank with a plan to pay them all back.

6

SEX WORK

At the beginning of 1990, my friend Judith from WISE was offered a new job working on national HIV/AIDS projects. This meant that her position as manager at WISE was up for grabs and she asked me if I would like to throw my hat in the ring. The job involved driving around to Canberra's fourteen brothels twice or three times a week with large quantities of condoms, lube, sex education material and, very discreetly, needles for a needle-exchange program.

As a fashion designer, I was now well known among Canberra sex workers, many of whom would have a strong say in who got the job. They'd seen me attend a few WISE meetings with Judith and hold my sex worker fashion parades. Moving to WISE would mean quitting my fun gig at Country Road and working late nights with sex workers and brothel owners. It also meant a drop in pay. I reckon I thought about it for at least a minute and then jumped at the chance.

At the time, WISE was funded by the federal Department of Health with matched funding from the ACT government. Under an agreement with the Commonwealth, all states in Australia had their own schemes under different names, but the national association of sex workers, the Scarlet Alliance, acted as an umbrella group for all the various state and territory groups.

None of these programs would have been possible except for the vision of then federal Health Minister, Neal Blewett, and his counterpart, Liberal MP, Peter Baume, back in the mid-1980s. As the AIDS epidemic started to spread, there was a fear in the community that one of the main potential transmission routes was the nation's unregulated and illegal sex industry. Given that 60 per cent of men who visited brothels were married or in long-term relationships, the spread of HIV into the heterosexual community was considered a real possibility. The fact that a large percentage (30 per cent) of men who visited male sex workers identified as heterosexual and were married or in relationships with women made this prospect even more scary for legislators and commentators.

Blewett and Baume recognised that peer education was the key to prevent HIV/AIDS from spreading. The grim reaper television advertisement was an important part of the mix—it went 'viral' and started a lot of community and government conversations. But most of the education and money was allocated to harm-reduction. Australia rolled out needle and syringe programs quickly and without fuss. AIDS organisations were funded to provide peer support and education for people with HIV/AIDS—mainly gay men. Intravenous (IV) drug user groups were funded to provide education about stopping the spread of HIV and there were sex worker organisations like WISE.

Whatever the public perception about the spread of HIV/AIDS, sex work was never going to be a huge transmitter in Australia because sex workers had always looked after their health. In fact, they were the first group to heed the warnings about HIV. Condom use was almost universal in the industry by the mid-1980s. On reflection, I think that the rush to judgement by politicians around sex work was the main reason these initiatives were funded so well. I mean, how could you trust a woman who has sex for money to protect herself, let alone her client? Notwithstanding these age-old discriminatory attitudes, Australia still led the way in harm reduction around HIV/AIDS, along with the transmission among the gay community and the IV drug using community.

Initially, WISE operated out of the AIDS Council offices before moving to its own digs in Fyshwick at 152 Townsville Street. Many of my working days were twelve hours or more, but I loved it. I was also still making clothes and had set up my industrial sewing machine in the new stationary room.

Sex workers would drop in to my office with any number of issues. Counselling and talking to women about sex work took up most of my time. Within the first month, I authored my first submission to government, published my first WISE newsletter and had my first complaint to the health minister from a brothel owner about the standard of my attire. The complainant was an older woman, trapped in 1970s fashion. Her establishment, the Touch of Class, was my least favourite Canberra brothel because it was the only one to have all workers on show whenever clients walked in. I gave her complaint short shrift.

The second month began with a visit from the Transport Workers Union (TWU) wanting to sign up sex workers in the ACT. On one level, it seemed like a good fit. Transporting clients to greater levels of pleasure. Moving bodies to blissful states. I could see the manifesto for the new relationship writ large on the walls of every brothel waiting room . . . The union reps argued in more pragmatic terms. Their members drove taxis and delivered laundry and other personal effects that were necessary to run brothels, and if a brothel owner started to mistreat sex workers, they would have them blacklisted. This last suggestion made me feel distinctly uneasy.

Most people think of brothels as men's spaces, but they're not. The rooms are designed for women to work in. The men are visitors. In some brothels, like the Northside Studio, I regularly counted over twenty women. It was incredibly rare for men to misbehave with such a weight of oestrogen in the building, and I only ever heard of two violent acts at my entire time at WISE. One occurred at a brothel in Mitchell that was hosting a large buck's night with strippers. Someone made the mistake of bringing in a couple of male security guards for the evening. Everything was going fine until the buck accidentally knocked over a vase and smashed it. To the madam and the girls, he was apologetic, and was beginning to offer to pay for it when the security guy got in his face. The buck resented it, his mates backed him up, the second guard came over, the testosterone flowed and in an instant a brawl erupted.

Most sex workers that I spoke to just weren't all that interested in joining a union. Most of them guarded their anonymity very closely—such was the stigma attached to the job—but equally important was that almost none of them saw their job as a sex worker as a lifelong career. It was a job to pay some bills, amass a nest egg or save for an overseas trip. Most women went into the industry with the intention to work for six months, though the average tenure was around two years.

Sex shop workers and shop assistants, on the other hand, laboured with the opposite problem: they couldn't get a union to take them on. Traditionally, the Shop, Distributive and Allied Employees Association (SDA) would have represented them, but this union, strongly influenced by Catholicism and praised by right-wing politicians, refused to have anything to do with people working behind the counter at the local adult shop.

Eros Foundation surveys in the years ahead would show that the adult retail industry had by far the largest number of LGBTIQ shop assistants (around 50 per cent) and this may have contributed to the homophobic union's refusal to take on our members. Porn, butt plugs, nipple clamps and pony tails, on the other hand, were probably not going to excite the local SDA officials to drop in for a chat as much as a display of semi-hard Dutch gouda or a stack of Stroopwafels.

In the early 1990s, the Australian Taxation Office started to move on sex workers because many of them weren't paying any tax. It was a sizeable industry (only a few years later, I would commission a study for the Eros Foundation that looked at the average number of clients a sex worker would see multiplied by the number of sex workers in the country. It showed that Australia's brothels and single sex workers catered for around twelve million visits a year, and generated $1.2 billion dollars in revenue. This equated to an average of 2.6 sex worker visits per year for every man in the country).

Most sex workers will tell you that while the job itself is pretty easy, what is hard is telling people what you do for a living. The main reason sex workers didn't want to pay tax was that without any guarantees of privacy they didn't want to disclose to a government agency how they earned their incomes. Another important reason was that the profession was not recognised in law. While being a sex worker may have been legal, running a brothel certainly wasn't, which made working in one a grey area. It wasn't like telling someone you were a psychologist or a personal trainer. Most sex workers had felt the sting of discrimination in ways that people in conventional jobs never would. So while many told me they were happy to have 20 per cent taken out of their earnings each week, they simply could not take the chance of being outed. But since they used the roads and their kids went to school, I told them they should really be paying tax, too. On the positive side, they could claim deductions for clothes, hair, makeup, fitness regimes and even their watches (time is very important to sex workers).

However there have always been questions about whether sex workers are employees or whether they are self-employed. The ATO was keen for brothel owners to pay the super for their workers because it was easier for the bureaucrats to collect. But most sex workers I spoke to were adamant that they worked for themselves and were no different to a contract landscape gardener who might have three or four clients at any one time.

Although my job was primarily outreach and designed to make the work in brothels as safe as possible, the health department tolerated a holistic approach, which meant I could also do a reasonable amount of lobbying for the decriminalisation of sex work. I was there to represent the best interests of sex workers and having the profession legal was in the best interest of all. Not long after this, I became the main conduit between Canberra sex workers and the

ACT Legislative Assembly MP Michael Moore. He was aiming to present a bill to the new parliament to legalise sex work, which meant authoring all sorts of submissions.

The more I spoke to people about sex work, the more I realised they really had no idea about the industry. I decided to hold an 'open brothel day' as a way of showing what was behind those closed doors. It worked a treat. The majority of Canberra's brothels opened their doors for a few hours on a Saturday and the public poured in. Most were surprised that they were clean, modern and more like a five-star hotel than the den of iniquity they had always imagined. The visitors were mainly women and they were curious, asking a wide range of questions. Some, I suspect, were considering whether they would apply to work.

The job was full of drama and intrigue. Driving back to my office one night, I noticed an ambulance out the front of the Crystal Palace on Newcastle Street. This was never a good sign: most of the time they came for clients who'd had heart attacks. So I chucked a u-ie in my canary-yellow Mitsubishi Sigma and angled into the driveway that led to the rear car park. I walked in the back door to see if there was anything I could do.

Inside I was confronted with a very plump sex worker lying on a gurney and looking for all the world like a wench from a Monty Python sketch. She had an ambo on either side and she was groaning—but not in a good way. She was well known in the business for her medieval dress-ups and was a member of the local medieval club. No doubt she had a number of clients also into that scene. After they wheeled her out, I was told that somehow, and for some reason, she had hauled herself up into the ceiling cavity in her work room and fallen through. Fortunately, she had fallen on the only sofa in the room and was later pronounced fit for her next gallant.

Heart attacks in brothels are more common than you would think. Men in their fifties and sixties who live otherwise sedentary lives are prime candidates when they get down and dirty with a twenty- or 30-year-old women and engage in an hour of frenetic sex. They might as well run a marathon. The moral issues can be as important as the medical ones. It raises a lot of issues around counselling for families of men who have a heart attack at the local brothel, but sex workers, too, need counselling. It's distressing to take a $250 fee from a client, make friends over a glass of wine, have an intimate conversation, sex, orgasm, and then suddenly he has a heart attack and dies on top of you.

Hypocrisy was never far from sex work in the national capital, and the World Council of Churches international conference held in Canberra one weekend in late 1991 proved no exception. As the conference was getting underway on the Friday night, I visited the Northside Studio, which was upstairs and open 24 hours. As I got out of the car, I noticed a small gathering just inside the brothel's front door. There were about twenty men of various ages and dress styles queuing up the stairs. As I walked up, I saw that their group leader was speaking to the manager. The one thing that they all had in common was a little white calico bag with *WCC* stamped on the side. Inside, more men filled the waiting rooms. Later in the evening, the story was the same at other establishments. It was the busiest weekend that Canberra's brothel owners could ever recall.

If the clients of sex workers were many and varied, so were the sex workers. Although many women I worked with closely were in their twenties, there were still plenty of older women. One who stood out had been a regular at the Touch of Class for over a decade. She was quite matronly, in her fifties, and wore box-pleated skirts with Fletcher Jones blouses. She had a regular clientele that included wealthy older men who regularly booked her for dinner and conversation. But I was amazed at how many younger men booked her as well. During her time in the industry, she had put her two boys through private schooling, bought a house and created a comfortable lifestyle for her family. When she finally retired, she told me that it was only because her eldest son had turned eighteen. Her greatest fear was that he would see her there or have one of his mates try to book her.

It wasn't a far-fetched scenario, either. One night at the Northside Studio I was sitting in the girls' room pulling condoms and lube from my bag when I heard a loud male voice coming from the waiting area. As a place to meet clients, it wasn't best practice in the industry and most other brothels had some sort of two-way mirror or other scanning device to stop husbands, boyfriends or university lecturers from discovering who worked there. With no way to vet clients, however, that night one of the girls had suddenly come face-to-face with her father. He immediately started screaming at her. The girl was dying of embarrassment and felt awful.

As I walked out to see what all the fuss was about, one of the other workers piped up to the father: 'Well, what are you doing here?' At this point he burst into tears, and father and daughter retired to a more private space to talk. Not long after they both left separately after exchanging promises that neither would return or tell her mother.

* * * *

'Jumping the counter' is a euphemism used to describe the moment a receptionist in a brothel decides to become a sex worker. Generally this happens because the receptionist sees how much money her sisters are making and wants a slice of the action. As the manager of an outreach program for brothels, I wasn't really in a position to jump any counters, and yet about six months into the job I fell into part-time sex work.

My first job wasn't really about money, either. I had been visiting one of Canberra's original brothels, Tiffany's, which was situated between the Tool King and Hoods Carpet Court on the corner of Barrier and Isa Streets in Fyshwick. It featured the traditional red-light neon out the front, lots of 1970s timber veneer and original shag pile carpets. On the night in question, I had just climbed the rusted-up staircase at the rear of the building that was used by workers to avoid clients and arrived in the girls' room with my bag of tricks. Everyone was busy and I sat chatting to the receptionist as I waited for the women to finish their jobs, but two of the four women working had extended their bookings. This was a problem for the receptionist: she had a client waiting that she had assured would be attended to shortly. I poked my head around the corner to take a look at him. I hadn't had a lot of sex lately and was horny, so I said to the receptionist that I would do the job if he was interested. He was.

'What's your name?'

'Peter.'

'Hi, Peter. I'm . . .'

Suddenly, the narrow path I was walking down opened up into a broader vista, and in a flash I knew I wouldn't give Peter my real name. Perversely, it was my granny's that tumbled out of my mouth.

'I'm Heather. And what do you do, Peter?'

'I'm a plumber.'

'Ah ha . . . Okay, then. Would you like to come with me?'

And with that I lead Peter down the hallway and into the first vacant room I could see. It just happened to be the spa room, which I thought was fitting for a young plumber.

I turned on the taps, squirted some bubbles, and said, 'Now, how long will you be staying tonight, Peter?'

'An hour would be fine, thanks.'

'Okay. That will be $150.'

He fumbled around in his King Gees and pulled out a small clip of notes, peeling off three fifties.

'Make yourself comfortable and I'll be back soon.'

Back out in the front room, the receptionist looked at me and smiled as I handed her the cash.

'Smooth,' she said. 'I'll buzz you in 50 minutes.'

Sex with Peter was enjoyable and I left Tiffany's that night with an extra $100 in my pocket and a new income plan. Over the next six months, I ended up doing a few shifts. During that time, I never had a request that was weird or disrespectful, and I met quite a few interesting and engaging men—most grateful that I was prepared to have sex with them and not ask for their phone number afterwards. Most men get that. They are after a one-hour relationship with a woman who is always pleased to see them, never has her period and is looking forward to having sex with them.

There is often not a lot of sex in a one-hour booking. First there is the welcome, including a physical STD check, then the transaction and a bit of small talk. So many men just wanted to talk and the sex gave them a reason to do that. Of course, some men were looking for the latest *Penthouse* model, but most of them just wanted a woman they thought they would get along with. This was brought home to me when I did an impromptu survey of clients one night at Tiffany's for WISE. I asked them what they were they looking for, what attracted them in a sex worker, and even about what clothes turned them on. Most of the comments were ordinary: 'I look for the best smile' or 'A girl with a bright dress stands out.' No pretensions to film stars or goddesses here!

Sex workers are believed to know every trick in the book and to a large extent it's true. They swap stories and experiences of sex at a far greater rate than women in other occupations and they deal with sexual responses from a wide variety of men each day. Working at WISE, we coined the term 'sex workers are the sex educators of the world'. The health checks and general discussion around sex led many clients to be a lot more informed about sexual-health matters. When they were doing something uncomfortable or clumsy, sex workers would suggest a better technique. There were times when men would tell me that their wives weren't interested in having sex with them and I thought, 'Well, if you're doing that, no wonder they aren't.'

I continued to learn things each week I was in the industry. A couple of my regulars were young guys in their early twenties who would often come in early on a Friday or Saturday night before heading out on the town. I asked them how they went if they cracked on to a girl after being at the brothel only a few hours before. That was the idea, they said. If they had sex before they went out, they were much more likely to get a girl because there wasn't the same pressure to score. With that out of the way, girls were much more interested in them, they claimed. My mother, the queen of reverse psychology, would have loved them.

Though many sex workers were of one mind on most of the political issues of the day, one issue that divided them was the old debate over sex work and porn. Most sex workers I knew would recoil in abject horror at the thought of appearing on film or in a magazine, open to the gaze of potentially millions of people. Likewise, many porn stars I had met were equally horrified at the thought of having sex for money with a stranger.

For the record, my definition is that sex work is sex with strangers in a private place, while porn is sex with someone you know in a public place. Of course sex workers often see the same client many times, sometimes over years, and a relationship develops, while porn stars, conversely, will occasionally end up in front of the camera with someone they just met. But, by and large, the two professions have quite different sets of criteria even though they both involve sex for money. Governments have great difficulty understanding these differences.

I remember one English sex worker who made an X-rated film with her husband. They were both very attractive and the film had a certain style, even though it was a simple film depicting two people in love and having some great sex. It was natural and it sold well. One evening at the brothel she worked at, we were all discussing the film. Other sex workers were appalled. How could you do that? Put yourself in the public eye? The thought of being public about enjoying sex with your husband was unthinkable. Personally, I was bemused by the reactions. I didn't have a problem with porn or sex work. When the infamous US porn star Nina Hartley came out to Australia in 1992, she told me she could never be a sex worker.

She'd had many offers but just couldn't do it. She thought it was beneath her. Nina and I hit it off famously, but I could never understand her attitude on this—along with her owning a gun!

The issue of sex slavery and trafficking was gaining a lot of traction in the media around this time. Scarlet Alliance and other groups were hearing that allegations of widespread trafficking were frequently made up by the growing number of 'saviour' groups around the world receiving lucrative government grants to help 'trafficked' women. In this, they were supported by conservative male politicians who were generally misogynistic. To Australian sex workers working alongside foreign sex workers, it was obvious that these practices were rare in Australia—they had an eye for their colleagues' welfare and could understand why they were working in Australia and how they got there. Sex worker advocacy groups were in the brothels seeing first-hand what was going on. It was clear that if governments wanted to reduce the opportunity for exploitation, they needed to allow overseas sex workers access to proper working visas that would enable them to work legally in our brothels, to pay tax and to earn superannuation. Under an open system, crime gangs that wanted to traffic women would find it impossible to get a toe hold in the industry.

But it was going to be an uphill battle. When Pru Goward became head of the Office of the Status of Women in 1997, she called a roundtable discussion on sex slavery. In attendance were police, immigration officials, public servants, academics and representatives from international agencies. Almost all of them were anti-sex work and came to the table with preconceived ideas about the industry. Many thought it was distasteful and women in poverty should work in factories and learn to sew rather than do sex work. In their eyes, there was no way for a woman to consent to come to Australia to work as a sex worker. These attitudes still haven't changed—Temporary Skill Shortage (TSS) visas are available to all legal industries except sex work.

Most of the international sex workers I met during my time at WISE in the early 1990s were permanent residents or from the UK and New Zealand on working visas. Some of the women from Asian countries found that rather than entering a legitimate contract with a broker to work in a brothel in Australia for a fixed term, these terms had changed on arrival and never in their favour. For a few, this meant ending up in illegal brothels, often under horrible conditions with long hours, limited freedom of movement and, in some cases, unprotected sex. I heard of many sex workers found to be breaching visa conditions who refused to admit to immigration officials that they had readily agreed to move to Australia as a sex worker (usually they were sex workers in their home countries).

In a meeting with then Attorney-General Philip Ruddock years later, in 2006, I put it to him that because the government could not bring itself to issue working visas to bona fide sex workers, crime gangs had moved in and organised mainly student visas for sex workers and found them places to work. These gangs were demanding fees of $50,000 a year from the woman from her $100,000 earnings. The criminals organising these deals also made the sex worker pay the $50,000 before she could take her remaining $50,000. Frequently, this meant that if the worker was busted in the first six months of her stay by immigration and sent home, she would not get any money at all, while the black market operators still pocketed their share. Many sex workers from poor Asian backgrounds were still willing to do this, though, in the hope that they could take home some money. Ruddock's reply to my suggestion was that he would never get a proposal to grant legitimate working visas for prostitutes through Cabinet.

In early 1992, I became president of the Australian Sex Workers Association, the Scarlet Alliance. Because Scarlet was a delegate of the Australian Federation of AIDS Organisations, I also became a member of the board of AFAO. My six months as Scarlet Alliance president was a challenging time with some moments of hilarity.

It came to a sudden end when a group of young lads that I knew had tricked up an old 1964 EH Holden and entered it in Australia's longest running charity motoring event, the Variety Bash. They had sourced sponsorship from a number of X-rated video companies and I had organised a brothel sponsorship as well. The car was emblazoned with a dozen brightly coloured logos for companies like the Mature Media Group, Leisuremail and Channel 69. Before setting out on the trip they had removed the back seat and filled it full of X-rated videos and stuck brothel vouchers in the glove box. During the trip they used these items to barter petrol and accommodation with almost every venue happy to trade. I put out a media release on WISE masthead promoting the event and the fact that the charity was being sponsored by adult industry companies. The employee-based sex worker group, however, saw me as sleeping with the enemy and promoting the interests of the bosses, not the workers. They weren't happy and that was the end of my time with Scarlet and WISE.

7

SOUL MATES

I had first noticed my soul mate, Robbie Swan, in a newspaper headline in 1988. We had been circling each other for years on the outer orbit of two large groups of friends without ever meeting. We both studied at Canberra University—he in the early 1970s and me in the 1980s. Neither of us finished our respective courses and we had left under slightly scandalous circumstances in our second year. Robbie was busted for growing 600 marijuana plants while doing a creative writing course and received a suspended jail sentence for his efforts. The profits of his crop were destined for the Vietnam moratorium movement. Sick of being shadowed by police, and tired of the Canberra drug scene, he moved to Switzerland in the early 1970s. Here he became a florist and studied at the Maharishi's meditation ashram on Lake Lucerne. Arriving back in Canberra in the mid-1970s, he set up a meditation centre and a health food shop.

In the early 1980s, he was the editor of the glossy alternative-lifestyle magazine, *Simply Living*. He then co-founded the irreverent and heavily sued political humour and satire magazine, *Matilda*, where a couple of my friends had hung out, and before joining forces with the merchants of porn in Canberra he produced Phillip Adams' radio show on 2UE in Sydney. He also had two young daughters from an earlier relationship. For the best part of ten years, I interacted with people who had done his meditation courses or were friends with him. But still I never met him.

It was a front-page story in the *Canberra Times* in 1988 that first brought him to my attention. He had just become a lobbyist for the Adult Video Industry Association of Australia and was trying to save X-rated videos from being banned. He figured that the debate had been hijacked by religious types and forced into a moral-panic mode. Needing to lighten the debate somehow, he sent a bunch of X-rated videos to federal Cabinet members, all handpicked for their portfolios. Treasurer Paul Keating got an X-rated accountancy film called *Liquid Assets*, Gareth Evans as Minister for Foreign Affairs got *Lust on the Orient Express*, and the National Party leader, Ian Sinclair, got a video called *An Unnatural Act*. I thought it was hilarious. Later that year his campaign was successful when a meeting of the Labor Caucus refused to back a proposed ban that had been pushed by the Catholic bishops. Prime Minister Bob Hawke was cagey when door-stopped outside the party room meeting. 'There are no deep throats around here,' he said. The decision was widely reported, and over the next couple of years I started to follow the debates around censorship as I was lobbying for legal prostitution.

In 1989, Robbie was in the news again. The ACT's first Labor government had fallen while they were trying to apply a retail tax to the burgeoning X-rated industry. The new chief minister, Trevor Kaine, had described the tax as a 'franchise on flesh' and 'loot from lust'. In the parliamentary debates that followed, the balance of power party, the Residents Rally, drew attention to the fact that Robbie had handed over a cheque for $8500 to the ALP on the day of the previous election. It was a line-ball call as to whether it should have been declared in the returns for that election or the next. The Rally's leader, well-known Canberra human rights lawyer, Bernard Collaery, thought it scandalous that Labor would take a donation from the porn industry, and he withdrew his party's support for the Labor government and it collapsed. Collaery's party then joined the Liberals to form a new government.

Once in government, they wasted no time in announcing their own tax on porn. Their 40 per cent wholesale tax, however, was nothing other than a de facto ban. The porn industry was in disarray because, unlike a retail tax, a wholesale tax of that size would have quickly sent everyone broke. The industry quickly mounted a High Court challenge (the now famous Capital Duplicators case), which ended up threatening the foundations of federal government revenue from excises around the country. The porn industry was ultimately successful, but it cost the main protagonist, John Lark, dearly. The legal fees almost bankrupted him, and as he was the major player in the ACT's X-rated industry, everything was suddenly on shaky ground. A few months later, the ACT's second election loomed with porn a major issue and me still blissfully unaware that I was about to make my debut into this political cock fight.

In the run up to this second general election in February 1992, I received a phone call from Robbie's best mate—a popular-music entrepreneur around town. I already knew Gavan Evans quite well, and when he asked me if I would like to meet Robbie and have dinner with him I thought it was a joke of some kind or a terrible blind date. But, always up for a challenge, I agreed. You can imagine my surprise when, on the Friday evening of the dinner, Gavan and I pulled up outside an older-style red brick house in Hooker Street, in the vice-regal suburb of Yarralumla. As far as I could see, I was the only hooker there. It was the first of many serendipitous markers around our relationship.

Robbie greeted us warmly and we followed him along a path lined with primulas and pansies to his front door. We all sat down at an enormous antique table that looked like it had once been used in a mechanic's shop. It went from one end of his dining room to the other and on either side were two equally long antique church pews. The walls sported advertising signs for a magazine called *Raiders Country*, 'the official organ' of the Canberra Raiders rugby league team. This was a magazine that Robbie and his co-publisher at *Matilda* magazine had collaborated on along with the porn industry's leader, John Lark. Photos of writhing and sweating Mal Meningas and Laurie Daleys lined the hallways interspersed with cover shots of a very different magazine called *Ecstasy*, which showed writhing and sweating porn stars like Ginger Lynn and Jamie Summers. The lounge room walls were covered with framed photos of the earth from outer space and constellations of stars like the Pleiades. A large photo and quote from Albert Einstein hung above an ersatz Nick Scali black leather lounge. I was struggling to come to terms with the personality that lay behind it all.

At this point, Gavan took his leave and Robbie brought out some food. Tofu and rice. I was expecting steak and chips from a bloke with a gold chain around his neck. Instead I was being waited on by a long-haired hippy in hemp pants. Later, over coffee, we smoked some incredibly aromatic weed that he had grown himself in the backyard and cured in cade oil. It was like smoking a lump of coal, but the THC worked a treat.

'So, how's it going legalising sex work?' he asked.

'Pretty good, actually,' I replied. 'I think we'll see a bill in the Legislative Assembly before the election.'

'I was going to ask you about that. Are you running a campaign against the Libs?'

I told him that WISE was producing pamphlets and writing letters and the usual lobbying stuff.

'And do you think there's a way to expose their hypocrisy around sex?' he asked.

I didn't really have an answer to this. Besides, I had noticed that he was zeroing in on me. It was a hot summer's night and I probably wasn't wearing anything under my yellow silk frock. The combination of male attention and good weed was beginning to make me sweat a little.

'Have you thought about running as an independent yourself?' he then asked. 'There's plenty of people who'd back your campaign.'

'What? You want me to run on a porn ticket in the election?'

'Well, it would be a civil liberties ticket that would focus on porn and prostitution. But it would also be about other basic freedoms, like freedom of trade and freedom of expression.'

I'd never thought of going into politics. I'd had sex with a politician, but that was politics going into me . . . The thought of me pushing my agenda into the local parliament was not unattractive, though. We talked a bit more about the nuts and bolts of a campaign, and by the end of the night I was sold. We shook hands. I could tell he wanted to shake more than that, but I wasn't having a bar of it. I had been going out with a handsome Manuka restaurateur and I was pretty happy with that. Still, something lingered after the handshake that I wasn't sure would easily wash off.

* * * *

Robbie called me a week later and we went to lunch at a popular Manuka club. After the meal, he asked me back to his place for coffee. I knew the invite for what it was. Strangely enough, my relationship with the restaurateur had flattened somewhat since that first dinner and I could feel myself shifting gears. At 27, and with a dozen relationships under my belt, it was a feeling that was more than just changing boyfriends. It was a whole-body experience. The vision of a new career that Robbie was putting to me was frankly much more attractive than the thought of a new boyfriend. I also wasn't going to just fall into bed with him like a client. He wasn't paying me. So, over coffee, I challenged him in a way that I knew would also challenge me.

'I'd like to wait for a couple of months until the election's over,' I said. 'Then I'll fuck you.'

Most men don't get the complex emotional and intellectual mechanisms at play when a sex worker says no to sex with someone they actually care for but yes to someone they don't. I'm not sure he did either, but eventually he said, 'Okay. If that's what it takes.'

Political news travels faster in a pre-election period than at any other time in the electoral cycle. A week after I had agreed to run as an independent, I received a call from the local transport minister, Craig Duby, asking me to join his new party. He had formed the No

Self-Government Party and won three seats at the first ACT election in 1989. Canberrans, meanwhile, had begun to realise that however much they protested about being forced off the federal government's nipple, the ACT was now a separate entity and self-government was here to stay. Craig's party name was unlikely to win him a protest vote at the second election in 1992. Moreover, as Minister for Transport, he had twice been convicted of drunk driving and only a few weeks out from the election the *Canberra Times* reported that he had been taken into custody after running into another car and then released without charge. He needed a makeover badly and had registered a new party of independents called the Hare-Clark Independence Party.

Craig had another candidate already locked in with him, but they wanted a woman on the ticket as well. I met with him at his favourite watering hole—the Olympic Soccer Club in Civic—to thrash out a deal and soon became their number two candidate. His other running mate was a Thai Buddhist monk, and as the three of us took our campaign on the road the new party soon became known as The Drunk, the Monk and the Spunk.

Meanwhile, Hooker Street started looking more and more like General Joseph Hooker's military operations room with whiteboards, maps and butcher's paper everywhere. In among the politics of the place, I became increasingly aware of the presence of a much older woman. Frumpy dresses, large gloves and large orthopaedic-looking shoes kept turning up in the hall cupboards and in bathroom laundry baskets. My first questions to Robbie about it were met with what I interpreted as mild embarrassment. Maybe he was dating someone twice his age? I backed off.

Then one day I received a letter at my WISE office from a Ms Caroline Cumming-Sweetly professing love and admiration and asking to meet me. It was accompanied by a video of Ms Sweetly talking about censorship. She was a geeky-looking women in her mid-thirties with a thick eastern European accent and Nana Mouskouri glasses, and she was on the rampage about government censorship of her new magazine. She wore a grey flannel twin set and pearls with a fluffy rabbit's foot brooch. Even on her show reel she reeked of Chanel No.5. The only attractive thing about her was her sparkling eyes and her tousled blonde locks that were tied up in a loose-fitting bun. Then I noticed that she was wearing a scarf that had come from my shop! It was bizarre. I'd never had such a weird proposal from a stranger . . . and yet there was something familiar about her. I put the letter to one side and watched the tape again. Then, like a lens gradually being twisted into focus, I realised the truth. It was Robbie in drag!

He had been secretly dressing as a woman for six months as part of an elaborate hoax to promote his hardcore women's magazine *Ecstasy*, funded by John Lark's Mature Media Group. He had a female art director and a former policewoman writing agony aunt columns, but he couldn't find anyone to fit the role of editor. So he decided to do it himself. Gavan Evans had introduced him to my old friend, Chris Beige, from Channel 10's makeup department. Chris was able to transform Robbie into a convincing middle-aged woman who wanted to break new boundaries in publishing in Australia. They took photos and made videos extolling the new feminist porn magazine and sent them to various media outlets. Following an interview with Ramona Koval on 3LO, the hag was well and truly out of the bag and had shot to minor celebrity status within a few weeks. Jana Wendt even interviewed Robbie for *A Current Affair* without apparently noticing the gender bend. When an old *Truth* journo that Robbie had known for years called to ask 'Caroline' out on a date, he knew it was time to give it up. But before that could happen, Caroline Cumming-Sweetly aroused the interest of investigative reporter Frank Robson at the *Weekend Australian* magazine.

The exposé was brutal. Robbie resigned from the local school board, neighbours avoided him in the street and his kids were heckled in the schoolyard. The crusty old Tasmanian senator Brian Harradine claimed it was a national disgrace and in a speech in the Senate argued for Robbie to be banned forever from giving evidence to Senate Committees. He claimed that Robbie had sent a submission to a parliamentary committee as his alter ego arguing for women's access to hardcore erotica. 'How could you trust a man who would con the Parliament to deliver a message on filth and depravity?' he asked.

The only positive thing that came out of the exposé, Robbie later told me, were two phone calls from old girlfriends who wanted to have sex with him as a woman. This was my entrée into the porno *Tootsie* show.

* * * *

One of my major opponents at the coming election was the anti-sex crusader Dennis Stevenson. A former NSW police officer, he had the smarts, like Craig Duby, to see that half the ACT population did not want self-government when Bob Hawke and his Minister for Territories, Clyde Holding, forced it on them. He set up the

Abolish Self-Government Party and got himself elected in 1989. He then became famous for living in his Legislative Assembly office, converting the sofa that his constituents sat on during the day into his bed at night, and even having the milk and newspapers delivered to his publicly funded office. But it was his ability to convince the local Christian groups that he was really one of them and to use the X-rated debate to raise his profile that made him a worry. Besides, a six-foot politician who could take a bath in a basin was a force to be reckoned with.

In late 1991, in the wake of the Caroline saga, Robbie argued that acts of guerrilla warfare were a legitimate part of political campaigning, especially against crusty old conservatives who used incumbency and privilege to their advantage. He was no stranger to pulling political stunts. A couple of years earlier, he had set up a photo shoot on the steps of ASIO headquarters. Somehow he conned the ASIO security guards into allowing him to photograph two porn stars, one dressed as a spook and the other in a policewoman's uniform, groping and kissing each other under the ASIO house sign. He used the photos in a fictional porn shoot about two undercover agents that was later published in Australian *Hustler*. It was as audacious as it was stupid. He could have easily been busted for not much political advantage. I admired his courage and sense of humour in pulling these things off, but some of them were just a bridge too far for me. His plan to disrupt Dennis Stevenson's anti-porn rally in Albert Hall had me in two minds, too, but it went ahead.

Robbie and Gavan drove to Fyshwick on the afternoon before the anti-porno prayer fest where they purchased two small bottles of helium and a large blow up doll called Kylie from the Fantasy Lane adult shop. It was a scorching day, and as the cool of the evening descended they drove to the venue on the shores of Lake Burley Griffin and waited until it filled with the party faithful. As soon as everyone was inside, the pranksters moved in and hid behind the large cypress pines that lined the building. As Dennis Stevenson's soothing baritone voice started to fill the hall, they unrolled the painted plastic Kylie. They attached the rubber hose of the helium bottle to the nozzle on her anus and opened the valve. Kissed by the helium prince, she slowly awakened from her boxed slumber.

As she popped and crackled to life, her magnificent mouth pushed out into the perfect O. Hard and taut, she strained forward, and as Dennis began to wind up his crowd about the dangers of organised smut, Robbie and Gavan rolled her on to her tummy, cupped her silicone breasts and plastic pudenda with their hands and gave a mighty shove as they stood at the hall's open French doors. Kylie travelled flat like a stealth bomber for the few metres it took to get her inside, where she soared upward. The effect was electrifying. The miscreants didn't wait around to see her arrive at her final resting place—stuck somewhere up on the ten-metre high ceiling of the Albert Hall—and high-tailed it out of there as fast as they could.

15 February 1992 was election day, and it arrived with just a slight sense of ennui. It had been three months since I had met Robbie. We had worked together, swapped stories and drawn up plans. In the last week of the campaign, we had started kissing and engaging in some pretty passionate exchanges. Now I wanted the election over so I could either take up a seat in the parliament or move on to the next adventure.

The official tally room was located in the gym at the Canberra TAFE college only metres from where I had studied fashion design a few years earlier. We drove into the car park at the eastern end of the college and nudged Robbie's old charcoal grey 190C Mercedes under the gum trees that formed a border with St John's Church—the preferred place of worship for Kevin Rudd in the years ahead. We were reasonably well known to many of the MPs and journalists in the room, and I did a number of interviews as the results started to tumble in.

At about 8 p.m., my vote was not looking bad, but not great either. There was still a chance they hadn't counted the inner-city booths where I would do much better than out in the nappied valleys. By 10 p.m. it was clear we weren't going to win, even though my vote was respectable. Later, an electoral official would confide that I had got the fourth highest personal vote.

I was feeling good and enthusiastic, but I'd had enough of politics. And, besides, I had a pledge to honour. As the night wound down, I grabbed Robbie's hand and lead him back out to the car park, waving at well-wishers and friends along the way. Robbie unlocked the car and we got into the back seat, laughing and happy in each other's company. I rolled a big three-paper joint that we smoked while recalling the night's events. I like to think that what happened next was an exchange of marriage vows, the first delivered draped over the front seat with my hands on the steering wheel, the second on the backseat with my feet out the window, and the final 'I do' uttered while straddling Robbie in the passenger's seat.

We hadn't won the election, but it was a helluva after-party that lasted well into the next morning. Almost immediately, Robbie and

I fell into a deep and abiding relationship. Just a few weeks later, the former bass player for The Go-Betweens, John Willsteed, formed a new band called the Drunk, the Monk and the Spunk. It was a fitting epilogue to my first tilt at politics.

8

BIRDS OF PARADISE

As often happens after a life-changing event, my elevated mood started to plateau in the weeks following the election. Making an emotional commitment to Robbie meant a major shakeup of my lifestyle and an involvement in politics that I was beginning to have doubts about. I was still only 27 and wasn't sure I wanted to be locked into anything. I kept recalling my childhood dream about God wanting me to become a nun and how I pleaded with her to just let me have another year of fun. It was clear that Robbie and I had strong feelings for each other, but also clear that we both wanted an open relationship that guaranteed each of us space.

By the end of March 1992, my mood had worsened and I was beginning to get the migraine headaches that I thought I had left behind in adolescence. I knew I had to flee Canberra and just sit on a beach. Cairns would do nicely, I thought. My best friend, Judith, lived there now and I was owed three weeks' annual leave from WISE.

Because the beaches can be loaded with stinging and biting things at that time of year, I booked a scuba-diving course as a means to spend time in the ocean.

Cairns is home to many colourful birds known collectively as Birds of Paradise. The males of the species sport intense, iridescent blocks of colour on their plumage, framed by the deepest velvety blacks. They flaunt these colours, and even make them appear to ripple and then disappear in sexualised dances designed to attract females. The name also applies to a popular flower around Cairns: the equally colourful Strelitzia or Bird of Paradise flower. It's so named because it displays intense oranges, purples and reds. Like the birds, the plant is an unusual sexual strategist because it uses sunbirds to help it reproduce rather than insects or wind. The birds alight on a spathe that sticks out from the flower, meaning they can easily feed on the sweet nectar that Strelitzia produces. As they land on this sprung perch, they force the flower open, stimulating the stamen to 'ejaculate' pollen all over the bird's claws. The bird feeds, then takes off and lands on a different plant. At the point of impact, pollen granules are forced into the air and swirl all around the flower. Some of them are fortunate enough to land on the flower's lady part (the pistil), which means they germinate and fertilise the ovary from whence the seeds for the next generation are born.

In the early 1990s, Cairns was home to a third species of Birds of Paradise: an escort agency. And although it didn't house many iridescent birds or brightly coloured flowers, there was a fair bit of preening and plenty of pollen being shunted around. Most of it wrapped in latex. The agency was owned by a woman in Canberra who I knew from my outreach work. She ran Club 77 in Fyshwick for quite a while and she was an organised and honest person. I had prearranged a few weeks of work with her at the escort agency so I would have some money to pay for my scuba course and a comfortable stay in a four-star hotel. My first client was an ordinary young bloke who had been working out in the mines and was staying at a cheap motel on the south end of Cairns on holiday. He was fairly typical of most clients up that way.

****

At the beginning of the second week, things took a more unusual turn. One job led me to an upmarket block of serviced apartments not far from the wharf. The client was an average-looking middle-aged man who greeted me at the door, and after paying his $130 he introduced me to his son sitting in the living room. I thought it a bit unusual but wasn't unduly worried by his presence; I had developed a good antenna after only a couple of years in the industry. I said hello to the son and headed off to the bedroom with his dad. After his hour was up, we walked out to the living room and before I could say goodbye he asked me if his son could book me for another hour. I have to say I did baulk at the vaguely icky sense of the father sharing his intimate experience. I couldn't imagine my father or brother in this situation, nor any of my uncles or older male friends. But he wasn't my son and, besides, out through the front windows I could see the harbour and the dive boats anchored, calling to me. So it was back to the bedroom for an hour with a rather awkward and embarrassed young man.

It was a serendipitous time for me to be doing escort work in Queensland. The state was beginning to gear up for an election and prostitution was a big-ticket item. It had figured prominently in major police corruption according to the Fitzgerald Inquiry in the late 1980s and was the subject of a Criminal Justice Commission (CJC) Issues paper in early 1991. Later that year, the commission produced its landmark report on the industry where it established that there were 3500 visits to sex workers each week throughout Queensland, making it a multimillion-dollar black market industry. The Birds of Paradise was one of 86 illegal escort agencies being run in Queensland, and the report estimated that there were a further 26 illegal brothels and 36 illegal massage parlours scattered around the state. The CJC had recommended decriminalising the industry as a way of taking it out of the hands of organised crime and corrupt police, as well as allowing best practice for the control of communicable diseases like HIV/AIDS. Their preferred model was for small brothels of no more than ten workers to be permitted to set up around the state, and they also allowed for single sex workers to work legally from their own homes.

For the reformist Labor premier, Wayne Goss, the recommendations seemed tailor-made. He was happy to decriminalise homosexuality, abolish the corrupt police special branch, introduce far-reaching discrimination laws and actively put more women into the top jobs. Agreeing with the 63 per cent of Queenslanders who supported legalising brothels in the CJC report was the logical thing for him to do. Incredibly, he faltered. Not only on sex work, but on abortion, too. Many blamed his Catholic upbringing, but he managed to mix enough sex-negative feminist rhetoric into his media comments to appear reasonably secular on the subject. Still, it didn't add up, and Goss remained remarkably quiet about his reasons for going against the recommendations of the CJC.

Although I was not aware of it at the time, Kevin Rudd was Wayne Goss' chief-of-staff and had earned the nickname 'Dr Death' for his take-no-prisoners approach. Goss took advice from Rudd on policy and it's my belief that Rudd had a lot to do with formulating the government's response to the CJC report on prostitution. As prime minister in the years ahead, Rudd was exposed as a deeply religious man who even defended the right of Church lobbyists to influence governments on social policy.

By cherry-picking the CJC recommendations, Goss and Rudd made brothels much darker places than they had ever been under former premier Joh Bjelke-Petersen. The only recommendation they allowed was for single sex workers to legally operate from their homes. If a second person was found on the premises while they were working—whether it was a cleaner, a security guard or even the girl's mum making scones in the kitchen—they were deemed to be running a brothel and thrown in jail. It didn't take long for psychopaths and rapists to figure out what it all meant.

Within a few years, three young sex workers had been brutally murdered in their homes and many more assaulted and raped after opening their doors to men who knew the government had mandated that they would be alone. On the same day as Goss's new Prostitution bill was announced, the *Courier Mail* reported the rapes of three Brisbane sex workers in the previous week. And the seven-year prison sentences that Goss legislated for clients found guilty of a third offence of 'being found in a place suspected of being used for prostitution' were longer than those normally handed out to men found guilty of rape.

In Opposition, Goss had never hinted at these new laws, and the CJC report had been emphatic that decriminalisation was the way to go. A few years later, I would write to Wayne Goss and accuse him of having blood on his hands. He responded with a denial of any culpability for the deaths or rapes of sex workers. I probably should have sent the same letter to Kevin Rudd.

Goss left as much of the industry in the hands of organised crime and corrupt police as his predecessor. Nothing changed except that sex workers were in a more dangerous workplace environment. His new laws around porn were no better. He said he would reform censorship laws by introducing the federal government's classification scheme instead of continuing Bjelke-Petersen's archaic system of having the police take cases of obscenity straight to the courts. It sounded reasonable, and the adult retail industry believed what they were told. But as so many duplicitous Labor leaders had done in the past when promising to regulate sexual goods and services, Goss introduced the federal classification scheme for Queensland but then deleted all the adult categories from the Queensland laws. This meant that if you sold porn from the Gold Coast you automatically went to jail, unlike retailers across the NSW border in, say, Tweed Heads, who were free to trade. In retrospect, Bjelke-Petersen's method of dealing with porn was much fairer. He basically left it to the police to carry out a raid every now and then on an adult shop and then get a magistrate to determine, using old-fashioned obscenity law, whether the material was likely to 'deprave and corrupt' the citizenry. More often than not, the magistrate would have seen something similar in his youth and would acknowledge that it hadn't corrupted him, meaning a not guilty verdict was more likely than a guilty one.

Under Goss's new laws there was no chance to go before an independent arbiter about whether a magazine or video was likely to harm people. If it showed a certain level of nudity or sex, it was automatically declared to be harmful by a group of public servants with little or no understanding of the issues. Magazines that promoted war, animal hunting, boxing and other blood sports—even 'famous murders and rapes'—were all perfectly legal because they showed no nudity or sex.

With all of this still swirling around in my head, I finished my three-week stint with the Birds of Paradise, pocketed a cool $2000 and boarded a twelve-berth dive boat at the Cairns wharf. From the moment we got past the reef and I entered the water for the first time, everything seemed to make sense again. My glee was so evident that I did a series of underwater somersaults with my tanks on—much to the consternation of the guides. 'Exuberant', I think they called me. At the end of the five days, I had my scuba diving certificate and it was clear that I was going back to Canberra and moving in with Robbie.

9

LAUNCHING EROS

John Lark, dubbed the 'king of porn' by some journalists and 'Australia's Larry Flynt' by others, started his empire as a young student in the early 1960s at Cranbrook School in Sydney's prestigious Bellevue Hill. In his sixth year, he started running a book on the twelve-metre yacht races held on the harbour, which were easily viewed from the many vantage points around the school. He would take bets from his fellow students and set the odds against what he'd read in the newspapers. With the proceeds of this enterprise, he started photocopying single pages from old black-and-white porn magazines and selling them to his mates for a shilling a piece. At Cranbrook, that was lunch money. Soon he started buying in his own porn magazines, and when he was eventually caught he headed up a long line of his customers waiting outside the headmaster's door to be caned. He was then expelled, but not so much for the gambling, or the porn, but for the fact that he refused to bend his arse for the headmaster's rod.

Launching the Eros Foundation from a cruise boat on Sydney Harbour, in the shadow of Cranbrook, was a hat tip to John's early business acumen and the wonderful opportunity that the harbour (and a privileged education) had afforded him. It was also a great place to have a giant piss up and launch a new adult industry association. In many ways, John had been the driving force in getting the adult retail industry to where it was by 1992. He had run what was arguably the largest adult company in the 1980s and formed the industry's first lobby group—the Adult Video Industry Association (AVIA).

The industry now needed a more inclusive association where everyone was contributing. The bill that I had worked so hard on to legalise sex work in the ACT was finally moving towards enactment, but in other states things were going backwards. I had called as many sex industry traders as I could in the week before the launch and alerted them to the fact that given attacks on the industry were increasing at an alarming rate we needed a truly national industry association. It didn't matter what part of the industry you were from; our opponents were the same, and politicians did not want to sit down in a restaurant with a porn producer or brothel owner for fear that they might be accused of taking a bribe or, worse, of being labelled prurient. Meeting with a professional independent industry representative was far more strategic.

I arranged for popular US feminist porn star, Nina Hartley, to become the 'matron' of Eros. Nina was a former nurse who was just starting to make her celebrated sex education video series, including *How To Perform Fellatio* and *How to Make Love to a Woman*. With her signature baby-blue eyes, curvy figure and shining intellect, she was a great ambassador. Later in her career she would go on to play the part of 'Little' Bill's profligate wife in the 1997 hit movie, *Boogie Nights*. She also played Hillary Clinton in the classic porn movie parody, *Who's Nailin' Paylin?*

On the morning of the launch, 10 November 1992, about 100 adult shop owners, brothel owners, porn producers, porn stars, adult magazine reps, sex workers, strippers and therapists all gathered together at Pier One on Sydney Harbour to vote in office bearers and approve an initial budget for the Eros Foundation. Also present were the Enema Survivors Association, the Cavalry Club, Salon Kitty's Bondage and Domination House, and *Wet Set* magazine. With the formalities over and done with, we all boarded an older style private cruise boat and headed out on to the harbour for a lobster lunch and plenty of champagne.

* * * *

A year earlier, the federal Opposition had launched its 650-page economic manifesto called Fightback!, which was intended to propel the Liberals into government after nearly a decade of Labor rule. It was still in the headlines. We had been working on our own manifesto for a few months and decided to unveil it at the Eros launch. Sex Fights Back was an impressive 40-page booklet that outlined what Eros was about and what its policies were. Chief among them was the legalisation of X-rated videos and sex work around the nation, as well as the creation of anti-discrimination laws to protect people in the industry. We mailed a copy to every politician in the country together with a survey about their attitudes to sex and violence. Unsurprisingly, we didn't get a single response.

The morning after the launch, the *Sydney Morning Herald* ran a front-page story announcing the arrival of the new lobby group.

The article reported that the organisation would be headed up by 'former sex worker' Fiona Patten. I hadn't counted on that. I thought I'd told the media I was a former fashion designer. My parents, who were happy with me being a lobbyist for free speech, were shocked to see my secret life writ large on the front page of their morning newspaper. I had hoped that because they were now running a bed-and-breakfast in a sleepy little hollow in the Bega Valley they wouldn't see it, but of course one of their friends just had to fax it to them.

I was upset, but not because I had been outed by a journalist keen to get a bit of spin on his story. I felt guilty for not having told my parents and now they were being ambushed by their friends at the Candelo general store. I called Mum to try and explain. All she could say was, 'How could you?!' over and over in her British accent. She was embarrassed for me, even though I wasn't embarrassed.

I went down to see them not long after that to calm things down. My father didn't want to talk about his daughter's professional sex life, but after the initial shock started to wear off, Mum asked me what it had been like and what sort of conditions I had worked under. 'What if you had to be with an old man?' she asked, recoiling in horror. As she said it, we both became aware that my father had nodded off in his old armchair in front of the open fire at the other end of the room. His false teeth had fallen slightly forward in his mouth, giving him that distinctive Chad Morgan look. We both caught it at the same time and broke into hysterics. After that, we never discussed it again.

Following the launch, Robbie, Nina and I drove back to Canberra, stopping halfway at the Antique Centre in Mittagong for a coffee and a cinnamon bun. There we discovered an old Rubens print of 'Cupid and Psyche' that would have been about 90 years old and out of copyright. With the line 'Logical Perspectives on Love and Sex' underneath the image it would make a fabulous logo for the new association. Cupid and Psyche had been appearing in artworks since before Christianity. The beautiful Greek god and goddess represented the combination of heart and mind. A few years after the launch, the Reverend Fred Nile would accuse us of encouraging child pornography by adopting the logo. He thought Cupid, or Eros, was a little kid about to engage in sex with the adult women in the drawing. It was a warning to me of just how unhinged politicians could be in pursuing an agenda. In keeping with our logo, we decided to adopt the definition of pornography as defined by Dr Alison King from Reading University: 'Pornography is sexually oriented material of a graphic nature designed for recreation rather than education.'

Three days later, I launched our first National Oral Sex Day at Gorman House on the fringes of Canberra's CBD. Only a few years earlier I had exhibited and sold my clothing range there, but now I was attempting to open up public discussion about taboo sexual subjects, as well as have a bit of fun. We published a small booklet that outlined the facts and the myths around oral sex, and Nina and I organised an oral sex competition using dental dams as a safe-sex promotion.

Around a dozen contestants assembled to go down on Nina in front of a crowd that included journalists from the *Canberra Times*. Each person had a couple of minutes each and had to show good technique, appropriate sounds and a working knowledge of the female vulva. I stood next to Nina with a microphone while she provided a running commentary on the hopeful 'cunnylinguists' as they did their thing. The winner was a local woman in her late twenties who

Nina said was wise beyond her years and also wise between her ears. Later over drinks with the contestants, I heard her say, 'Now I'm working with women who are younger than my breast implants.'

After Nina returned to the US, I spent a couple of months organising our new secretariat at Robbie's Hooker Street house into a modern office with an effective war room. The internet was just appearing and I was interested in how we could exploit that in our work. My mother and father had both moved into communications technology businesses in their mid-forties so I was a lot more aware of new technologies than most. Around the same time, I bought Apple's early laptop, the PowerBook 150 (which I still have and still works) even though there were rumours that they would release a new model with a colour screen in the next twelve months.

Early in 1993, the office was complete and ready to function as a working secretariat. On a Friday afternoon in late February, I started to get frantic phone calls from a number of Melbourne adult shops claiming that police were raiding their premises. Some adult cinemas were also being raided. Doors were being bashed in, office staff were forced to 'stand away from the cash register' and premises were searched.

* * * *

Australia's largest porn raid, Operation Jack (police humour for 'jack-off') had just commenced. It had been initiated by the prudish Victorian attorney-general, Jan Wade, after only being in the job a few months. She also held the other key portfolios for the adult industry of Women's Affairs and Fair Trading. She had the sex industry in her sights and the raids were clearly a reflection of her personal moral agenda rather than any widespread community complaint.

My first job was to find out just how extensive the raid was. If it was big, then it was most likely political, and I would need to focus my attention on both the politicians and the media. By the next day, however, it became apparent that the police resources that Wade had thrown at this operation were staggering. A total of 22 teams of police took part, and although they claimed to have seized 10,000 videos, industry sources put it closer to 20,000. They had arrived at some venues with large black trucks to transport the huge amount of confiscated porn. It was on the same scale as a terrorist operation. Guns had been drawn in one situation and pedestrians had given a wide berth around shops being raided.

The policeman I spoke to at Russell Street claimed that they were looking for child pornography, but not even the police conducting the raids believed that. Reports from store owners said the police were being told to sweep Melbourne of pornography and to get every video they could find, regardless of what it was.

As it turned out, the raid was focused on Victoria's largest chain of adult shops and distributors: the Club X/Calvista group. The business was owned by the avuncular Ken Hill and his brother Eric. They came from humble beginnings in the working-class suburb of Reservoir in the 1950s and had originally started out by acquiring a few mainstream cinemas and drive-in theatres. When the video boom took off in the late 1970s, they sensed the technology shift better than most and set up a number of successful R-rated adult cinemas in the Melbourne CBD. Later they turned unwanted retail space in Melbourne into adult bookshops and set up the Club X chain.

It was my observation that the Hill brothers had a strong moral compass hanging over their empire most of the time. They were committed family men who disliked violence, and, apart from quality red wine, had few other vices. They were generous with their time and money, and well-liked by a wide circle of people including Rotary and other community-based organisations. They had little time, however, for politicians with religious and prudish agendas, and as soon as the dust had settled on the first few days of Operation Jack they made it their business to beat the attorney-general at her own game.

* * * *

As the legal arguments for the industry started to be heard, I tried to make an appointment to see Jan Wade. She refused. Surprisingly, she would be only the second member of parliament to ever refuse me a meeting (the other being then ACT Liberal leader and now Senator Zed Seselja). I immediately sensed a level of insecurity in her position. The issues were big ones. Not only was she attacking the long-established adult retail network, she wanted further restrictions on legal adult magazines sold from newsagents and convenience stores. Her agenda even snaked into adult services where she was trying to ban table-top dancing venues and peep shows by broadening the definition of prostitution, which at that stage was still illegal in Victoria. If she failed, it would not look good for Premier Jeff Kennett's first term, and knowing Kennett to be a bit of a pragmatist and a 'lad', I couldn't see how her actions had been directed out of his office, either. In fact, I was much more successful in approaching Kennett's office directly. One of his staff arranged for me to meet with his justice advisor. He agreed that Wade was going over the top, but as the state's first female attorney-general they were reluctant to interfere.

Banning erotic dance and the viewing of adult peep shows was an extremist position that technically made some forms of masturbation illegal. Knowing I had to at least try and put my members' arguments to Wade, I went undercover and made an appointment to see her as a constituent at her next round of suburban electoral office meetings. I arrived at her office for a mid-afternoon meeting and sat down in front of her. She wore a grey suit with a tight bun of grey hair that made her look like one of those black-and-white Edwardian cameos. She was clearly ill at ease with strangers and I sensed she was suspicious of me before I even spoke. When she realised who I was she quickly sat back in her chair, crossed her arms and frowned.

I started with adult magazines:

'Minister, I notice you're wanting to put Category 1 Restricted magazines in blinder racks in newsagents to stop people from being offended, but I don't think you realise that those magazines already have to have unrestricted covers and plastic bags under federal law. Why would you also want to put them in blinder racks? It's censoring what's already been censored.'

I pulled out the latest copy of *Penthouse*'s Category 1 Restricted magazine shrink wrapped in plastic and a copy of *Plumpers* and put them on the table in front of her. She recoiled as if I had slapped a turd on her desk.

'I don't care' was all she said.

'Okay, but if the industry takes this into the courts, your logic will come under scrutiny.'

'I don't care,' she said again. 'I can do this and I will.'

I rarely lose my temper with people I don't know, but I was ready to boil over. It was so infuriating to sit there and hear someone as educated and qualified as she was being so unintelligent and wilful. I moved on to table-top dancing and peep shows in order to keep my emotions under control.

'Minister, can you tell me in legal terms how a man sitting in a chair watching a naked woman dance on a catwalk two metres above him can be called prostitution?'

'No.'

'Or an adult viewing sexual acts on a screen? How can that possibly be equated to an act of prostitution?'

Her monosyllabic answers turned into a stony silence and she just glared. Then the door opened behind me and I was ushered out.

In the end, the year that it took to finalise Operation Jack turned out to be Wade's *annus horribilis*. All the charges against the Hill brothers were successfully defended. The court ordered the 10,000 seized videos be returned. All costs were awarded against the police. The cost to the taxpayer ran into hundreds of thousands of dollars. Ken Hill, his brother Eric, and their streetwise lawyer, Peter Allaway, had beaten the attorney-general and cost her many times over what she had already spent.

It was a bitter blow for Wade, but it didn't stop her obsession with the porn industry. A few years later, in 1996, she ordered another twelve shops to be raided under similar circumstances. A number of people were charged with selling X-rated films and this time the police brought in a senior prosecutor normally used for murder trials. They also engaged a QC at considerable expense to avoid another embarrassment like Operation Jack. The legal case lasted for six years, with the taxpayer footing a bill estimated at around half a million dollars. After two appeals, the case was abandoned on the advice of the Director of Public Prosecutions. It was another huge win for the Hill brothers and their legal team. It was also a huge win for common sense and public opinion, which would have undoubtedly been against the spending of so much taxpayer money on chasing porn that was already legal in two other jurisdictions.

Raids like Operation Jack, however, continued in other jurisdictions for many years. One month out from the 2007 NSW election, Kings Cross police raided several adult shops and confiscated about 6000 DVDs. It was Valentine's Day and a state election had been called for 24 March. It was not the first time that a porn raid had been timed in this way and ended up all over the front pages of the newspapers. This particular raid was under the command of Andrew Scipione, who became NSW Police Commissioner only six months later. As in Operation Jack, the police said they were looking for child pornography, but no one was ever charged with it. By now it was becoming obvious that the police were using this excuse to deter civil libertarians who objected to the use of police to enforce laws on adult porn. Eros estimated that the total cost of the Valentine's Day raids to the taxpayer was in the hundreds of thousands of dollars, while hundreds of police hours were spent in processing and classifying material.

10

LIVING IN THE SIN BIN

Fyshwick is one of Canberra's most iconic suburbs and probably the only one that has been designated by a government as a 'suburb for sex'. Between 1987 and 2000, Fyshwick's postcode became one of the busiest parcel post offices in the nation. Millions of X-rated videos were being sent around the country from the post office. This curious situation first came about through a series of political trade-offs in 1989 when the then ACT Attorney-General Bernard Collaery had a casting vote on whether or not to ban X-rated videos in the ACT. Caught between his natural civil libertarian inclinations and a need to placate the religious right who were baying for a ban, he decided to restrict sales to the industrial suburbs of Canberra. Effectively, this meant Fyshwick, although it also included the smaller and less serviced industrial suburb of Mitchell. Up until that time, Fyshwick had been a suburb for light industrial activities and the home of Canberra's white goods retailers.

In 1992, when prostitution was legalised in the ACT, the government chose to regulate the other 'sin' industry along similar lines and only allowed brothels to be set up in the industrial suburbs. The vast majority chose Fyshwick. The idea behind designating a suburb 'industrial' was so that industrial waste and noise would not pollute people's living environments. The kind of industrial waste and noise that came from brothels and X-rated video production houses hardly qualified—clearly the government had added a new caveat to businesses in Fyshwick. Out of sight, out of mind. Strangely, that notion would work to the commercial benefit of the industries in the years ahead.

****

Fyshwick was named after a Tasmanian politician, Sir Philip Fysh, with the 'wick' part being ye olde English word for a village or borough. Some of his personal attributes appeared well matched with aspects of the future sex work and porno mail-order businesses that would flourish in his suburb. Phil Fysh was a businessman before he came to Australia and was twice premier of Tasmania in the 1800s. He was a follower of liberalism, and a champion of small business and freedom of speech. Fysh was an instrumental figure in establishing Federation and did a lot of work around reforming customs issues between the states. Following Federation, he entered federal politics and became Post Master General in 1903.

At the end of the First World War, the government built an internment camp in what is now the old part of Fyshwick between the railway line and Canberra Avenue. It was called the Molonglo Internment Camp after the Molonglo River that marks the eastern border of the suburb. It was to house 3500 Austrians and Germans expelled from China and was often referred to as Australia's very first concentration camp. The prisoners never arrived, but the large campsite ended up housing 150 German internees who had been transferred from a camp in Bourke and were sent home after the war. Although the camp buildings were eventually sold off, the infrastructure was used as the basis of the new suburb of Fyshwick. As the American architect Walter Burley Griffin's plan for Canberra took shape in the 1930s, the suburb was earmarked as Canberra's industrial hub and the bureaucrats determined that all the streets would bear the names of Australia's great industrial cities.

* * * *

By the end of 1993, Robbie's Adult Video Industry Association (AVIA) group was facing difficulties. The 40 per cent wholesale tax levied on X-rated videos by the new Liberal government was crushing the porn industry, and AVIA's funding was now affected.

Although we weren't living together, I was starting to spend more nights with Robbie. Sometimes this would see us drive up to his mountain retreat on the edge of Kosciuszko National Park, where he had a yurt that sat on the edge of a mountain stream. But mostly it was at his Hooker Street house, where both of us would rise early most days and head straight for Fyshwick. I still had my WISE office out there, while meetings with Eros clients would often last late into the night. Driving back to Yarralumla was the last thing we wanted to do.

Finding somewhere to live in Fyshwick wasn't easy. Census after census showed that there was never more than 50 people living in the suburb even though thousands of men and women spent many hours lying on beds each night. After a few weeks, however, we found a beautiful 1930s French-style open-plan house snuggled into bushland behind a mechanics workshop and an art studio. The owner was an eccentric inventor who had just patented a new birth-control device that was pushed into the eye of a man's cock before sex, but eventually negotiations on the house went the same way his invention did.

My aunty Evelyn's restaurant where I held my fashion parades for sex workers had recently closed and the whole of the top floor was now vacant. I called her and got the keys so we could check it out. The first floor of 41 Whyalla Street was a huge 1960s loft with hardwood floors and a large bank of continuous north-facing windows. At the eastern end it had a kitchen and toilet with a space for a bathroom. With a little modification, it would make the perfect home/office/showroom/entertainment space. It was within a kilometre of most of the brothels and X-rated outlets, ten minutes to Parliament House and fifteen minutes to the ACT Legislative Assembly.

Robbie gave notice at Hooker Street, we signed a five-year industrial lease and immediately started to make the loft our home. We cut a hole in the roof, laid a huge sandstone slab on the floor and brought in an old Rayburn wood stove that would burn all night. We bought two huge old barn doors from a local second-hand merchant and hung them on giant hinges from each side of the building to open and close off the living space from the working one. Then we brought in all our furniture, including Robbie's three-metre antique pine table and church pews, which formed the centrepiece of the main office space. I put my industrial sewing machine, fabrics and mannequins in a sunny corner and we covered the walls in erotic art from a recent exhibition that we had been asked to store. A friend who had a litter of ducklings asked if I could look after them for a while, which gave us pets. Finally, we needed a bath. Fyshwick was home to half-a-dozen antique traders and we soon located a very large antique cast-iron bath complete with lion's claws. We grabbed a couple of friends and the four of us pushed and coerced the beast up the stairs and into the vacant bathroom space.

Before moving in, we had failed to notice that the printing company in the unit directly below us displayed the 'Christian fish' on his window. When the owner saw furniture, erotic art and now a bath going up above him, he rang the landlord and told him that we were installing a gay sauna. The landlord was soon beating down the door and demanding to know what was going on. After a cursory glance to reassure himself that he was not inviting Sodom and Gomorrah on to the premises, he stopped at the top of the stairs on his way out and said, 'You know you can't live here. It's not zoned for residential.' We assured him that we wouldn't be living there, although we worked late every night and started early. It was an interesting intellectual exercise for us later in deconstructing what 'living' actually meant, and we decided that as long as we talked about work before we went to sleep and immediately upon waking we were probably complying with the lease purpose clause.

The Christian printer (who serviced many of Canberra's revivalist groups) was not the only neighbour we had to worry about. As soon as we moved in, we planted three marijuana plants in large earthenware pots under the sunny north-facing windows. A few weeks later while watering them, I looked out the window into the laneway below to see half-a-dozen men in black drill outfits and hobnail boots.

They were hiding small parcels in various places and inviting three or four young dogs to sniff them out. Freak out! We were living about twenty metres from a customs' dog-training facility. After the initial shock, we reckoned that if they hadn't sussed out the dope smoke and the plants by now, we were probably pretty safe, but it was disturbing nonetheless.

As we settled in over the next year, '41' became a regular destination for a wide variety of groups and individuals. Sex workers still came up there for fashion parades and to chat. The X-rated traders dropped in on a regular basis for work and recreation. Members of parliament, like ACT Chief Minister Kate Carnell, Attorney-General Gary Humphries and Minister for Health Michael Moore were all visitors. Federal MPs like the Deputy Speaker, Ron Edwards, and Tasmanian MP Sid Sidebottom came up to see the political cartoon collection on the walls that Robbie's magazine *Matilda* had bequeathed. AIDS Action Council and the Australian Federation of AIDS Organisations (AFAO) members had meetings there and media personalities like Phillip Adams came to visit. Journalists including the late Peter Blazey and cartoonists like Geoff Pryor and Bill Leak were also regular visitors. *GQ* magazine came up and ran a cover story on the place. They photographed us in some bizarre and sexualised poses. One with me in my scuba gear and Robbie naked with his thighs in between a large book press and me screwing down the big screw. In between all this madness and mayhem, we managed to make it feel like a home as well and Robbie's two daughters, Angie and Georgie, would often come over and spend nights up there.

Canberra had only ever had one escort agency that was pitched to federal parliament and the diplomatic corps. Universal Escorts had operated out of a house in the Weston Creek suburb of Rivett during the late 1970s and the 1980s. It was a unique operation where some of the sex workers belonged to the Children of God/Family of Love religious sect and were known as 'happy hookers for Jesus'. It had closed down during Bob Hawke's first term of government. It had always amazed me that no one had ever tried to set up such an establishment again. When parliament sits, there can be up to 5000 people working in the building, with many of them flying in for the sitting and flying out again when parliament breaks. Another 2000 work in ancillary agencies. Big FIFO events wherever they are always bring with them a contingent of horny men away from home. I have to admit that Robbie and I had thought about creating such an establishment on a number of occasions.

We were approached by a Sydney-based group looking to join Eros and get help opening a new upmarket brothel called the Parlour-ment House. They had secured first-storey premises on the corner of Geelong Street and Canberra Avenue, only a few hundred metres away from our loft.

The new owners spent up big on the fit-out and together we worked out a marketing plan aimed at an upmarket clientele that included parliamentarians and their staff. They put in a bar with plush white shag-pile carpets, a mirror ball on the ceiling and the latest chiropractic mattresses from David Jones. A large blue and white circular neon sign with the words 'Parlour-ment House' was cleverly mounted to the outside of the building so that at certain times of the day it reflected the electricity pole opposite to vaguely resemble the flagpole on top of the real Parliament House. The second floor of the 1970s modular building had two large windows that looked out over Canberra Avenue towards Queanbeyan and were tinted just to add to the mystery of the place. Unfortunately, there wasn't much they could do about the hamburger shop underneath them.

Not long after we had moved into No. 41, Robbie and I started bemoaning the fact that Australia did not have a major sex industry trade fair. So we sat down one night in front of the open fire with a joint and a glass of wine and sketched the outline of a show that we called 'Sexpo'. After a few weeks it became obvious that the concept was far too big for us to pull off in Canberra so we handed it over to Ken and Eric Hill from Club X who subsequently brought it to life as the most successful adult industry trade fair in the world.

During our first year together, I introduced Robbie to many of my sex worker friends and he began to get a more personal view on the nature of sex work. Up until then, he'd pretty much been a 'rub 'n' tug' kind of guy. At the same time, he introduced me to the business of porn. I thought I had a reasonable understanding of the nature of this beast until the day he took me to one of the largest porn magazine distributors in Australia. We were there to meet the owner, a gnarly old ex-cabbie and racehorse owner, to talk about ways of distributing a future industry magazine.

As we walked into the sprawling warehouse in Sydney's Rockdale, we discovered the floor covered with around 200 pallets of various magazines, all with one or two boxes open. As we walked past each row, I was astounded to see just how many aspects of life and how many body types were part of the collection. As well as the standard nudie mags like *Playboy*, *Chic* and *Hustler*, there was an astonishing array of fetish and explicit-sex magazines. Fat and skinny. Dwarfs and giants. Interracial and cross cultural. Schoolgirls, MILFS and grannies. Big boobs, small boobs, hairy and shaved. The treatments ranged from gonzo gangbangs to sickly sweet romance. No part of the anatomy was left out, either, with boobs, cocks, feet and vaginas the most popular. Never before in my life had I seen an erotic magazine devoted to the beauty of ugly girls. There was even one for amputees! To top it off, many of these market segments were broken down into straight, gay, lesbian, bi and trans.

I flicked through a few magazines from the open boxes. Apart from those that set out to be offensive as their selling point, the vast majority were respectful and even reverential towards their subject matter. Was this the ultimate anti-discrimination business or was it a tawdry excuse to exploit vulnerable minorities? Before I could even think about such philosophical considerations, my eyes started feasting on a stack of old black-and-white 1960s mags. The beehive hairdos, the heavy black eyeliner and the knee-high boots. And over there—the *Rubberist*! A magazine devoted entirely to dressing in rubber. Porn was even a fashion statement.

After ten minutes of meandering through this lubricious labyrinth, I could feel myself becoming quite aroused by the plethora of sexual images. By the time we'd sat down and discussed our magazine distribution, the feeling had become overpowering. I moved my foot and tapped Robbie's shoe, and as he turned to me I rolled my eyeballs towards the door. Soon we were out in the car park where we renewed our vows in the backseat of our red Ford Courier on a side street in downtown Rockdale.

11

CONTEMPT AND OTHER CHARGES

Contempt of parliament is a serious business. Before 1987, people who were found guilty could be locked up at Her Majesty's pleasure, pretty much without trial and without legal representation. New laws around contempt in that year moderated things considerably, but still left people open to fines of $5000 and six months in the slammer. Being charged with contempt is pretty much the only charge in our legal system that denies a person the right to bring in a lawyer to defend themselves in front of the all-powerful Committee of Privileges, although defendants can appeal a judgment to the federal court.

In politics, everyday words can take on meanings that would never be attributed to them in daily life. The explanatory memoranda and the definitions section of parliamentary bills and legislation manipulate the meaning of many words that form part of our everyday lexicon, often causing ordinary people to misinterpret legislation that affects them. Pauline Hanson's 'please explain' moment was absorbed by millions of Australians who sympathised with her against the use of elitist language in political discourse. All too often the public sees parliamentary debates degenerate into the most bitter and acrimonious slanging matches. Politicians who defame and threaten colleagues in a parliamentary debate can also use 'privilege' to attack members of the public who question them about their behaviour or decisions.

Without much of an understanding of these issues, Eros's first year of operation opened explosively. An animated media interview suddenly whooshed up into a wildfire that threatened to burn my new lobby group to the ground. Only weeks after Eros officially launched, I wrote to the Senate Select Committee on Community Standards Relevant to the Supply of Services Utilising Telecommunications Technologies (there's that jargon at work again) about their recommended ban on phone-sex lines on the 0055 network. This would seriously impact many of my new members. It would also rob many housewives around the nation of their livelihoods. Eros estimated that thousands of women were earning a good wage just from talking dirty on the phone while they did the ironing. I commissioned a legal opinion that said the recommendation was seriously flawed and attached it to my submission. I finished it by writing, 'Please be advised that traders who have been disadvantaged by the Committee's rulings in this area will contemplate damages actions in the courts unless some reassessment is done.' I was fair, firm and polite. I waited for a reply.

Four weeks after lodging my submission, Robbie and I received a late-night phone call from a politically savvy shop assistant at the Fantasy Lane adult supermarket in Fyshwick. With only a few days to go before the federal Coalition was to hold a joint party-room meeting to vote on whether to formalise a ban on X-rated videos, a senior National Party member was caught on security camera buying X-rated videos. Normally it would have been a 'so what?' conversation, but I knew the member in question would vote with his colleagues to ban the products he had just purchased. He even told the shop assistant that 'he couldn't see what all the fuss was about', which only made it worse. I made sure the film footage was put in a safe place and then sat down with Robbie to discuss it.

Was it anyone's business if politicians engaged in personal behaviour that contradicted their stated policies, or was this a case of moral hypocrisy that the public was entitled to know about? Especially as the policy these politicians were endorsing could see people go to jail and pay thousands of dollars in fines. As attorney-general in Bob Hawke's first government, Gareth Evans had said that he regarded this sort of hypocrisy as one of the most damaging charges a person could bring against a serving politician. Politicians are a privileged class of people and the only ones who can effectively make or change laws. If they are going to make a law that punishes people who can't change that law, I believed that they should abide by that law or go public with their grievance if they intended to break it.

* * * *

The following morning, Robbie did a phone interview with ABC radio journalist, Matthew Abraham while we were staying at his mother's house. During the course of the interview, Abraham (a fairly devout Christian who never divulged his religious leanings during interviews) pushed him on the rights of politicians to ban erotic material that they found offensive. Robbie exploded and asked

Abraham if that included politicians who actually bought X-rated videos and then voted against them. Abraham said Robbie had no evidence of that and was making unsubstantiated allegations. I could see Robbie starting to straddle that thin line between reason and rage. It was the middle of winter and he was standing naked in his mother's kitchen, so he wasn't as calm and thoughtful as he usually was on radio. Suddenly, he jumped for the more visceral approach. Eros had video evidence, he said, of the MP in question, and would consider releasing it if he voted to ban X-rated material.

The media went into a meltdown. They called us 'sleaze bags' and 'blackmailers'. Guilty of abrogating the sex industry's basic principles of discretion and confidentiality. Kiss but don't tell. Ethics and social commentators argued over the rights and wrongs of outing hypocrisy among politicians. Lauchlan Chipman, an academic who published extensively on philosophy and jurisprudence, called it 'Fantasygate' and 'an indecent exposure even our more wayward politicians do not morally deserve'. The Opposition spokesperson on legal matters, Peter Costello, said that 'profits from porn will decline if the Coalition is elected and we will not be deterred by blackmail or stunts'. He was also adamant that he would 'not push for their prosecution in trying to intimidate politicians—a practice banned by the Crimes Act'.

Margo Kingston reported in *The Age* that Canberra brothels had information and credit card details about two Liberal backbenchers, and a very senior Liberal figure who had been banned for life for 'roughing up the girls'. She quoted me as saying that the brothel industry 'would only release the information as a last resort to save the industry'. Derryn Hinch invited me on to his TV show, *Hinch*, to talk about the issues and asked me directly if the MP in question was so and so. He wasn't in the slightest bit worried about outing anyone, but still I declined to name names.

Meanwhile, the Eros Board had become involved and was worried about the association's standing. Robbie would have to stand down, they said, if only for a short period. I issued a media release saying his position had been terminated and that he had been thoroughly spanked with a member's product. And then salvation came from a most unlikely quarter. A Liberal backbencher from Victoria, Russell Broadbent, issued a press release outing himself as the MP in question, but claimed that he had merely bought the X-rated videos for research purposes. It wasn't him but it was manna from heaven for us. How many more were there?

The following day, we issued another press release denying that it was him, but thanking him for his honesty. We then asked for all conservative MPs who had made the trip to Fyshwick to come forward. None did, but there was no hiding the collateral damage for the conservatives. The issue soon died as the media started to realise that the hypocrisy probably ran much deeper than one or two backbenchers. It felt like a win of sorts.

* * * *

A few months later, Robbie and I fronted the Senate Committee on Telecommunications to give evidence, but before we could even start the Chair of the Committee, Senator Margaret Reynolds, read out a statement telling us that we had both been charged with contempt of parliament for threatening members and senators with legal action in my letter and for threatening to out an MP caught buying X-rated videos. They made no mention of the threat to out MPs who had misbehaved in brothels.

If it was a contempt to interfere or coerce witnesses to a Senate Committee, then the Committee had just done that to us by introducing these trumped-up charges just prior to giving evidence. It put both of us off our submissions. Later that week, we received an invitation from the Committee of Privileges to put forward our case, and in December the Committee came down with a 'not-guilty' verdict on both charges. They warned us, however, that if we tried to out an MP again under the same circumstances, the outcome would be different.

The whole thing was a charade. If MPs are immune from prosecution for the decisions they make under privilege, then why was I dragged before this star chamber to answer a charge of 'threatening' them with legal action? They are cocooned. And why was Robbie dragged in as well for threatening to expose sexual hypocrisy? It's not like there wasn't much of it in the parliament. As a lobbyist for the sex industry frequently in and around the place, I'd heard many stories about the sex lives of politicians. Like the story about the well-known female journalist who was having a long-standing affair with a recent Prime Minister. It just wouldn't go away. Or the one about the ABC cameraman in the 1990s who was contracted by the local porn industry to film a few sequences and ended up becoming the 'stunt cock'.

Years later, in 2007, Oswald Hancock, the husband of South Coast Liberal MP Shelley Hancock, was outed by Channel 9 for having made an appearance in a commercial porn movie. The film was one of a series shot by John Lark in the early 1990s. Lark had rented the Hancocks' holiday resort (the H Ranch Hotel) for a week to make three films and had paid the Hancocks around five thousand dollars. Oswald Hancock claimed he had appeared as an unwitting actor in one film, playing cricket. He also appeared in rushes of the other two, holding a horse from which a naked actress slides off into a sex scene and then at the back of what looks like an aviary where another sex scene was taking place. The Hancocks claimed that they had no idea that the ironically named Parliament Video film crew were making porn; they thought they were making a documentary, but when they found out, they told them all to pack up and leave. According to John Lark, however, the crew, the porn actors and directors all stayed on the premises for the whole week and were never asked to leave.

Then there were the unsubstantiated but persistent rumours, like those around a former conservative senator who was well known for his homophobic views, but who, according to many gay groups, was a frequenter of popular gay beats.

I'd heard a few stories that involved me as well. One had Robbie and me in a threesome with the leader of a particular party in a particular jurisdiction. It never happened, though I can understand how an imaginative mind could have come to that conclusion.

* * * *

The sex industry is never far from politics. Politicians make it this way by creating laws on sex and sexuality that they can't live up to in their own private lives. 'Do as I say, not as I do' seems to be the sexual credo under which many MPs enter parliament. When these indiscretions are revealed, the electorate is rightly upset and becomes cynical of legislated sex and morality. My moral compass on these issues tells me that exposing someone's personal life, particularly a member of parliament, is only ever justified if there are matters of what I would call 'criminal hypocrisy' at stake. That's where a politician injures an aspect of someone's life or robs them of their wellbeing or dignity by callously and maliciously doing or saying something that they have publicly railed against or decried in the past. Then, I think, the electorate has a right to know.

US pornographer Larry Flynt's 2011 book, *One Nation Under Sex*, examined the way in which sex scandals have shaped the history of his country. He revealed many previously unknown scandals, including Benjamin Franklin's role in seducing women in the American Revolution, Abraham Lincoln's predilection to sharing men's beds, Eleanor Roosevelt's lesbian relationships, James Buchanan's gay love affair, Woodrow Wilson's girlfriend, the Kennedys, Bill Clinton, George W. and many more. Over the years, Flynt took out full-page ads in broadsheets asking readers to contact him with information that would link members of Congress or the Senate to illicit or hypocritical sex scenarios. He offered million-dollar rewards for documented evidence, and these forays led to resignations and the exposure of plenty of hypocrisy. His most recent offer is US$1 million for video or audio recordings of US President Donald Trump engaged in 'illegal behaviour or acting in a sexually demeaning manner toward women'. The recent publication of a story in the *Wall Street Journal* about Trump's lawyer paying porn star Stormy Daniels US$130,000 to shut up about a sexual encounter with the president could mean Flynt might be close to paying up.

In Australia, we don't have a robust tradition of outing sexual hypocrisy, even though Australian MPs have had their fair share of illicit relationships, sex scandals and even sex crimes. The most visible and outrageous transgressor is one who is never called out for his sins. It was our tenth prime minister, Joseph Aloysius Lyons. In 1992 (the same year Eros came into being), Lyons had his name nailed to the masthead of a new religious faction in the federal Coalition known as the Lyons Forum. Founding members included Eric Abetz and Kevin Andrews. The Forum dealt mainly with family and sexual issues, and appeared to revere Joe Lyons' wife, Dame Enid, as some sort of Australian Madonna. How they could possibly hold that view given Enid was only seventeen when she married the 35-year-old Joseph is beyond me. From many reports, Lyons had been courting Enid since she was fifteen. In what universe is it acceptable, or even legal, for a 33-year-old politician to date a fifteen-year-old girl and later have a group of social conservatives hold up the relationship as a paragon of family values and virtue? Lyons Forum members, like former arch-conservative senator and now Tasmanian state MP, Guy Barnett, still run articles on their home pages praising Lyons for 'falling in love with a seventeen-year-old girl'. This same group then goes on to decry adult same-sex marriages as an abomination and the first step toward legalising sex with animals. We'll never know if Joseph and Enid had sex before they were married, but if they did, Lyons was also quite possibly our first and only paedophile prime minister.

On a far more acceptable note, former prime minister John Curtin had a long affair with Isabella Southwell, the owner of Canberra's historic Hotel Kurrajong, while his successor, Ben Chifley, had a long affair with his secretary, Phyllis Donnelly, and probably with her sister as well. There's nothing inherently wrong with these adult relationships, either. The problem is that these two PMs presided over laws and public morality that did not support these illicit relationships.

To his credit, Curtin told a Catholic priest to bugger off as he lay dying in The Lodge, and to his credit Chifley stared down his detractors in the same Church to marry a Presbyterian, Elizabeth McKenzie. Both actions would have had some small effect in loosening the stranglehold religion had at the time. However, for those who didn't have the foresight or the social position to keep similar affairs quiet, awful discrimination would have been suffered in those days had they been outed. In my opinion, leadership is all about having the courage to put your personal convictions out there for everyone to see and to live by those same convictions, no matter how politically incorrect they might be.

The list of scandals didn't end with Curtin and Chifley. Below is a list of other prominent politicians' so-called indiscretions on the job:

In 1986, Prime Minister Malcolm Fraser was found naked and confused in the foyer of a Memphis Hotel. His minders tried to suggest he'd been slipped a 'mickey' by his mates, but southern state sex workers in the US told another story.

In the mid-1980s, Bob Hawke was having an undisclosed relationship with his now wife, Blanche d'Alpuget, while still married to Hazel, and threatened to sue *Matilda* magazine when they wrote about it.

In the mid-1960s Harold Holt had a long-standing affair with Marjorie Gillespie, a woman who owned a beach house close to his. His wife, Zara, admitted he had a number of affairs while prime minister.

In 1987 former Opposition leader Billy Sneddon had a fatal heart attack while he was having sex with his son's ex-girlfriend.

In 2007, then federal Opposition leader Kevin Rudd was found drunk in a New York strip club while representing Australia at the United Nations.

Then federal Treasurer Jim Cairns had a sexual relationship with his principal private secretary, Junie Morosi, in the 1970s.

One-time Australian Democrats leader Janet Powell had an affair with fellow Democrat senator Sid Spindler in 1991 which helped bring about her downfall as leader.

In the late 1990s, One Nation leader Pauline Hanson alleged she had an affair with her advisor David Oldfield, who consistently denied the claim.

In 2009, NSW Health Minister John Della Bosca resigned after a six-month affair with a young woman.

In 2013, NSW Opposition Police spokesman Nathan Rees had an affair with a single mother over five months that was carried out mainly in his electorate office and in public parks.

In 2009, a Parliament House barmaid claimed to have had a lengthy affair with the South Australian Premier Mike Rann in a *New Idea* interview. Rann denied the allegation.

Then Foreign Minister Gareth Evans and Democrats leader, Cheryl Kernot, had a five-year affair that was denied in parliament in the 1990s. The affair was outed by someone who should have known better. Evans was the architect of the X-rated film rating that challenged social conservatives in a way they had never been challenged before. He was a great civil libertarian and social reformer, and he was having an affair with a woman who was every bit his equal in age, intellect and status. They had a right to privacy. Jim Cairns and Junie Morosi were probably on the same level: both were libertarian socialists, and despite the fact that she was employed by Cairns they were more than equals. Morosi even went on to write a book called *Sex, Prejudice and Politics* and together they worked on alternative-living communities that were progressive and non-judgemental around relationships and sex.

Unfortunately, I can't say that for most of the others. I can't see where any of them have said 'let's legalise sex work' or 'let's legalise gay marriage' or even 'let's discuss the issue of extra-marital affairs in politics'. The only positive outcome for any of them fell to Kevin Rudd when 85 per cent of respondents to a *Herald Sun* Galaxy poll taken after his indiscretion revealed it made them feel better about him and proved he 'was a normal bloke'.

Most political hypocrites generally sow the seeds of their own undoing. This was the case with former Deputy Prime Minister and National Party leader Barnaby Joyce, who alleged that his rival in the 2016 federal election, Tony Windsor, was having an affair. When the inevitable happened, Joyce's own outing of his illicit affair with a junior staffer who became pregnant to him came at the same time as he was doing his utmost to lobby for a 'No' vote in the same-sex marriage plebiscite. Joyce's actions almost amounted to criminal hypocrisy under my definition of the term. The plebiscite that he championed resulted in widespread vilification of LGBTIQ Australians. The Black Dog Institute, QLife, Diversity ACT and many independent counsellors all noticed a dramatic spike in calls for help from LGBTIQ people after the first two weeks of the campaign. Posters calling on people to 'Stop the Fags' and describing the gay community as 'a curse of death' went up all over Sydney and Melbourne.

Meanwhile, Joyce's consistent rejection (even criminalisation) of practices that threaten traditional marriage and the nuclear family (X-rated films, legalising abortion, cervical cancer vaccines), and his public support for the morality favoured by the Catholic Church of which he is a staunch supporter, makes his transgression even more egregious. Only a month before the *Daily Telegraph* story, Joyce opened a $3.3-million taxpayer-funded upgrade to St Nicholas School in his New England electorate. In his speech, he told the hundreds of parents and teachers present that their children would really need a good Catholic education in their formative years to set a good moral compass for themselves as adults. He said all that knowing full well he was involved with another woman. If he had any moral fibre, he would have fessed up then and there, done an Edward VIIIth and abdicated his position, divorcing his old wife and marrying his new partner.

During the debate on same-sex marriage, he told the parliament that he had 'separated' from his wife and that he had not 'come to this debate pretending to be a saint'. He stopped short of telling the parliament any of the details of the affair that had led to his separation. Joyce had already got the message via social media that his support for traditional marriage looked pathetic when he couldn't uphold the 'till death us do part' and the 'forsaking all others' aspects of his own marriage.

In an interview with 2GB the day after his mea culpa, he said he had made the revelation because he didn't want to look like a hypocrite. In fact, it made the hypocrisy even worse.

Labor's reluctance to enter the debate at all, calling it 'private life' business, only reinforced the fact that they had a hypocrite or two in their senior ranks with a similar degree of culpability.

Jennifer Wilson, a journalist writing for *Independent Australia*, went further and attacked parliamentary press gallery journalists who refused to write about Joyce's affair. As she described it, the convention never to explore the private or sexual lives of politicians is selectively applied, and I suspect there are a few reasons for it. First, it's a way for some press gallery journalists (and their bosses) to shift attention from their own indiscretions as far away from Parliament House as possible. Second, a number of senior press gallery figures are just plain prudish and won't comment on sexual matters whether they pertain to parliament or anywhere else for that matter. Third, there is a fear in the press gallery that by reporting sexual affairs and indiscretions, serious journalists will end up looking like gossip columnists. Criminal hypocrisy, however, is not insignificant when perpetrated by a member of parliament, and can profoundly affect the lives of hundreds of thousands of people. It happens in state parliaments and at local government level as well. Righteous and religious MPs, many in real positions of power and influence, uphold and create morality laws that punish ordinary people, while often maintaining an illicit affair of their own . . . I could write a book on it!

Then there are MPs who exhibit the most bizarre sexual behaviour just because they are in positions of influence and authority. Again, in the teary apologies that follow these brain snaps, there's never a mention of moving the goalposts on other issues around sexuality in our society.

In 2006, Len Kiely, a Northern Territory deputy speaker once asked for a kiss from a security guard, telling her, 'I have a very long tongue and I could use it on you and make you a very happy woman.' Then, in 2016, NT Sports Minister, Nathan Barrett, a man who campaigned on 'family values', filmed himself masturbating in his office and then sent the film to a female constituent with whom he had a relationship but not 'that sort' of relationship. In 2013, Queensland state MP Peter Dowling stood aside as Chair of the Parliamentary Ethics Committee after taking a photo of his penis in a wine glass and then sending it to his former mistress. WA Opposition leader, Troy Buswell, sniffed the chair of a female staffer in 2005 and started writhing in mock sexual ecstasy in front of a group of stunned staffers. Previously, he was alleged to have snapped the bra strap of a Labor staffer. In 2010, the Reverend Fred Nile's office computer was found by parliamentary authorities to have had 200,000 hits on porn web sites. Nile denied 'perving at internet porn'. And on it goes.

Last, but not least, are those MPs who have committed sexual crimes. Interestingly, all of those reported involve children. In 2008, NSW Minister Milton Orkopoulos was found guilty of 33 counts of child-sex offences and drug possession, while in 2000, Queensland Labor MP, Bill Darcy, was sentenced to eleven years' jail for child-sex offences. In 2012, Terry Martin, a Tasmanian independent, was convicted of creating child pornography and having sex with a twelve-year-old girl, and, in 2015, a former South Australian police minister and Shop, Distributive and Allied Employees Association (SDA) assistant secretary, Bernard Finnigan, was found guilty of child-porn offences. The most high-profile case was that of morals campaigner and former Member for Capricornia, Keith Wright, who in 1993 was found guilty of one count of rape, one count of indecently dealing with a girl under fourteen, and four counts of indecently dealing with a girl under sixteen. Before their convictions, each of these men would all have cited adult pornography, adult sex work or gay and lesbian relationships as the main moral dangers in our society.

12

SAVING X

In early 1994, a couple of years after being appointed CEO of Eros, the solid ground that the X-rated film industry stood on began to shake. Since defeating the Catholic bishops' push to ban the X-rating in 1988, the industry had grown exponentially. X-rated companies rented or owned large amounts of real estate in Fyshwick and were now the largest export revenue earners for the national capital, pulling in $34 million a year from other states. They were the largest clients of Australia Post Express Courier in the ACT and the local economy was booming on the coat-tails of erotica. The possibility that Labor's thirteen years in government might come to an end at the next federal election, however, seemed a real possibility. A Liberal win would mean a ban on X-rated videos federally and the end of the ACT's thriving porn industry.

Given that states in Australia had now banned the sale of X-rated films, the ACT's X-rated industry stood out like a beacon against the tide of censorship that had swept across the nation. The porn industry had taken advantage of Section 92 of the Australian Constitution which said that if a product was legal to sell in one state then it was legal to send across the border into another state. The wording of the first resolution on Section 92, at the Constitutional Convention in Sydney in 1891, actually stated that 'trade and intercourse between the Federated Colonies, whether by means of land carriage or coastal navigation, shall be free from the payment of Customs duties . . .'

'Trade' and 'intercourse' is what X-rated films were all about. Furthermore, once a film had been sent interstate, the Constitution also appeared to confer legal rights on people in those states to possess it, regardless of the local laws. Western Australia did pass a law that attempted to ban possession of X-rated films, but it was never tested and to this day no one was ever been prosecuted, and in the early 2000s they removed the prohibition on the possession of an X-rated film in response to legislation dealing with online content.

For moral conservatives like Reverend Fred Nile and Senator Brian Harradine, the ACT completely undermined the states' bans on X that they had worked so hard to achieve. In 1993, Paul Keating had brought some long-overdue insight into the censorship debate and introduced a new MA15+ rating for films that were mostly violent. There was nothing unusual in adding or modifying a new classification, but generally it was a process that involved Cabinet, the Office of Film and Literature Classification (OFLC) and possibly a parliamentary committee.

Deputy Chief Censor, David Haines, and others at the OFLC had been working on a new MA rating for a while, but Keating decided to act on it after he had seen his kids watching a very violent film that was M-rated. His hand was pushed on the issue after the OFLC started to give films like *Crocodile Dundee* the same M rating as *The Silence of the Lambs* and *Cape Fear*. If children wanted to see an MA15+ film, they would now have to be accompanied by an adult. It was a popular move. Most parents wanted advice about the content of a film so they could decide if it was suitable for their child. In most countries, this is the sole reason for government classification, rather than censoring what adults can and can't see.

However, when John Howard became leader of the Liberal Opposition in 1995, he set his sights on sex, and a year out from the 1996 federal election it was clear that if he became prime minister the X-rated film industry was toast.

Howard was a dour Methodist who showed little evidence of humour or sexual awareness. Unlike Catholics, who took a more doctrinal attitude to porn, I always suspected that it was the visceral nature of the beast that offended Howard rather than anything that challenged his pragmatic religious beliefs. Within weeks of becoming Opposition leader, he publicly reaffirmed his commitment to wipe out the ACT's X-rated industry if he became prime minister. What he hadn't counted on was that there were still some in his party that strongly believed in the old Liberal adages of personal freedom and personal choice without the nanny state breathing down their necks. Some of them would actively work against Howard to uphold these philosophies and make sure they were not usurped by the steadily rising tide of religiosity and wowserism within the party.

One of these old-style Liberals was Malcolm Fraser's former press secretary David Barnett. I had never met anyone like him before. An arch conservative on most issues, he argued that conservatism was about small government and that meant not employing 'thought police' to chase down dirty pictures in the community. He was a tall and muscular man with greying hair that was beginning to recede—unlike his white Albert Einstein moustache that sat defiantly hirsute on his face like a relic from the early 1970s. In his earlier days, he would have been a very handsome man. A deep, commanding voice and soft, clear blue eyes made him all the more enigmatic. He occupied a unique place in the federal parliamentary press gallery. Officially he was a correspondent for the *Bulletin* and a freelancer for half-a-dozen other media outlets, but he was often wheeled out on TV current affairs shows as the token arch-conservative in the same way that his friend Gerard Henderson now appears on the ABC's *Insiders*. Most importantly for me, he had Howard's ear.

David's office, situated almost opposite the press boxes in the parliamentary press gallery, was a sort of curmudgeon's corner. When you knocked on his permanently open door, he would bark at you like an angry animal to 'Enter' without even looking up. His walls were papered with hate mail from bleeding-heart lefties and others who found his conservative views reprehensible. The more confected the outrage, the more prominently they were displayed. He seemed to thrive on upsetting people; I think he measured his success by it. Together with his wife, Pru Goward, they would later write John Howard's biography.

I had first met David while I was campaigning in the 1989 ACT election campaign. My anti-censorship, pro-sex work platform was in stark contrast to the wowserish policies of the ACT Liberal Party and others who wanted bans and restrictions. David was incensed at their incursion into free speech and sought me out for a couple of interviews.

As the 1996 federal election loomed, he came to visit me at Eros, and while chatting over coffee I told him we had one of the largest direct mailing lists in the country. His interest was piqued and he immediately engaged me in finding out more.

'How many people in total?' he asked.

'Well, we know from our surveys that 70 per cent of them are buying for a partner as well, so it would be over a million adults all up,' I said

'That's incredible', he said. 'Do they come from all over the country or are they concentrated in places like Kings Cross and St Kilda?'

'Oh no. They're evenly distributed around the country, although I suspect that Queensland might be over-represented. But sex cuts across all political and social backgrounds.'

A few days later, he came over for our now famously strong coffee again and quickly turned his attention to the mailing list.

'If you can find a way to break that list into federal electorates, I can guarantee you a cover story in the *Good Weekend* magazine,' he pledged. 'This will take the issue up to Howard in a way that he won't like and it will alert many in the Liberal Party to the folly of this sort of censorship.'

I poached a couple of my Eros members' staff and we started the arduous task of putting the postcodes of X-rated video buyers into federal electorates. After two weeks, the results were nothing short of astounding. Across all electorates, an average of 7.5 per cent of voters had purchased an X-rated video from Canberra. Although many South Australian electorates only showed 2–3 per cent on our radar, Queensland more than made up for that: unbelievably, 11 per cent of Arch Bevis's seat of Brisbane had signed up to buy porn, while other Queensland seats like Lilley and Dickson had 9 per cent and 7 per cent respectively. Many of these seats would turn on less than a few per cent in an election.

When I showed the figures to David, he was astounded. Within a few days, he had consulted with *Good Weekend* editor, Anne Summers, and had a cover story booked. On 28 October 1995, it appeared under the title, 'X-Rated Politics: How the Results of the Next Federal Election Could Be Determined by the Porn Industry's Marginal Seats Strategy'. It was a turning point in the debate and it shocked many politicians and party executives who had been used to lobby groups running marginal seats strategies against them with less than 2 or 3 per cent of voters on their mailing lists.

Some of the individual names on that list gave me a broader insight into the sex life of Australia. I found three Knights of the Realm (why would you call yourself Sir or Lady Muck when buying porn?), half-a-dozen members of parliament (again, why would you use your real name?) and a number of well-known judges and lawyers, eminent persons, academics, celebrities, media people, sportspeople and others.

* * * *

In the years following the *Good Weekend* article, a number of press gallery journalists dropped over to discuss it in more depth. It went without saying that the names on the list were completely confidential and would never be disclosed. There were, nonetheless, a couple of 'off-the-record' discussions where a couple of names may have been alluded to . . . The list had also passed through a number of hands at the X-rated companies themselves, so it was not absolutely water-tight. In fact, its permeability was ably demonstrated one afternoon in the spring of 1998. It came via a phone call that we talked about for years afterwards. Robbie answered the phone.

'Hello, Eros Foundation.'

'Arhh . . . Hello. This is Tony Abbott.'

Robbie paused. 'Yes. Hello . . . It's Robbie Swan here.'

'Hello, Robbie. Can I talk to you about your X-rated video list?'

'Sure.'

'Arhh . . . Look, this might sound like a strange request, but I've noticed your campaign for X-rated videos, and a little birdie told me that . . . arhh . . . you might be able to help with some information.'

Robbie gesticulated wildly for me to get over close to the phone.

'Yeees. And what would that be with, Tony?'

He came straight out with it.

'Well I did hear that [Mr X] was on that list and I was wondering if you could confirm that for me?'

We looked at each other in amazement and then with mock outrage.

'Well, no, Tony, we're not going to do that. You know that the adult industry doesn't give out names.'

He waited for a moment and then just said, 'Okay, thanks, then. See you.'

And with that he hung up. I had to admire his mettle, if nothing else. Not many politicians of his persuasion would ring the porn industry to try and gain an advantage over a rival.

* * * *

Strangely enough, I had met Tony Abbott's 'Mr X' quite by chance only a couple of months earlier at Aussie's coffee shop in Parliament House.

It's probably the most restricted coffee shop in Australia, where only pass-holders and their guests can place an order. It's the place to be on a sitting day when you are guaranteed to find yourself next to a mover and shaker on any of the twenty little tables out in the Senate side corridor. On this particular day, I had just sat down for a coffee after visiting a couple of Democrat senators. Just to my right was Mr X, who leaned over in my direction and immediately engaged me in a conversation about vibrators. *Sex in the City* had just aired its famous Rabbit Vibrator episode. I was surprised that he knew who I was, although my profile had grown following publication of the *Good Weekend* story. After a brief discussion about politics, he shuffled his chair over to my table and lowered his voice an octave. I could feel a personal anecdote coming on.

'You know, my wife and I like those remote-controlled ones.'

'Okay, yep, they're good,' I said.

'We like it when I'm on one end of it controlling it a bit. Like making the choo-choo train go into the tunnel.'

'Okay, yep, that's good too.'

I can't remember any more of the conversation but a vague existential malaise swept over me at the prospect of his party having any electoral success in the years ahead.

* * * *

Back on the election trail, David Barnett had told me not to waste my time trying to lobby Howard on the eve of an election but to deal with the man who was charged with getting them elected—Liberal Party federal director Andrew Robb. I tried to make an appointment to see him, but to my surprise he was more comfortable coming out to our X-rated loft in Fyshwick. Armed with the *Good Weekend* article, he looked around our political-cartoon gallery and my dress-making corner while Robbie got the tea and biscuits. He appeared to ignore the dope plants (or maybe he didn't see them) and asked questions about some of the crazy antiques and primitive furniture. Then we settled down to business and he asked us what we wanted.

We didn't say we wanted Howard to drop his promise to ban the X-rating. Eating humble pie gives most politicians a degree of indigestion. Instead we asked him to help us get a new category in place for sexually explicit, non-violent films called Non-Violent Erotica (NVE). This would make a permanent change to the way politicians viewed the product rather than trying to put out spot fires on the X-rating forever. We told him we could accommodate some changes to the X guidelines, like heavy bondage and the few offensive fetishes that were still in the category. This would allow the parliamentary wing of the party to defend NVE as genuinely a new category. If Robb would give us a promise to do this, we would not mail out to the average 7.5 per cent of each electorate that bought X-rated videos advising them to vote against the Coalition. Robb thought it over for a few minutes and then said that we had a deal, but we couldn't bring it up as an election issue. Neither could we mention it in the media. On this, he said we would just have to trust him. We shook hands. It was a gamble, but our intuition was to go with it.

* * * *

NVE was the perfect 'out' for the Coalition because they could still ban X and appear to be cracking down on porn. We knew that every state government would not ban a new category called NVE because it allowed them to keep their bans on X and placate the diminishing moral minority. I'd spoken to the NSW and Victorian attorneys-general, Bob Debus and Rob Hulls, and they had both indicated to me their general support for the move. Andrew Robb then approached the new federal attorney-general, Daryl Williams, following the Coalition's win in the 1996 federal election to begin the process of creating a new classification called NVE. This was in line with the 1988 Senate Committee recommendations, as well as a sunset clause in Victoria's Classification Act that said if NVE ever came into being the state would automatically adopt it. When Howard saw it, he declared his support.

Around this time, Pru Goward invited me on to her ABC radio program. She asked me about my time working in Canberra's sex industry. I liked her a lot. As an interviewer, she reminded me of my dad. She was forthright and worldly and didn't choke up on sex work. Following that program, she wrote an editorial for the *Good Weekend* in which she made the bold admission that she would prefer to see her husband visit a sex worker than have an affair with his secretary.

The fallout continued for weeks as commentators argued the morality of commercial sex and on talkback radio, wealthy and long-suffering wives admitted to dumping their older husbands at brothels while they did the weekly shop. Following the interview, Pru and David Barnett asked Robbie and me over to their Manuka house for a cocktail party. It was a brave move to invite a couple of sex industry lobbyists to a soiree set among a sea of blue rinse and royal-blue politics. Cabinet ministers and backbenchers mingled with press gallery members and other familiar faces, however, as soon as our presence started to be noticed by the guests, two older couples grabbed their coats and walked out in a huff. I just couldn't believe that anyone would be so rude to their hosts, let alone to fellow guests. But I was getting used to this sort of behaviour.

* * * *

The 1996 election was a huge success for Eros. I had given my word to Andrew Robb that we would not campaign against the Coalition and they had won. We were also free to support some individual candidates from other parties. We were seen as genuinely non-partisan. So we had sent 3500 letters into the Tasmanian electorate of Bass recommending a vote for Warwick Smith, the small-l Liberal candidate who had lost the seat at the 1993 election and who had been supportive of NVE. He had won. I mailed 230,000 letters advising a vote for the Democrats and/or Greens in the Senate and then another 270,000 letters advising a vote for the Democrats only. The Democrats vote was substantially up. I sent 3000 individual letters into Labor candidate Wayne Swan's electorate of Lilley, advising members not to vote for him because he had been an advisor to Wayne Goss on the draconian censorship and sex work laws in Queensland in the early 1990s. Swan lost by a handful of votes. I also sent a further 3000 letters into the federal seat of Herbert where former Eros vice-president and Democrats candidate, Colin Edwards, was running. Ken Hill from Club X produced thousands of G-rated videos in support of Colin and we mailed them into his electorate, too. He doubled the Democrats vote in that seat without winning it. We felt like we had politics by the balls.

13

THE PUBLIC CERVIX ANNOUNCEMENT

In February 1996, I received a surprise phone call from US porn star turned performance artist, Annie Sprinkle. She had just done an interview with Sharon Krum for the *Weekend Australian* about her remarkable career, covering her transition from a shy Jewish girl, Ellen Steinberg, to a sex worker, cable TV host, magazine editor, porn star and eco-sexual activist. She wanted advice and a bit of help with her new show, *Post Porn Modernist*, which was about to go on tour around Australia. It would kick off at the Adelaide Festival, then on to Melbourne, and finish in March at the Belvoir Street Theatre in Sydney. In the US, the show had been slated as 'a sewer of fetishism, depravity and pornography' by right-wing Christian commentators who had been in contact with Fred Nile in Sydney. He had subsequently issued a media release calling on the show to be banned. Annie was worried that the police would come along and arrest her.

She was right to be worried. This show was nothing like *Kinky Boots* or *The Book of Mormon*. In fact, it was the most explicit live show ever performed in Australia. *Post Porn Modernist* was a two-and-a-half hour autobiographical stage show that used costumes, slides, music and live performance to tell Annie's life story and bring it to an amazing climax. On stage, she explained to the audience that 'Ellen was excruciatingly shy. Annie is an exhibitionist. Ellen wore orthopaedic shoes and flannel nightgowns. Annie wears six-inch spiked high heels and sexy lingerie.' Later on, she even told the audience she had done the maths on the number of penises she had sucked on in her lifetime: their combined length exceeded the height of the Empire State Building.

The show included her signature 'Public Cervix Announcement'. This involved Annie sitting on a sort of mocked-up throne at the edge of the stage, flattening the top part of her torso on the seat, and spreading her long white legs out like a starfish in front of her so that her feet dangled over the edge of the stage. She then hiked up her skirts high around her thighs, slowly inserted a large shiny metal speculum into her vagina, and invited members of the audience to take a small torch and have a look at where they came from. She also welcomed patrons to pull out their cameras and take a photo along-side her opened vagina.

Looking inside a women's vagina all the way to her cervix is a huge taboo in most societies and is generally reserved for gynaecologists and a few extreme kinks. Even couples in the strongest and most loving of relationships will usually baulk at this degree of intimacy. This view of the sexual world flows through into our censorship laws, which wrongly equate explicitness with offensiveness. This means that an explicit sex act viewed from a distance of ten metres will generally get a lesser rating than an explicit sex act viewed from only a metre away from the action. But an act that takes the spectator inside the belly of a woman just goes off the Richter scale. When the gaze is said to be medical, the law exempts it from being obscene, but it somehow becomes obscene when the gaze is inquiring, curious, titillated or even confused.

So while all this was going on, Annie continued to speak about the various aspects of her biology that she was asking people to view, like a running commentary on the function and pleasure of the cervix, womb, clitoris and vagina. She welcomed the spectator's gaze as she did this, and in so doing rejected thousands of years of cultural conditioning that tells women they should feel shame and displeasure at the male gaze on this area.

She called me to ask if I would attend this show because the news on the ground was that the plods would buy a ticket, mingle with the audience and, at the appropriate time, jump up and arrest her. She wanted me to be there in case an expert witness on obscenity law was required at short notice—and possibly even to bail her out.

Robbie and I welcomed the challenge. I arrived about half an hour before the show to mingle with the crowd and establish if there was a police presence. I engaged a few patrons as they sipped champagne and found that most people were expecting nudity and sexual commentary of some kind. Most had seen Annie in a porn film before. Standing away from the entrance to the theatre, I spotted a couple of likely lads with close cropped hair and grey suits. To say they looked out of place was an understatement. They kept to themselves and I didn't try and engage with them. When it came time to take our seats, they sat in the centre of the theatre.

Annie did her thing and talked about her transformation. She moved purposefully around the stage, playing with her props and appearing in various states of undress. About an hour and a half into the performance, she sat down on her throne for the Public Cervix Announcement. I shot a look at the two vice squad detectives. They had been looking relaxed until she drove home the lubed and glistening speculum.

When Annie beckoned the audience to grab a torch and 'come on down', the rest of the audience froze. You could feel the weight of thousands of generations of collective taboo hanging heavy in the proscenium arch, ready to descend with crushing force on the first hapless soul prepared to get out of their seat. And then it happened. After an agonising two minutes, one brave woman towards the back rose and started the 'walk of shame' to the stage. Within a minute, a man down the front had risen in his place. Then another and another. After a few more minutes, the queue was already snaking back up into the aisles, and most people were shifting in their seats in a will I, won't I mode—except for the gents in grey suits and short back and sides in the centre of the theatre. They sat motionless and expressionless to the bitter end. No warnings or arrests. No summonses or legal notices. They just disappeared into the night as quietly as they had come.

* * * *

Annie Sprinkle's show was a catalyst for explicit sex education around the world. Like the egg that can't be unscrambled, it blurred the line between art, porn and sex education. She dared the world to look beyond the folds of her vagina. She took men's obsession with genitals by the balls and transcended it by showing them something more taboo. Most people who peered up into Annie's cervix probably didn't even notice her vagina. It was simply the doorway to a new holy of holies. The porn industry noticed it, though, and medical porn, fake-doctor porn, cream-pie porn and all manner of internalised content started to become more noticeable in new films. The mainstream sex education industry also noticed it. In 2006, Channel 5 in the UK screened a documentary series on sex called *A Girl's Guide to 21st Century Sex*. They inadvertently changed the course of porn forever by showing a challenging five-minute film of two people having sex: by positioning one of the new, high-tech, keyhole cameras inside the women's vagina, they filmed a sex scene, complete with money shot, from the point of view of the cervix. These scenes were filmed using Australian-born Elizabeth Lawrence and English-born pornographic actor Stefan Hard.

When the UK's TV regulator got the inevitable complaints from the morals brigade, they replied by saying, 'In our view, the portrayal of sex in this program genuinely sought to inform and educate on sex. Whilst the visuals were explicit at times, nothing was transmitted in a manner that could be construed as having the potential to harm people under the age of eighteen.' It was true. No minors would have been harmed, and many minors who saw it would have had a great educational experience. But to infer that this was not porn was arguable. Millions of men around the world pulled their pud even harder to what was, without a doubt, the most explicit sex scene ever filmed in the history of pornography. Since 2006, hundreds of porn distributors have hi-jacked this little film and added it to their sites.

Into this category fall many other purloined items from mainstream medical programs, such as the Channel 4 show, *Embarrassing*

Bodies. When 'Claire's Labiaplasty' went to air in 2011, it was immediately stolen and put on to thousands of porn sites. It lasted for years on BooBooTV.com before being taken down. Material like this is now regularly added to sites from around the world and forms an important genre of crossover media. The question of whether it's porn is largely irrelevant. Under recommendations from the Australian Law Reform Commission in 2011 (yet to be adopted by a federal government) the platform becomes irrelevant and content is everything.

Security cameras that show people's private parts to a select audience of customs officials are another contentious area. Is an X-ray image of someone's penis or vagina, viewed on a security scanner at an airport, a necessary form of pornography or just a small invasion of privacy for the public good? What about the Belgium neo-conceptual artist Wim Delvoye's famous X-ray photos of a man being given a head job? Could they be said to have medical or other educational qualities because they show in graphic detail the anatomy of sex in negative?

My feeling is that sex education and porn have been altered forever by their intermingling. You can't unlearn basic biological information once it has been cut with the pleasure principle, and why should we? In ten years' time, porn as we know it will be dead and what replaces it will feed the mind more than the senses.

14

JANICE

As my media profile started to expand, so did my role as CEO of Australia's peak sex industry association. In 1994, a couple of years after Eros had been formed, the back alleys and the side streets of the industry began to knock on my door to see if Eros would stand up for their rights as much as we did for brothels and adult shops. So too did some areas of mainstream society that had no sexual voice and were desperately seeking one. Disability was one of them.

As a society, we have progressed our understanding of the issues that disabled people deal with in ways that were never dreamed of only a few decades ago. The National Disability Insurance Scheme (NDIS) is but the latest step forward. On one front, though, disabled people still remain stuck in the dark ages. Despite the best efforts of some very brave disabled campaigners, sex remains the great taboo for people living with disability, even though it has the potential to liberate many lives just as much as medication and technology have.

During my first year at WISE I was introduced to a young woman with cerebral palsy who was one of the most courageous and tenacious people I ever met. Our friendship developed throughout my time at Eros and culminated in her appearance on a national TV show in 1997. When we met, we were both 26. In fact, Janice and I were born within days of each other. Both our fathers were in the navy and they vaguely knew each other. She was the eldest of three and, like me, she had a younger brother and sister. When I was born, my mother told me that I was a bit stubborn about breathing properly, but then I did in time to stop any complications. Janice didn't. As a consequence, her brain was damaged and she was destined to spend the whole of her life as a quadriplegic. By the time we were ten, we had both travelled around the world a couple of times, she in a wheelchair and me in a deckchair.

We met by chance. Janice had been to see Family Planning for a regular check-up and while she was there a counsellor asked her if there was anything more they could do for her. She told them that, like most women her age, she wanted to get laid. Knowing that I was running WISE and that I had just finished a sex-educator's course with Family Planning, her case manager called me to see if I could help. They thought I might be able to source some appropriate sex toys, maybe an erotic film or two, and maybe possibly even explore avenues for Janice to meet appropriate men for sex and even love.

I arranged to meet Janice at the disabled facility where she lived in suburban Canberra. I was quite open with her about her options, and after hearing her story and how she was feeling about sex I thought the best thing would be to get her a vibrator like a Hitachi wand that, with a little practice, she might be able to use herself. I also raised the possibility of finding a male sex worker for her. She jumped at this. Any personal contact, though, would have to be in a brothel or outside her home. It was clear from my first visit that the institution she lived in didn't even like male visitors spending time alone with female housemates, let alone having sexual contact with them, and when Janice did have visitors, the staff preferred her door to be left open.

It was obvious that what Janice really wanted was to have a relationship and to find love, but she was also realistic enough to know that that would not happen overnight—whereas having sex with a man just might. Back in those days, there were not many male sex workers seeing women and even fewer who would countenance the thought of seeing a disabled woman.

I didn't want to feel sorry for Janice because I knew that we had the beginnings of a genuine friendship based on a shared set of values. She also liked cigarettes and loved a drink, but after one try she had decided that marijuana wasn't for her. She loved to party as well, so in the months and years after we met we started going to the occasional nightclub together, and every now and then we would visit a sex shop. She'd never been to either before. It was fun, but I couldn't say it was easy. Even though she only weighed between 30 and 40 kilograms, I had to lift her in and out of her wheelchair, take her to the toilet, change her pads and wipe her arse. I didn't mind doing all this, but at the end of the night I just wanted to go out and party myself! Sometimes she would catch a cab over to my place where we would just watch telly or have a drink.

After many months of searching, I finally found a male sex worker who was willing to see Janice and was sensitive enough to cope with her disability. I had three or four others say they would do it, but when push came to shove they just couldn't deal with that level of disability and backed out.

Guy was a tall, blond, good-looking, mid-thirties man with a sensitive but pragmatic side. He was perfect for Janice and agreed to charge her only $90 for the hour, which at that time was half the standard rate for an able-bodied woman. I contacted Crystal's brothel about using one of their rooms, which they were happy to let us use free of charge. Some of the other sex workers also volunteered to help Janice get undressed and take her to the toilet. I bought her lingerie and adjusted it to fit her tiny frame.

She was pretty excited about the whole idea, and after her first time she glowed for days and couldn't wait to do it again. All her muscles relaxed after sex, her mood lightened and she didn't rely on medication as much to get through the day. Guy was the ultimate professional. He didn't have penetrative sex with her straight away, instead preferring massage, cuddling and masturbation. After her first few appointments in as many weeks, it was beginning to look like an expensive habit for my friend and I just couldn't afford to fund it every week. At this stage, too, I could also see she was starting to fall in love with Guy. It was understandable: this was the first time a man had been romantic and sensuous with her. He was handsome and loveable, but he was a professional and not there for love. I stepped in and had a chat to Janice. She understood, but it was very hard for her. As you would expect from someone who had lived in a wheelchair in an institution all their life, she had very limited relationship knowledge.

Janice saw Guy about half-a-dozen times over a six-month period. After that, we put an ad in the *Canberra Times* personal section trying to find men who might like to date her. A handful of men phoned me about the 'position' and I organised interviews with each one at an upmarket hotel lounge in Barton. Most of them were genuine and Janice loved it, sitting there with a cocktail on her tray. After each interview, she was beaming. She preferred younger men and made it clear that she expected roses and a bit of romance with the sex. She ended up seeing an older guy who was in town because his son was playing in a hockey tournament. I booked a hotel room for them, dropped her up there, and booked a taxi home for her. I'm not sure they ended up having sex, but she was happy because he was a nice man and they got naked together.

I also introduced Janice to my friend Cindy who owned Chrisindy's massage parlour. Cindy hosted a Sunday roast for all the staff at the brothel and Janice would come over and socialise with her and her staff. Cindy also gave her therapeutic massages and taught her how to use a vibrator. Soon Janice was enjoying orgasms like thousands of other women of her age around the country.

Janice's desire to have a sex life, however, was at odds with the prevailing philosophy within the caring community. Her care home rang me and accused me of exposing her to moral danger. She would be raped in the street, they said. I suppose there was always a chance that hooking up with strangers could lead to a range of disasters as happens with able-bodied women, but how else was she supposed to find love? Janice and I stood our ground. She had the right to experience dating just like anyone else.

Janice and I went shopping one day and I bought her a vibrator. It had slide controls rather than button ones. She just needed someone to pass it to her when she was in bed. But the staff at the residential facility refused. It was so mean-spirited, and I could feel my anger levels rising every time I went into the place. Here was a mature and intelligent young woman whose body just didn't work and they were treating her like a child. They were happy to wipe her arse, dress her and feed her, but wouldn't hand her a vibrator when she was in bed. In the Netherlands, disabled people were able to access sexual services on their equivalent of Medicare, but here in Australia her carers wouldn't even pass her a vibrator.

During this time, Eros was doing a fair bit of work with Channel 10's *Sex/Life* program and I suggested to their reporter, Dave Richardson, that they might like to do a story on Janice. I spoke to her about it first because if she went ahead it would mean her parents would see it, as would just about everyone she knew. She didn't hesitate. We talked about what she wanted out of the publicity and how she wanted to show herself to the nation. She decided that she would like to have a series of glamour shots taken and the cameras could follow her through the process. Of course this meant lingerie, so we went shopping again. There wasn't a lot out there in her size range, but we ended up buying an electric-blue lace outfit that I took in for her on my industrial sewing machine.

On the day Dave and his camera crew arrived, Janice felt a bit shy but incredibly excited. She had her hair and makeup done and I helped her into the lingerie. I would have been a lot more nervous than she was if I was about to have a national TV crew see me in a G-string. It was the first time the glamour photographers had done a shoot with a quadriplegic woman.

As all this was happening, a journalist on a national newspaper became aware of my relationship with Janice and the issues we were coming up against. She wrote a heartfelt article called 'Janice Looking for Love', in which she described the emotionally vexed issues around a young disabled woman trying to have a sex life, but the story was spiked by the editor, who sounded like the carers who had criticised me. How did the journalist know that Janice was not being manipulated by me or placed in mortal danger? Everywhere I looked there was fear and loathing about disabled people having sex.

If the internet had been around, finding love and sex for Janice would have been a lot easier. Sites like dating4disabled.com have made things so much more accessible, and as a result of this attitudes have softened, too.

* * * *

Not long after the *Sex/Life* program, I was approached by the Victorian disability and advocacy organisation, Yooralla. Dr George Taleporos was a young man in a wheelchair with spinal muscular atrophy. He worked with Yooralla and had done a thesis on sex and disability. He asked if I would speak to his organisation about what the adult industry was doing for the disabled. From those discussions, we set up a group together called Accsex and I was a part of the working group. I then talked to the owners of Sexpo and asked them if they would be happy to donate free space to the group so they could explain sex and disability to the tens of thousands of Sexpo patrons and hopefully start a broader dialogue. George explained how difficult it was for disabled people to have a sex life. When he first started to experiment with sex in his wheelchair, the only way he could get off was to put the chair up against the washing machine when it hit the spin cycle and feel the vibrations coursing through his body.

15

DRAWING THE LINE

'We must grit our teeth and see for ourselves. We shall come out unscathed.'

Elderly British morals campaigner, Lord Longford, on hearing that his government committee would have to go to Amsterdam in the late 1960s to see what a regulated porn regime looked like.

The 1990s and the 2000s in Australia saw some of the most vigorous censorship debates since the London *Oz* trials of the 1960s. As the CEO of Eros, I was involved in many of these through Senate Committee hearings, industry statements, media appearances and meetings with the chief censor and other staff at the Classification Board (formerly the Office of Film and Literature Classification [OFLC]).

The debates centred on four main areas. Explicit X-rated sex, material that was degrading or demeaning to women, censorship of the internet, and the line between child porn and art. In many of my submissions, I asked politicians to articulate whether they thought sex or violence should be on the top level of the censorship-ratings scheme. Apart from Eros's, there were almost no calls to consider violence a problem in entertainment media. In 1984, a ban on the ultra-violent R-rated slasher film, *The Texas Chainsaw Massacre*, was overturned. Just a few months later, in 1985, almost every state in Australia had banned the non-violent, sexually explicit X-rating. It was a portent of things to come. The publicity around the X-rated bans created a smokescreen under which the cult of video violence bred exponentially and was ignored by morals campaigners and politicians.

Australia's twenty-year-old state and federal Classification Acts are riddled with inconsistencies, untruths and unpopular notions. For the average person, they are impossible to read, and many lawyers even struggle with them; I frequently backgrounded defence lawyers trying to pull cases together for clients who had been busted with X-rated videos or unclassified magazines. The Classification Code, upon which the Act is based, uses the 'reasonable adult' as the final arbiter in most matters, and it promotes a morality scale where this reasonable adult says that real acts of non-violent sex are more 'offensive' than real and/or depicted acts of murder, rape and serious assault. It does this by restricting depictions of explicit, non-violent sex acts far more than acts of (seemingly) explicit violence. The truth of the matter is that this reasonable adult doesn't exist in the homes of ordinary Australians. They only exist in the parliaments of Australia.

* * * *

Sensing an approaching censorship storm, we decided to put down some stronger roots and buy ourselves an office closer to the designated national associations area of Deakin West. We went back to the vice-regal suburb of Yarralumla, which was the adjoining suburb, and in 1995 purchased a lovely little 1950s weatherboard cottage only a stone's throw from Robbie's original Yarralumla house in Hooker Street. After being denied a housing loan by the four major banks because we worked for the sex industry, we finally borrowed the money from the Police Credit Union—later to become the Police Bank. Over the years many people would wink knowingly when hearing that the sex industry's headquarters were bankrolled by the Police Bank.

When the first federal Classification Act came into being in 1996, it legislated language in the X-rated category more prescriptively than in G-rated cartoons. Any language in an X-rated film that suggested violence or non-consent had the effect of causing the whole film to be banned, even if the bad language had nothing to do with the sex. You could still say 'fuck me' in an X-rated film, but you couldn't say 'fuck you'. It was now called 'assaultive language' and was said to be a form of sexual violence—even if it occurred while the actor was portrayed having an argument with the pool guy.

Equally, the new rules around violence in this non-violent category were ridiculous alongside the violence that was permitted in the MA and R classifications. If a knife was on a table in a room where two people were having sex, the whole X-rated film could be banned because someone *could* have reached for it and stabbed their lover—even if the knife was only there to butter the toast. It came at a time when X-rated producers overseas were starting to respond to the many calls for realistic and plot-driven porn rather than vacuous, mechanical sex scenes.

Of course most dramatic, action or comedy films have a modicum of bad language and some aggression. The new laws meant that most of these more creative films never made it to Australia and porn was dumbed down again, this time by the policy-makers and not the porn moguls.

During the early years of Eros in the 1990s, it became obvious that Kerry Packer's Australian Consolidated Press (ACP) was making more out of porn than anyone else in the porn industry. His two 'P mags', *People* and *The Picture*, actually shaped the porn industry until the advent of the internet. By 1996, *The Picture* magazine was selling more than eight million copies a year, and along with *People* pulling in more ad revenue than *Cleo* and *Women's Weekly*—most of it from porn videos. Although most of the X-rated video companies produced their own monthly catalogues, *The Picture* and *People* were effectively national X-rated catalogues and included interviews with porn stars and even a bit of politics surrounding the industry. At around the same time, Rupert Murdoch's empire was making more money from prostitution than any brothel ever did by advertising sex workers and brothels in the *Daily Telegraph* where, in the absence of effective discrimination laws, they could charge five and six times the amount that they did for ordinary ads. Murdoch would later also profit handsomely through Foxtel's adult channel in hotels.

My first real interaction with the OFLC happened back while Eros was still preparing to launch in 1992. *People* magazine had just run a cover with a young woman on all fours with a gold-plated dog collar around her neck, tethered to a chain made of pearls. A small cover note read, 'Woof! More Wild Animals Inside.' It was a landmark publication in Australian censorship debates. At the time, a young advertising executive in ACP, Craig Ellis, had taken

Packer's publisher, Richard Walsh, to task over the cover during pre-production, saying in his opinion it was offensive and he could foresee a major shit storm over it. Walsh told him to concentrate on advertising and leave the editorial decisions to him because he had personally authorised it. Craig Ellis would later take over the second publicly listed adult products company in Australia, sharonausten.com, and become a lifelong friend.

When the magazine went on sale, feminist groups around the country went ballistic. They walked into newsagents, tore up offending copies and picketed Packer's offices on Park Street in Sydney for days. They claimed that the cover would fuel all sorts of hate speech and sexual assaults on women because it made them look like animals and at the beck and call of men.

At the same time, the cover of *People*'s stablemate, *Cosmopolitan*, had featured the black supermodel Naomi Campbell with a cover note saying, 'You too can have a body like this'. There was no protest here. I argued in the media that this was actually a far more damaging and enduring image for women than the dog collar, which was a bad-taste spoof at worst and would disappear just as quickly as it appeared. Richard Walsh didn't help his cause much, either, when I heard him argue on radio that *People* magazine was an important addition to the literature of the nation and that without it the working man would have nothing to read.

Packer convened an urgent meeting of his executives on the issue. Also feeling the heat over the issue was the Chief Censor, John Dickie. He called an emergency meeting of all parties to his offices in Darlinghurst to work out a way to placate those who had been offended. Eros was invited because Packer's adult magazine section, and indeed most of the major adult-magazine distributors in the country, had joined us.

Sensing an opportunity to get a step ahead of their adult counterparts, the mainstream magazine distributors Gordon and Gotch (who also distributed some adult titles) proposed a system of compulsory classification for any magazine that was deemed 'beyond the pale'. Eventually this became the dreaded 'Submittable Publication', which was defined in Section 23 of the *Classification Act 1995* as: 'A publication that contains depictions or descriptions likely to cause offence to a reasonable adult, is unsuitable for a minor to see or read, or is likely to be refused classification, is required to be submitted.'

After 25 years of operation, this law has only ever been applied to sexual content—and then mainly to that published by the adult industry. This has resulted in major publishers like Penguin being able to republish novels and coffee table books with content that would never be allowed in an 'adult' magazine. For example, Anaïs Nin's classic erotic anthology, *Delta of Venus*, opens with a graphic short story about a 40-year-old man having sex with a twelve-year-old and her fourteen-year-old sister. It's beautifully written, but how is this not 'unsuitable for a minor to read' when a benign topless photo of a 30-year-old woman is said to be unsuitable? A hunting magazine that shows a smiling shooter cradling a freshly slaughtered deer with blood running down its neck . . . How is that not 'unsuitable for a minor to see'? I'm not arguing for more censorship here, and certainly not of Anaïs Nin. However, a level playing field would be nice.

* * * *

Some of the discussions I had with censorship authorities at that time were just mental. In the early 1990s, South Australia, Western Australia and Queensland all maintained a separate state censorship office running alongside the federal government's OFLC. The cost to the taxpayer was huge and unnecessary. Frank Morrissey was the WA State Censor. He was a nice, softly-spoken man in his early forties who looked like he had a wardrobe full of brown cardigans. In late 1992, I received a call from the advertising manager at ACP, Mike Byers, to say that Frank had just banned an edition of *The Picture* magazine in WA and would I go over there and try and sort it out? The offending article was an eight-framed photographic cartoon of the magazine's ace reporter, 'Tubs Grogan', and his adventures with a stuffed beaver.

Tubs Grogan was in fact Pat Sheil, a respected journalist who would run Column 8 in the *Sydney Morning Herald* in the years ahead, and also run for the Sex Party against Malcolm Turnbull in Wentworth. The cartoon showed Tubs and the beaver heading off to the Hellfire Club one day where the beaver is put through a range of sado-masochistic practices. As I sat in Frank's pokey little Perth office, he tried to tell me that the cartoon represented an act of bestiality and was therefore offensive in the State of Excitement.

'But, Frank, it's a stuffed beaver,' I said. 'It's not alive. It has no existential configuration, so it can't be said to feel anything.'

'Doesn't matter,' he said. 'Dead or alive, it's still bestiality.'

Then he reached down into the little locked cabinet from whence *The Picture* magazine had come and pulled out a copy of *Australian Sexpaper*. This was a Category Two restricted publication that was all about explicit and crazy sex. Frank gingerly opened it to a page that showed a woman in her kitchen with a large zucchini inserted into her vagina. I looked at it and pulled on that frontal lobotomy look that people have when there's nothing really to say but they think there should be.

'What about that?' he asked. 'I'm banning it because it's an unnatural act.'

I'm not much of a size queen (the largest thing that had been in my vagina was probably a Jimmy Jane Whopper Dong one night after a lot of alcohol) so for a moment there I pondered the occupational health and safety aspects of the monster vegetable. Then, for some clarity, I asked, 'Why is it unnatural, Frank? It's no bigger than a baby's head.'

For a moment he seemed flummoxed, as if he had never thought about childbirth being a natural act. Then he turned his gaze away from me, deftly placed the two magazines back in their special cabinet, and showed me the door.

* * * *

The debate over women's labial lips first came to me in 1999, after the OFLC introduced revised guidelines for publications. Some Eros members who published unrestricted magazines with nudity started to be selectively banned because of what the OFLC called 'relished' nudity—and, no, it didn't mean the models were covered in chutney. It was just more jargon from the censors. 'Relished' nudity existed, they said, where there was too much 'genital emphasis'. If a nude photo showed a model with neatly fitting labial lips that butted up together to form a tight crease, the image was said to be incapable of causing offence because that represented 'discreet genital detail'. However, if the inner labial lips protruded in any way through the outer lips (called an 'outie'), the image was said to be 'emphasised' and therefore capable of causing offence. I issued an urgent media release claiming that under this spurious logic, a circumcised penis should also be capable of causing offence because you could see what was under nature's little tarpaulin. Male penises, they said, could only be held to be offensive if they were erect.

It was a ludicrous proposition. To get around the censorship imperative, the editors of these unrestricted magazines started airbrushing their model's vaginal lips together in a process that became known as 'clamming'—so called because the vulva was made to look tightly shut like a clam.

Between 1999 and 2000, the number of banned publications in Australia rose by an extraordinary 600 per cent. In 2001, one of my Eros members, *Australian Women's Forum*, attempted to publish an article about the increasing numbers of women presenting for vaginal plastic surgery. To illustrate the story, editor Helen Vnuk included photographs of different vaginas to show women the wide variety of shapes and sizes, and that they were all normal. When she submitted her finished artwork to the OFLC, she was told that it was unacceptable for an unrestricted magazine and she would either have to take them out or 'clam' them. Failing that, she would get a Restricted Category 1 classification, which meant the magazines would have to be shrink-wrapped in plastic and subject to a reduced point of sale. Things went from bad to worse for *Australian Women's Forum*, and later that year the magazine closed because readers could not get the information they wanted in an unrestricted publication. Circulation dropped from 45,000 to just 16,000. Helen Vnuk later wrote a book on the whole saga called *Snatched: Sex and Censorship in Australia.*

* * * *

In the week following the hanging of the Iraqi dictator, Saddam Hussein, at the end of 2006, grainy video footage emerged of the event that was quickly all over the internet and playing on some news networks. The OFLC had previously classified a number of films that showed these sorts of executions as R-rated, the most famous a film called *Executions* that showed an hour of grisly real-life scenes of people being put to death in a variety of ways and offered up to the viewing public as entertainment. I thought that there was a need to house this material in a special restricted category of its own.

Only weeks before the Saddam video was released, one of my Eros members from WA, the listed company adultshop.com, had lost an appeal to have a stylish, non-violent, sexually explicit film called *Viva Erotica* reclassified as R. The decision was appalling on many levels. By insisting that the film carry an X-rating, the OFLC was saying that this film and its consenting, adult love-making had the potential to cause more offence than a film that showed people being machine gunned in the streets, hung from lampposts or fried in an electric chair. It was a reprehensible view of the electorate's values that was not supported by a Neilsen poll at the time: only 22 per cent of the national survey thought that the reasonable adult found depictions of explicit sex offensive, while 76 per cent said they should be available on a restricted basis to adults. The X-rating meant that *Viva Erotica* would be banned from sale in all states, whereas the OFLC had made *Executions* available everywhere.

So I thought I'd catch out their hypocrisy and their cant by submitting the three-minute film of Saddam's hanging for classification. When they gave it an R-rating (which they had to give it to be consistent with previous violent classifications), I would call them out over their decision. But in a four person to three judgment, they banned it with a Refused Classification rating. It was one of the most politicised decisions ever made at the OFLC. Clearly, they had seen me coming. Rather than take on a sex versus violence debate in the media, which threatened to make the then attorney-general, Philip Ruddock, look out of touch, they opted to fall on the sword of gross inconsistency in their classifications.

The increasingly forensic nature of classification in Australia did not stop here. Following the pioneering work on women's sexuality and female ejaculation by Professor Emerita Beverly Whipple in the United States, adult films featuring this phenomenon boomed. Whipple's book that described the phenomenon, *The G Spot*, was a bestseller and articles in the *New Scientist* and on Norman Swan's 'Health Report' on ABC radio, had also raised public awareness of this largely hitherto unknown aspect of female orgasm in Australia. But although Whipple appeared to say that female ejaculation, squirting and urination were three different physiological processes, each with their own distinct chemical markers, the Classification Board was having none of it. To them, it was all New Age nonsense. If you depicted any fluid coming out of a vagina in a book or a film (except blood but that was another fetish in itself), then it would be treated as 'urolagnia', which is the technical term for a 'golden shower'. Under the Classification guidelines, this is an offensive fetish and is banned. This flat-earth interpretation of basic female biology was then applied to potentially send people to jail.

In 2010, one of my members, abbywinters.com, was prosecuted for selling a Refused Classification film because it featured a depiction of what the Classification Board claimed was urolagnia. When

I saw the offending film clip, I realised the young woman who had brought herself to orgasm was clearly a squirter; this was a depiction of a form of female ejaculation, not urination. Under our classification laws, male ejaculation is not considered an offensive fetish and is not illegal to display in a restricted classification book or film. So why were women being discriminated against in this most visceral of ways?

It was no minor point, either. Abbywinters.com was the leading adult-content producer in the country at the time, with hundreds of young women and men producing hours of sexual content for the website. Garion Hall, who ran AbbyWinters, had purchased an old bluestone church in the hipster suburb of Fitzroy in Melbourne and turned it into a paragon of ethical porn production. I had been there several times and was impressed at how water was being recycled off the roof, staff were given regular breaks for exercise, and wholesome food was encouraged. Models and directors were handed a brochure on how to make ethical porn before going out on a shoot. It contained all sorts of advice, even down to a list of local hospitals and doctors if there was a medical emergency. This was something different and the punters were responding in kind.

The revenue streams and the basic illegality of selling porn in Victoria, however, had not gone unnoticed by a *Herald Sun* crime reporter, Keith Moor, who had it in for AbbyWinters. But prosecuting an online company for selling X-rated material where the transactions all occurred in another country wasn't easy. Finding a refused classification film on the premises was a much more serious offence—and an easier one to lay charges over. A film showing urolagnia would fit the bill, and when the police found the squirting film, Garion Hall faced a possible prison sentence.

Twenty-two people have made up the Classification Board over the years, chosen, as described on the website, for being 'broadly representative of the Australian community' and 'drawn from diverse areas, age groups and backgrounds'.

The squirting debate made a mockery of these statements. I'm not sure how widespread this phenomenon is, but I'll put my hand up to the odd squirt, and I have quite a few girlfriends who would as well. My rough estimate is that 50 per cent of women have had some sort of experience of it. By denying the existence of female ejaculation, the Classification Board members were almost saying that none of them had had personal experience of it. In any case, the public was not being represented. As a postscript to this story, Garion Hall was fined $6000 after police dropped most of the charges against him. The AbbyWinters company fled Australia days after they were prosecuted and relocated to the Netherlands where everything they did was deemed perfectly legal.

* * * *

Personal smear and character assassination were never far from the job of defending porn. It was something that just went with the territory and I tried hard in those early days as a lobbyist to develop a thick skin. Looking back, I don't think I did this as well as I should have, but I wasn't born a rhino and the barbs thrown by conservative politicians did take their toll. Des Clarke's reign as Director of the Classification Board from 2000–04 was cordial and without incident. Then in November 2007 the NSW MP Fred Nile made a speech in parliament that would have seen him sued by both Des and myself had he not been protected by parliamentary privilege.

> I have received copies of emails sent between Robbie Swan and his partner, Fiona Patten, of the Eros Foundation who are actively involved in the importation and sale of prohibited goods, which they bring into Australia and seek to put through Australia's classification system. The movies, on DVD or videotape, have been refused classification due to violence and underage actors. In some cases, they use actors of legal age who purport to be children and are intended to depict children.

Then he went a step further and alleged a criminal relationship between us and the Chief Censor, as well as the head of the ACT X Licensing Scheme, Tony Brown.

> There was a similar unhealthy relationship involving Des Clark, former director of the Office of Film and Literature Classification. Those relationships are a cause for great concern. When Des Clark was leaving his role, Robbie Swan of the Eros Foundation said, 'I will send him a nice, original, erotic Indian miniature painting as a thank you for what could be considered as a good term as director.' I am very concerned about these close relationships between pornographers and people in charge of film classification, or people working for the Commissioner for Fair Trading in the Australian Capital Territory. I call on the federal and state governments to investigate these relationships to ensure that public servants are not breaking the law.

I wish the ACT and NSW governments had taken Nile's advice and set up an investigation. It would have made fascinating reading and allowed me an opportunity to defend myself against his deceitful allegations.

In reply to the spray, the President of the NSW upper house, Amanda Fazio, did defend us.

'There is nothing sinister in industry groups giving small gifts to departing heads of regulatory bodies,' she said. 'The notion that an erotic miniature could be said to form the basis of an unethical and illegal relationship is an extreme point of view that is not sustained by normal business practices.'

She was right. A senior executive in Treasury might get a gold watch when they leave the job, and a former PM might get a leather-bound copy of his speeches. So what do you give the Chief Censor when he leaves? It was obvious. You give him a turn-of-the-century Indian erotic miniature painted on the back page from a 200-year-old copy of the Koran!

Nile's epitaph to this fiasco rolled on ten years later when a NSW Department of Parliamentary Services report showed that computers in his office had accessed porn sites up to 200,000 times. Nile told an enthusiastic press conference that his staff had been told to access the Eros Foundation and Sex Party sites to see if we had links to hardcore porn sites. Yep, 200,000 times, just to make sure . . . Of course, Nile didn't do any of the accessing, either. He told journalists that he had given his login and password to a junior researcher and that he'd never watched any porn in his entire life. It was a more damning admission than he could possibly have comprehended.

16

TAKING OFFENCE

Censorship by its very nature is a conservative practice. Always deleting, never adding. It should then follow that censorship officials would be very dour folk indeed, and that the Classification Board would be full of long-faced men in dark suits and finger-waving ladies in thick woollen skirts. I did meet a few Mrs Grundys in that office over the years, but I also met some people who worked like resistance fighters against their repressive political masters.

To this end, it was a joy and an utter surprise to meet David Haines in my first year as Eros CEO back in the early 1990s. He was into his sixth year of a nine-year appointment as Deputy Chief Censor. David came to Australia in the late 1970s from Bristol in the UK where he'd been a teacher. His first inclination in Australia was to be an actor. He appeared in a number of commercials (as diverse as ads for AMP insurance to ETA Mayonnaise) and a few TV series (including *The Timeless Land*) before becoming a member of the Film Censorship

Board. A few years later, he was appointed to the position of Deputy Chief Censor and, at the same time, Secretary of the Senate Standing Committee for Censorship Matters.

From my very first meeting with David in 1990 at a Greek restaurant just down the road from the OFLC offices in Darlinghurst, I had the feeling that he was sleeping with the enemy. He was a tall, handsome man who spoke like a BBC newsreader and dressed in grey pinstripe suits. His urbane manner reminded me of a diplomat, but the twinkle in his eye said something else. Over lunch, I found out that he was married to author Di Morrissey and that together they were writing children's television programs. He also told me that he had watched over 15,000 X-rated films in his job at the Board—many of them on fast forward.

David would never make the shortlist for the top job as his name had been tarnished by conservative politicians and morals campaigners. When he arrived at then federal Labor Attorney-General Michael Lavarch's office for the first time in the mid-1990s with Chief Censor, John Dickie, one of Lavarch's advisors greeted them with: 'Here they are—good cop, bad cop!' As they were shown into Lavarch's office, Dickie introduced David as his deputy. 'Ah . . . You're the one they call the Antichrist,' Lavarch exclaimed.

Defaming David was the specialty of the conservative Senator Brian Harradine, and apart from lobbying the attorney-general about David's supposedly immoral standing, he also convinced the government to bring in new legislation to limit the tenure of Deputy and Chief Censor to not more than seven years. He argued that it was to prevent appointees from becoming desensitised to the material. It was a ruse, of course, and designed solely to get rid of David, who at that point had been in the office for fourteen years with no end in sight.

After his term finished, David bought a Harley and became a censorship consultant to the entertainment industry. He helped set up the first adult pay TV channel, Nightmoves, and consulted to the largest X-rated company at that time, AXIS. But what he did next astonished everyone. In 1998, he abandoned any pretence at a respectable job and became the executive producer of Redstone Films, the newest and most visible producer of Aussie porn. His first production was the erstwhile *Buffy Down Under*, which received rave reviews in all the US trade magazines.

In an interview with Angela Catterns on ABC Radio about his extraordinary transition from Deputy Chief Censor to porn producer, he explained that there were three essential qualities that male wannabe porn stars had to have: they had to be able to deliver their lines, perform their parts and 'get their parts to perform as well.'

Before David, Janet Strickland was Australia's Chief Censor from 1980–1986, and although I never met her, I think she was probably the most enlightened Chief Censor we ever had. In 1996, she gazed into her crystal ball and told the *Sydney Morning Herald*:

> It's speeding up. It's going to get worse. God knows what kind of society we'll be living in in 10 years' time. It could be like Victorian times again with all the hypocrisy and double standards. Why is it that we are not allowed to be shocked and offended? Where is it written? It's good to be shocked and offended. It means we can still feel.

Strickland more than echoed the words of the world's most heavily censored writer, Salman Rushdie, who famously said, 'What is freedom of expression? Without the freedom to offend, it ceases to exist.'

Both their statements echo the debates we are still having today about whether or not it's okay to offend people and whether there should be criminal sanctions for doing so. Section 18C of the Racial Discrimination Act has been attacked recently by conservatives like Tony Abbott and Andrew Bolt for making it an offence to do something which could 'offend, insult, humiliate or intimidate' someone based on their 'race, colour or national or ethnic origin'. These critics claim that merely being 'offended' by someone's speech should not make that speech illegal and that this narrowing of the law discriminates against free speech.

While debate about causing offence to people in this particular way has been a relatively recent issue, using 'offence' or 'offensiveness' to prosecute people under federal and state Classification Acts has a long history in Australia. Prime Minister Malcolm Turnbull tried to pull the Racial Discrimination Act closer to the Classification Act by replacing the words 'a reasonable member of the relevant community' (the one being discriminated against) with a 'reasonable member of the Australian community' (ostensibly a much broader cohort). This is the same 'reasonable (Australian) adult' who is said to be offended by certain films, publications and computer games under the various state and federal Classification Acts.

It was only in 2010 that a man was sent to jail in New South Wales for selling a DVD that the state government had determined was 'offensive to the reasonable adult'. Over the past decade, hundreds of Australians have been prosecuted for similarly offending this reasonable adult. How can someone be said to have offended others by selling images of legal acts?

I believe in freedom of and freedom from religion. I think it is important that religious groups are not shielded from being investigated by legislation. I am uneasy, however, with where the changes to 18C are coming from because those politicians who are most vocal about getting rid of the 'offence' provisions in the Racial Discrimination Act are also the staunchest proponents of prosecuting people under the 'offence' provisions of the Classification Acts. Eric Abetz, Cory Bernardi, Tony Abbott and Guy Barnett are all strong supporters of strict classification schemes where non-violent, sexually explicit material is strongly prosecuted. Politicians like these have stopped some of the major recommendations for censorship reform made by the Australian Law Reform Commission in 2011 from ever reaching the parliament.

If you were to push these proponents of change to 18C to say what it is they find so offensive about consensual sex in the Classification Act, they would likely reply that it deeply offends their personal and religious beliefs. It's a hypocritical stand by any measure, but then it's the same old, misguided and inconsistent mindset that motivates these religious politicians to ban abortion and voluntary euthanasia but support capital punishment. It's okay to punish someone who offends your moral or religious beliefs where sex is concerned, but it's not okay to punish someone who calls Asians or Aboriginal people evil or unintelligent.

It's time that we stopped prosecuting people and sending them to jail for merely 'offending' people's sensibilities (mostly religious) with a film or publication. Sure, let's make it an offence to publish a book about how to make a dirty nuclear bomb or use Facebook to organise a gang war, but let's allow people access to consensual porn.

As Kevin Rudd's first term religious reign entered its final days in 2010, the moral rearmament unit of the Australian Customs and Border Protection Service embarked on a new crusade. They added a new question to the incoming passenger cards for returning travellers to Australia, asking if you had any illegal porn in your possession alongside firearms and weapons of mass destruction. Clearly, they were thinking in terms of videos and magazines, however they soon realised that laptops and mobile phones were also fair game. This meant that if you happened to have filmed yourself and your partner making the two-backed beast on your mobile phone, or even if you'd captured a 'stiffie-selfie' in the heat of some airborne toilet moment, you risked a jail sentence for carrying it back through customs.

What was 'illegal pornography', anyway? Most people coming through customs didn't have a clue. The word *pornography* doesn't appear in any Australian statute for good reason: it has been used to describe so many things over the years that it doesn't define anything anymore. The net effect of using such a nebulous term was that red-faced fathers were asked to reveal the latest edition of their US *Penthouse* magazine in front of their embarrassed families, while gobsmacked teenagers were asked to explain the photo of their vagina that they'd texted to their holiday lover—all in the name of national security.

It was so ridiculous that as the head of Australia's sex industry association, I decided to challenge the new laws using satire rather than logic. I ran a competition on social media asking for people's thoughts on a suite of new luggage stickers for travellers who resented this unnecessary intrusion into their private lives. The winning lines were then forwarded to my zany art director, Ilia Chidsey, who turned them into luggage tags. 'Hands off my sexcess baggage'; 'Get your own porn' and 'You can have my porn when you pry it from my warm sticky fingers' were some catch phrases that made it through.

A few months after the customs' campaign started, I was asked to address an adult trade show in the US. I decided to pack a few sample DVDs in my bag ready for customs' show-and-tell when I landed back home. My passenger card asked if I was carrying any goods that may be prohibited or subject to restrictions, and I answered 'yes'.

The DVDs I had were all vanilla US porn, but because Australia's classification laws around the X-rating were so strict (a depiction of a 'Dutch oven' had recently been considered an offensive fetish), almost every film that is classified X18+ in Australia requires a few edits to make it legal. My videos had not been edited.

When I tried to show the first customs official my films, I was quickly ushered on to another official. He checked my card and I was told to put the films away. All of my bags were then X-rayed and I was directed to a counter behind a screen, where I finally found an officer willing to see my porn. I placed the DVD boxes on the counter and he had a quick look at the back cover.

'This isn't what we're looking for,' he said. 'We're only interested in illegal pornography.'

'How do you know what illegal pornography is?' I asked.

'The pictures on the back of the covers.'

'Really?'

'Yes. If they're taken in proper recording studios it means they're okay.'

At this point he flipped over the top DVD box cover to show me what he meant. It was a Girlfriends Video spoof of *LA Legal* called *Lesbian Legal*. Slashed across the box cover was 'bald pussy, face-sitting and Bubble Butt', while the photos showed writhing lesbians with hands disappearing all over the place.

'But you can't tell what's on the disk because of the cover,' I said.

'Um, well, you can . . . We don't need to look at the film.'

By this stage he was beginning to turn bright red and didn't know where to look. I got the feeling that he had not viewed porn with a woman before. I felt sorry for him and decided to abandon my quest to force him to sit with me in a small, dark room in the bowels of the airport watching lesbian face-sitting.

Over at the cargo side of the airport, new operating rules within customs had thrown the classification of bulk shipments of X-rated films into chaos. Customs maintained that the industry could no longer import a film or publication that may be Refused Classification. For the past 30 years, this had meant that bona fide operators had brought in a master tape or disk from overseas, which was then modified and submitted for classification before being duplicated thousands of times. Now customs were saying that even a master disk had to be classified before it could be brought into the country, but how do you classify the film if you don't have a copy of it in the country? It was a catch-22 situation to stop all classifications of adult films around Australia. And here they were judging the content of my three DVDs by the images on the back of a box cover. I could have been bringing in master disks for someone else and they would have never known.

17

HOME MOVIES, PORN STARS

Photographing or filming your sex life has become one of the defining technological features of the last century. Forget Nietzsche and Sartre. The ability to record yourself having a good root is one of the great existential acts of all time. It's just you and the universe, stripped bare and doing what the animals do.

And while it may not be a spiritual experience for a lot of people, the advent of mini DV recorders in the mid-1990s certainly added a new dimension to the sex lives of many. Suddenly *you* were the centre of that action rather than some engorged porn star. People could now store last night's romp on the lounge room floor alongside the wedding vids and Nana's 80th birthday photos.

Robbie has a theory that the reason X-rated films are so popular is that people are hot-wired to watch other people having sex as some sort of subconscious confirmation that we're all doing it right. Like animals in the paddock or Neanderthals around the campfire, evolution has given us an X-rated gene that makes us want to watch others doing it. He reckons that before the advent of organised religion, sex as a spectator sport would not have carried any guilt or shame, but scripture and clergy changed all that. After religion, we all went off into darkened rooms to 'put the devil into hell'.

Like many of our friends, Robbie and I experimented with this new technology. Not long after we got together, we commissioned a sex worker friend of mine who was also a professional photographer to spend a night with us in a heritage hotel room at The Rocks in Sydney to record our official 'wedding photos'. They were tasteful but highly explicit black-and-white portraits that we looked at from time to time. Over the next few years, we recorded half-a-dozen home videos having sex in different rooms of the house, and once in the backyard. We thought they would be safe from prying eyes if we locked them up in our old cast-iron safe. Like our photos, it had a bit of style to it—a brass emblem, chipped Federation green paintwork and a long, slender antique key that fitted neatly into a sturdy old lock.

In July 2001, we had our new Eros Blueberry computer stolen in a rather daring raid. It contained a lot of sensitive adult industry information. Earlier, I had had my laptop stolen from a swanky Perth hotel where only the staff had a key. Australian Associated Press reported it as 'Erosgate' and speculated that it could have been politically motivated. The report said that a computer containing an exposé on state and federal MPs' attitudes to the sex industry was reportedly among the items stolen during the robbery.

About a week later, Robbie and I returned home from the airport one freezing night to find the front door of our Yarralumla house slightly ajar. As we walked in, a blast of cold air flew up the stairs from the rear door, which was wide open and the old safe was gone. One of the tiles on the back verandah had been smashed and I spotted a small amount of blood. The wheelbarrow was also missing from the backyard.

We called the police to report the burglary. They did a quick search of the property but came up empty-handed. We went to bed that night with a feeling of dread that our most intimate moments were about to be unleashed on the internet by some mad Christian campaigner.

Sensing the worst, Robbie hastily convened a couple of family conferences. The first was with his parents and siblings. They didn't flinch. They had expected it for years, they said. The second was with his two daughters, now teenagers, to warn them that the mother of all embarrassments might be heading their way. They came over that night and, once they were seated, he began to tell the story.

'Girls . . . I . . . er . . . have to tell you that we were burgled last night. The thieves made off with the safe and . . . well . . . there was something in it that you should be aware of.'

The girls looked perplexed. Robbie was starting to flounder. He needed rescuing, so I just put it out there.

'We made a few porno videos of ourselves and they were in the safe,' I said. 'We think they might end up on the internet.'

Their mouths flew open but no words came out. Then came the realisation of how this might impact their social lives.

'Daaaaad!' they howled. 'How could you!?'

It was hard not to laugh.

Thankfully, our stolen moments in the safe never showed up online, but as part of an escalating trend around the world at that time, others were not so lucky. As our drama was unfolding, US actress Pamela Anderson was being declared by *The Guinness Book of World Records* as the 'most downloaded star' of all time after her sex tape with then husband Tommy Lee was leaked across the internet. Their tape had also been locked in a safe that was stolen. And while porn star status eluded me, I did host the 'classics' section of Australia's first adult pay TV channel, Nightmoves. It was like being the Bill Collins of porn for an hour a week as I previewed and then introduced the classic porn movies.

Back then, Senator Brian Harradine had pushed the Coalition government to ban X- and R-rated porn from being broadcast on pay TV channels, but narrowcasting had been exempted and it was under this banner that Nightmoves operated. Narrowcasting was defined as a service that was limited through some means like a PIN number or other electronic firewall but could also be like the system for in-house movies in hotels.

I have met many local and international porn stars over the years. Although she was before my time, Ginger Lynn was probably the first famous porn star to visit Australia back in 1988. John Lark had brought her out here to champion the Joint Select Committee Report that recommended the new classification of Non-Violent Erotica. Her press conference, which Robbie organised on the steps of old Parliament House, was reported to be the largest since Gough Whitlam was sacked in 1972.

Following Nina Hartley's visit in 1992 to launch Eros, I invited a very different actress out here to address the National Press Club in 1994. Ona Zee was a dark and sensuous actress who specialised in bondage films, and it was a sell-out luncheon with her speaking out against censorship. Ona had an intriguing history: B-movie actress at twelve, *Playboy* centrefold at seventeen, first *Cosmo* lesbian layout at nineteen. Dancer who met her preacher husband at 30 and promptly started acting in X-rated films.

One of the first porn stars to start selling X-rated on the internet, Ona also said she was an incest victim who had used an adult career to work through childhood abuse and become empowered using sex. Most porn stars, however, didn't report this kind of traumatic early-life experience: Ginger Lynn always stated that the rates of abuse in the sex industry were the same as in the general community.

* * * *

My first international trip as a representative of Australia's adult goods and services industry was to the 1998 World Conference on Pornography at the University of Southern California. Nadine Strossen, President of the American Civil Liberties Union, opened the conference and all the luminaries and founders of the modern porn industry were there: Larry Flynt, Vanessa Del Rio, Al Goldstein and Veronica Hart. One of the most important books on regulating porn worldwide, *Porn 101*, was published from the papers that were delivered there.

In true US style, I was the only speaker from another country at this 'world conference'. With such unifying subject matter, I had hoped that there may have been a European or Asian representative, but, no, just hundreds of Americans—and me. I felt like a minnow in a big ocean, but to my surprise, all the female porn stars made me feel really welcome. On the first night, I had the good fortune to meet Jeffrey Douglas, the Free Speech Coalition's First Amendment lawyer. We smoked a lot of pot together in my hotel room. It was the first time I'd spoken to anyone who had a job like mine and it was the same for him. In fact, we were probably the only two people in the world with the jobs we had. We both felt the weight of the responsibility because adult traders were being sent to jail on a regular basis in the US and heavily fined at home.

We were accommodated at the Universal Hotel, which was used mostly by Universal Studios, and the trip happened to coincide with a twins convention. I don't know why, but it was a surreal thing seeing hundreds of sets of twins mingling among all the well-known porn stars. On the first night, there was a party for all the women in porn. We were ushered upstairs to a bar where Nina Hartley, Annie Sprinkle and a couple of others did a live performance. Under local laws, they weren't allowed to show their nipples, but their performance was played out with a compilation of many of their old adult movies projected on the wall behind them. Scenes of double penetrations, fisting, squirting and queefing (a practice where women suck air into their vaginas and then expel it like playing the bagpipes) were all there and, under local laws, all perfectly legal to screen. They just couldn't show their nipples on the stage.

* * * *

My good friend in vibrator sales in Australia, Sue Raye, had previously introduced me to the feminist pornographer, Candida Royalle, who at the conference in turn introduced me to the world's most famous porn star.

Ron Jeremy is an enigma not so much for being a porn star but because he has turned the fame monster on its head. When he first started acting in porn films in the early 1970s, he was a tall, dark and handsome man with a big moustache and a nine-inch penis. These days he's affectionately known as 'the Hedgehog' because of his hirsute and rounded stature, although his penis and moustache still mesmerise. Now 65, he looks like the primary-school janitor who should have retired many years ago; he is the antithesis of a sex symbol. And yet the older he gets, the more his status grows.

Ron is a very funny man to be out and about with, and has that same Jewish New Yorker sense of humour as Jerry Seinfeld, Lenny Bruce and Austen Tayshus. Not surprisingly, he's also fairly self-obsessed and loves getting things for free. There's something simple and uncomplicated about him, which makes him very direct when addressing other people.

Before getting into porn, Ron was a teacher and taught music to kids with intellectual disabilities. Unlike the stereotypical image fostered by porn stars like John Holmes and Hollywood movies like *Boogie Nights*, he doesn't drink or use any recreational drugs and is still an accomplished concert pianist. He can be charming towards women, but sometimes his frankness can be a little off-putting. He is extremely wealthy and has a large stuffed toy collection.

Following the live performance, Ron and I ended up having a few drinks together and got along really well. He asked me if I wanted to come and see a James Taylor concert with him at the Hollywood Bowl. He had a couple of backstage passes. I had heard James Taylor's famous anthem 'Fire and Rain' in my youth, but I was really an Elvis Costello kind of gal and not familiar with the west coast music scene at all. Never one to dodge a party, though, I enthusiastically agreed.

He picked me up at my hotel in a 1970s Ford Pinto hatchback with food wrappers littering the floor. He was half an hour late because he had been having his chest hair dyed. Everywhere you went, people recognised him. They'd start up chants and pump the air: 'Ron, Ron, Ron.' It was like walking next to an ageing rock star.

This would never happen at home. When Nina Hartley had come to Australia a couple of years earlier to launch Eros, I could sense that some people recognised her in the street but they were coy about letting on. Ron wasn't famous for just being a porn star, he was famous for being like no other, and like Paris Hilton he was now simply famous for being famous.

We arrived at the Hollywood Bowl with only a few minutes to spare and sat down in our premium seats about six rows from the stage. At interval, Ron got up and said, 'Let's go backstage.' As we walked down the corridor on the side of the stage, quite a few of the young guys seemed to know him. They were yelling out his name and high-fiving him. More 'Ron, Ron, Ron'. There were faces in the crowd that I'd seen before on television, but I had no idea who they were. Ron opened the door to James Taylor's dressing room and they shook hands.

'I love yer work, man,' said Ron.

'I love yours, too,' Taylor said back to him with a wry grin.

'James, this is Fiona from Australia.'

Ron was attentive and made sure I was part of the conversation.

'I love Australians,' said Taylor, and we had a conversation about Australia, especially the bushfires that had surrounded Sydney at the time and had received a lot of coverage in California.

On the way home, Ron pulled into a bar where Smashing Pumpkins were doing an acoustic gig. They asked Ron up on stage where he played keyboards with them for a few numbers. After a final solo performance, he came back to our table and put the hard word on me to have sex with him. I said no because I just wasn't attracted to him in that way—besides, I'd only known him for a day. Ron left his car and we got a taxi back to the hotel where we joined a party in someone's room. There were plenty of women there who wanted to flirt with him and play with his cock. He obliged for a while until we left and went back to the conference hotel where another larger party was happening. As we entered the bar, the singer called out, 'Ron Jeremy has entered the building.' I was getting used to it.

* * * *

On a later trip to the US, in 2008, I accepted an award from the Association of Sites Advocating Child Protection for the work Eros had done in making the adult industry aware of child porn and how to report it. The conference was organised by a new adult industry group called XBIZ and I was again a guest speaker. The award was a prestigious one and in years ahead would be won by many famous porn stars and industry supporters, including Stormy Daniels, the porn star who was paid US$130,000 by US President Donald Trump's lawyer during the 2016 election campaign to keep quiet about their alleged affair.

When Ron Jeremy heard that I was in town again, he called me and asked me if I wanted to go for a foot massage and a drink. He picked me up in his Ford Pinto (this time he was on time) and we headed for the Best Thai Foot Massage, somewhere in a cheaper part of west Los Angeles. It was good to see him and we connected immediately, but he chatted incessantly the whole way. He fell asleep in the chair and snored while getting his foot massage, though I was pleased because he had finally stopped talking. Everyone was pleased, in fact, including the woman doing his feet.

After the massage, he drove me back to my unit in Beverly Hills. It was rush hour and the traffic was slow. As we crawled to a halt on Sunset Boulevard, only metres from where Hugh Grant had picked up sex worker Divine Brown two years before, Ron suddenly turned to me, flashed a big smile and said, 'I dare you to give me a blow job.'

Gobsmacked, I looked straight ahead.

'Really? In the car? Now?'

'Why not?'

Though I felt a lot more comfortable with him now, and of course I was curious to see the legendary organ that had played on millions of video screens around the world, I still wasn't that into Ron as a sexual partner. In two minds, I leaned over and unzipped the legend. In heavy traffic on Sunset Boulevard, let's just say I took a dip with the world's most famous porn star . . . without getting wet.

* * * *

Ron was typical of many porn stars who often have a surprising other side to them and I have learned to expect the unusual. When a visiting smooch of US porn stars came to dinner at our place in late 2007 the big boobs, big hair and big nails had been replaced by big brains.

Bobbi Starr was first through the door. Like many young actresses entering this industry, she was brought up in an evangelical household. At 24, she had a music degree and played oboe, clarinet and piano with a particular fondness for Baroque music. I was amazed to hear that she played in a symphony orchestra, but I did wonder if the string section had seen her performances in *Romancing the Ass* or

Butt Junkies #2. Cute as a button and sharp as a tack, she represented the new crop of Generation-Y porn stars who seemed to reject the diva image in favour of a much more tribal thing.

Next was Roxy Jezel. At 25, she had a PhD in philosophy and ethics. She's the sort of porn star that hard-line feminists like Sheila Jeffreys and Andrea Dworkin would have just loved to hate. Try telling her she's being 'used' or that what she does is immoral, and you'll get a half-hour dissertation on Kant with cunt.

The minders from Australia's largest adult wholesaler, Calvista, who were hosting our guests tour down under were also there at the dinner, and so was Roxy's mum, who had come all the way from the UK to join the Magical Clitory Tour. She was a kind of spiritual advisor to the group who didn't say much, but when she did they were like pearls of wisdom from the streets. At first, she was a bit apprehensive of her daughter's lower chakra/higher education choices, but like the mothers of many porn star daughters, she finally got the hang of it and went on tour. Not so strange when you consider that another famous porn star, Belladonna, was raised as a Mormon and her Mormon mum was labelled as a producer for some of her films.

Next was the star of *Debbie Does Dallas . . . Again*, the diminutive Monique Alexander. Monique had arrived in Australia fresh from a nationally broadcast debate at Yale University as part of the American Broadcasting Company's *Nightline Face-Off* program. Hosted and moderated by the urbane Martin Basheer, Monique debated the positive aspects of a career in porn against an onslaught from a seasoned moral campaigner. She did him like a dinner. Back at the party, she confided to me that she eschewed relationships so she could get on with her career, but she also dreamed of having children post porno.

Then there was Jay Grdina, a former business and psychology student who had married and then recently become divorced from the world's most famous porn star, Jenna Jameson. They had just sold Club Jenna to Playboy for a cool US$35 million as part of their divorce settlement. He was the only millionaire in the world that I had seen with a mohawk. Jay was the most engaging male porno producer I'd ever met with a genuine warmth and interest in the other people around him. At last, a big dick with a small ego!

* * * *

What is it about female porn stars where so many of them are card-carrying members of People for the Ethical Treatment of Animals (PETA) and The Humane Society? Monique Alexander's Myspace site quoted her as saying, 'Save all the puppies from evil people.' Infinitely more sensible than the Christian clarion call of 'God kills a kitten every time you masturbate.'

Jenna Jameson joined forces with PETA to promote less, rather than more skin . . . Well, fur skin, anyway. She also championed the use of a new synthetic leather called pleather and was featured on a PETA promo poster looking vampish and encouraging people to 'pleather yourself'.

No doubt the porn industry has its fair share of cretins and arse-holes. But my experiences with the people I've met in it is that they are more ethical on the whole than those I have met in hospitality, fashion, business or politics.

18

THE LOVE BUS, THE EROTIC MUSEUM AND BEYOND THE FATAL PORNO

Eros was not your ordinary Motor Trades Association or Pharmacy Guild outfit. In fact, it was the only incorporated adult industry association in the world. It was also a think tank and a breeding ground for many interesting and commercially viable adult industry projects. These included, Sexpo, The Love Bus, the Adult Industry Awards and, of course, the Sex Party. All of these ventures started as ideas generated within the Eros office and later developed by Eros members and staff.

The Love Bus was a behind-the-scenes tour of the adult goods and services industry. It ran for six years up until 2000, and in that time gave over 6000 people an insight into the day-to-day operation of brothels, strip clubs, adult shops, wholesalers and duplicators that were all trading in Canberra's red light suburb of Fyshwick.

It started in 1994 when I received an invitation to be the guest speaker at a Fyshwick businesswomen's luncheon. I talked about the nature of the adult industry in Canberra and tried to dispel a few urban myths. Some of the women admitted that they had husbands and sons they felt sure had visited adult shops. After the meeting, some of them asked me if I would hold their hand while they visited an adult shop. I agreed, and the following week about a dozen women from the meeting piled into three separate cars and we set off for a guided tour of the Club X shop and peep show in the city, and the Hello Sexy adult shop in Fyshwick. It was a huge success.

A few weeks later, a group of Queensland politicians descended on Canberra to check out the national capital's brothels, legalised only two years before in 1992. At that time, Queensland was still wrestling with the issue of how to regulate prostitution and they wanted to see how the ACT model was working. These politicians contacted the ACT MP Michael Moore, who had tabled the ACT Prostitution Bill, and he asked me if I could organise a tour. I called a few brothel owners and organised an afternoon, but, with eight MPs on board, I told Michael to hire a minibus as we didn't want any of them to go missing. The bus headed off from the city and took in the Executive Studios, the Parlour-Ment House and my old training ground, Tiffany's. Standing at the front of the bus, I gave the MPs a running commentary on the details of the ACT legislation in between stops.

These men saw theme rooms and dungeons, talked to brothel owners and sex workers, and I gave them an information pack at the end of it. The tour lasted for three hours and when the bus pulled up outside the ACT Legislative Assembly to let everyone off, many commented that they 'didn't think it would be like that at all' and 'wow, that was fascinating'.

Meanwhile, I was getting more women who had heard about the businesswomen's lunch, asking me if I would take them on a similar tour. With the minibus of MPs still in my mind, I thought that if I hired the same bus and extended the tour to include brothels as well as adult shops, I could charge a small fee to cover the costs. It worked.

Within a week there were more than 30 women registered for the tour and it was time to get a bigger bus. A quick call to the local ACT government bus service, ACTION, secured a 45-seater. They'd even light up Route 69 on the destination window at the front for us. And, lo! The Love Bus was born.

The champagne flowed and the show bags were stuffed full of vibrators and condoms. It was run as a non-profit venture with tickets selling at about $40 for the four-hour tour. It was an instant hit and the bus was booked out for weeks. Hen's nights were by far the major demographic, but birthdays, weddings and other milestones were also part of the clientele. The wildest one was a booking from the local Rebels' motorcycle club.

News of the bus soon leaked to journalists and I started to get requests from celebrities wanting to take the tour. We trialled this with comedian Judith Lucy and writer Helen Razer. I packed them in the back of my old cream and red Mercedes 220SE and headed off to the Mustang Ranch and the Suckatorium. Naked male dancers swooped and swooned around them like trapeze artists; I think it was the first and last time anyone would ever see Helen Razer and Judith Lucy at a complete loss for words . . .

I closed the Love Bus down six years after it had started, but only because it destroyed most of my weekends during that time. Twenty

Crows Nest, the family home on The Peak in Hong Kong, during the 1930s.

The Street family in Sherbourne, UK, in the late 1960s. Me, my sister Kirsty and our parents are at the bottom of the stairs.

Even as a toddler I was a voracious reader.

My early-teenage tomboy phase.

School holidays at Bawley Point.

Family in the backyard of our Aranda house, with me looking like I would rather be elsewhere. Dad and Kirsty are standing, with my brother Ian, Mum and me sitting at the front.

My wrecked Datsun Sunny—this time I was lucky I wasn't wearing a seat belt, as I was tossed into the back seat.

Looking groovy with sister Kirsty in the height of 1980s suburban chic.

Body Politics fashion parade.

One of my 80s designs.

Tiffany's brothel on Ipswich St, Fyshwick.

My calling card from Birds of Paradise escort agency in Cairns.

Robbie as his alter ego, Caroline Cumming-Sweetly.

Posing for an outrageous *HQ* magazine article.

HQ Magazine

The cover of the *Good Weekend* magazine that launched our lobby campaign to save X-rated videos.

Our Fyshwick loft at 41 Whyalla St.

John Lark, Australia's King of Porn.

Robbie and me dining with US porn star and former nurse, Nina Hartley.

Getting a cuddle from Phillip Adams.

Getting my arse cast on the Sexpo stage.

One of my luggage stickers for those who were pissed off with the porn question on customs new incoming passenger cards.

Network Ten

Channel 10 promo for *Sex/Life* program featuring my friend Janice Burt.

Promo for Galaxy's *Nightmoves* program.

With expat historian and art critic Robert Hughes on the set of *The Erotic Adventures of Ned Kelly*.

Cover of *Hypocrites*—the first publication to call for a royal commission into child sex abuse in the church.

Ron Jeremy

With the world's most famous porn star, Ron Jeremy.

Robbie, Graeme and me having lunch.

Scuba diving on the reef at Cairns.

Winning a gold medal at the 2002 Masters Games in the 100-metre freestyle.

I wanted him!

Breakfast with Don Chipp and his family.

David Haines

Former Deputy Chief Censor David Haines on his new Harley.

With former ACT Chief Minister Kate Carnell.

The Pornstar PhD party at our old Yarralumla house.

Above: Robbie playing silly buggers in our Yarralumla bathroom. The old barber's chair I was sitting in was purchased by the Canberra Museum and Gallery for its historic qualities in the adult industry.

Left: With advisor and good friend, David Barnett.

Campaigning against Pastor Danny Naliah and Rise Up Australia on top of Mt Ainslie.

ifeelmyself.com

Sex Party candidates Zahra Stardust and Angela White make history by being the first two political candidates in the world to make a lesbian porn film together.

Making a point in the Legislative Council.

Working late at night on the chaise lounge in my Parliament House office.

Campaigning on the streets of Melbourne with our yellow-shirted volunteers.

Campaigning with The Basics band on the back of the truck.

Jorian Gardner

Well-wishers at Midsumma.

On the cover of News Limited's *Weekend* magazine.

Addressing a Darebin Council meeting.

Dean Beck

Standing alongside Victorian Premier Daniel Andrews, Mental Health Minister Martin Foley, Police Minister Lisa Neville and Planning Minister Richard Wynne as they announce the Medically Supervised Injecting Centre in Richmond.

years later, Eros was still getting calls from people who had heard about it wanting to take the tour.

* * * *

In 1999, expat art critic and author, Robert Hughes, came to Australia. He was involved in a near fatal car accident in Western Australia while filming his new documentary, *Beyond the Fatal Shore*, which alerted me and others to his presence here. I had taken a small interest in his work after reading a chapter from his fabulous book, *The Fatal Shore*, which chronicled the first night that the first fleeters had spent on Australian soil. Notwithstanding the fact that his version of events had been challenged by some historians, he claimed to be working off letters and other documents from the period in describing it as nothing short of a massive rum-fuelled orgy with soldiers, sailors and female convicts having drunken sex all over Sydney Cove until the wee hours of the morning. His characterisation of Governor Phillip standing on the bow of his ship and reading the proclamation from King George III to formally announce Britain's takeover of Aboriginal land is hilarious and at the same time deeply disturbing. His claim that it was the first political speech made on Australian shores is an eye-opener into our national character, where he can't see the native culture for what it is. It says much about modern-day racism and intolerance in Australia. Phillip's final rejoinder to the crowd was that if they dared to behave in that way again he would have them all flogged, which reveals even more about our attitudes to crime and punishment.

It came as a total surprise, then, to receive one afternoon in October 1999 a call at the Eros office from one of Hughes's producers. Hughes had recovered from his accident and was back in the chair, albeit a wheelchair. He had heard about an X-rated film that was in production called *The Erotic Adventures of Ned Kelly* and wanted to know if he might be allowed on to the set. Hughes found it fascinating that Australians would make their greatest folk hero the subject of a porn film and he wanted to record it for *Beyond the Fatal Shore*.

I was keen to help out, but the truth was that the film had been shelved a few months earlier when the production company, Redstone Films, had fallen on bad times. The producer was disappointed when I told him.

'Would it be possible to re-create a scene for us?' he asked.

I thought about it for a few minutes and bravely said, 'No problem.'

It took me a week of talking to producers, local porn stars and film crews to get a makeshift porn production company into a vacant paddock on the outskirts of Canberra's northside industrial estate of Mitchell. On a cool September morning in 2000, I met Hughes and his team at the gate. His greeting was warm and friendly. He'd dressed in a dark blue sports coat and brown chinos for the occasion. His sculptured silver-handled walking stick laid across his lap and his sunglasses sat loosely on his face. He looked like an antipodean Larry Flynt on the set of a *Hustler* movie. I walked beside him as he worked his wheelchair over the bumpy terrain to the centre of the paddock. We stopped in front of the makeshift porn set and talked while we waited for the epic to begin.

On a large rug in front of us lay the naked 'Ned' facing his girlfriend 'Madeline'. The director, 'Jerkoff Jeff', had been co-opted for the re-creation scene and his crew bore down on Ned from above while

Hughes's team took the wide shot. 'Action,' called Jeff. But Ned wasn't quite ready. The absence of a fluffer and the presence of a celebrity was causing him some performance anxiety. So he fluffed himself to one side and then attempted to mount his girlfriend.

Hughes was clearly enthralled. Ned failed to consummate the union a second time and was beginning to beat himself up. Jeff called time-out and leaned over to apologise for Ned's 'no show'. Hughes didn't seem to mind.

'I've never really seen this done before,' he said. 'I mean, it's the first time I've seen someone have sex in front of a camera.'

'You get used to it,' I replied.

Our chit chat was cut short by Ned's sudden resurrection. Like Lazarus rising, he mounted Madeline and began humping her like a stallion. A few minutes later, it was all over. Like spectators at a footy match, we turned from the action and, with bowed heads, ambled back to the gate. When we stopped to undo the chain, Hughes looked up at me from his chair and with a mixture of wonder and confusion said, 'You know, that's the darnedest thing I've ever seen!'

I liked his attitude to Ned Kelly and the porn industry. The way he saw Australia's attitudes to censorship in *The Fatal Shore* was devastating:

> In the midst of all the constraints of a penal colony, the native born had developed for themselves a sense of physical liberty and kinship with the landscape—like Australians in the 1950s, accepting all manner of censorship, Grundyism and excess police power, but feeling like the freest people on earth because they could go surfing at lunchtime.

Today, as a member of parliament who attends and loves citizenship ceremonies, all I get to hand out is a small, bare-rooted eucalypt and a plastic, Chinese-made Australian flag bearing the Union Jack. We should be handing new citizens a copy of *The Fatal Shore* for all its honesty and understanding of the Australian way.

* * * *

My experience with Hughes contrasted wildly with Robbie's experiences with another great historian, the late Manning Clark. Before I had met Robbie, he had attended a morning tea at Clark's home at the invitation of Griffith University historian and future Sex Party candidate, Professor Ross Fitzgerald. Ross had written widely on his alcoholism battles and Clark had recently confided to Ross on his own struggles with the demon drink. They were coming together this day to talk about the possibility of co-writing a book on alcoholism in Australia that would revolve around their shared love of Henry Lawson's work and the fact that he also had been alcoholic.

As they made their way into Clark's 1950s bungalow-style house in the leafy Canberra suburb of Forrest, Clark's wife, Dymphna, was making scones on an old wood-burning stove in the kitchen. After twenty minutes of talking about their new project, Clark turned to Robbie and asked what he did. Robbie told him he was the editor of the recently defunct political humour and satire magazine, *Matilda*.

'So what are you doing now?' Clark asked again.

'I'm a lobbyist for the porn industry,' Robbie replied.

Clark paused for a minute and reflected. Ross said later that Dymphna looked like they had invited Dracula to dinner. Clark then slowly rose in his chair and walked to the kitchen where he chatted to his wife for a few minutes. When he came back down to the living room, he extended his hand to both Ross and Robbie.

'It's been good to see you,' he said and showed them the door.

Dymphna turned her back on them as they left, without even offering a scone.

* * * *

Crazy people were never far from Eros's day-to-day work. As Sexpo entered its eighth year in 2000, the organisers were hunting around for something new to keep the crowds coming in. We had recently heard of a bizarre exhibit in a Russian museum that could be the Holy Grail. It was the Mad Monk's pickled penis. No, not Tony Abbott's briny budgie smugglers, but rather the preserved penis of the famous Russian monk, Rasputin, a political lobbyist in the court of Tsar Nicholas II. Like many church lobbyists, he hadn't been all that popular and he had been murdered by a group of noblemen. Before they threw him into the Malaya Nevka River, someone had detached his massive thirteen-inch penis and took it home as a keepsake (or a doorstop)—or so the story goes. There are many other stories including one claiming that it was never detached at all; one that a group of Russian women living in Paris had acquired it and worshipped it as a religious symbol; and another that it had been auctioned by Bonhams whereupon the new buyer then discovered it to be nothing more than a sea cucumber!

Whatever the object, it was now in the possession of a well-known Russian doctor, Igor Knyazkin, and was on public display at the Russian Museum of Erotica in St Petersburg. From all reports, people were flocking to see it. So I rang the good doctor and asked him if his exhibit was available for hire. Yes, it was, he said, but it could not leave his side and would require a first-class seat alongside him on a flight from Russia to Australia and a fee of $10,000 for the four days of Sexpo.

With a price tag of around $25,000 now attached to the venture, Sexpo organisers thought better of it. They could get Ron Jeremy's nine-inch penis for a quarter of that amount and it was still attached to its owner. So the idea quickly folded and Ron Jeremy arrived later that year for the first of his many Sexpo appearances.

* * * *

Vibrators have been around in various forms since the Victorian era, but the modern portable electric vibrator really only came into commercial production in the 1960s in Europe. Early 8mm adult films that had been smuggled into Australia during this period sometimes showed these new pleasure machines being used to bring women to orgasm and the race was on to get some into the country. The problem was that not only were the X-rated films illegal to import into Australia, but the vibrators were also prohibited. In 1966, when a young Lane Cove lad, Jim Hamill, first realised the seriousness of the situation, he decided to build his own. Using the famous Coles-brand Embassy torch, a Scalectrix slot car motor and a piece of electrical wire, Jim worked out the basis for the vibrating component of the machine. He then fashioned from his own penis the 'dildo' part of the unit, using a lead mould and some Ansell prosthetic rubber compound. After making his initial prototype, he went into production and made over 1000 pieces, which he sold mainly to soldiers on army bases for their wives and girlfriends.

After buying a new car and putting a deposit on a house with the proceeds, Jim's business started attracting some unwelcome attention. One night at a military establishment in south-west Sydney, he had just begun his sales pitch to a group of young soldiers when the doors burst open and two of Premier Robert Askin's vice squad detectives entered the room. They told everyone to leave except Jim, then put a gun to his head and told him that if he ever sold another vibrator he would be in serious trouble! At that point, Jim decided his luck had about run out and he quit the business. He is now retired and lives on the Queensland central coast. He donated his still functioning prototype to my National Museum of Erotica in 2003.

19

BRIBES, BENEFICENCE AND BALLS

There is a theory about corruption in government that says it tends to filter upward. So federal parliamentarians are said to be less corrupt than state parliamentarians, who are in turn less corrupt than local government officials who are the most corrupt of all. Because local government tends to get the least public scrutiny and federal politicians get the most, this makes some sense. During my time at Eros, one debate in particular captured the worst of it.

In the mid-1990s, commercial sex was starting to make use of new technologies like never before. As leader of the Labor Opposition, Kim Beazley followed in the footsteps of his moral rearmament politician father by banning commercial phone sex on telephone lines that used the 0055 prefix. These numbers had been widely used to broadcast sports results, competition results, weather and other information, and charged the consumer a fee for every minute they stayed on the line. Having an uninhibited woman talk about her sex life or her fantasies to an anonymous caller was worth about three dollars a minute. Most guys who were listening to these lines were, of course, fapping furiously on their end while the women were usually doing their nails or the ironing. The men didn't really care, even if they suspected it: they were there to have an intimate moment. The average time for each call, from my members' anecdotal evidence, was about ten minutes, costing each man about $30, and hundreds of thousands of men were happy to pay it. Over and over again. Although the business impacted brothel revenue, it also opened the door for more women to engage in a different form of sex work. At the height of the phone-sex revolution in the late 1990s, hundreds of women were earning a pretty good wage working at home but also from purpose-built call centres.

I had lobbied hard to have Kim Beazley's wowserish ban on 0055 phone-sex lines reversed without success. In retrospect, it was a minor loss because most of the phone-sex companies soon found a new home on the 1900 platform. Calls to these numbers were much the same as 0055 lines, but a bit more expensive and they could be re-routed if necessary through other countries like Vanuatu who were not too ashamed to take their cut from the millions of dollars being traded.

By the end of 1997, phone sex-lines were turning over a staggering $10 million profit a year. On the back of this new-found revenue stream, a young Western Australian surveyor, Malcolm Day, bought a failing mining company and did a backdoor listing. He turned it into the first publicly listed adult products company in the nation. Adultshop.com took in $24 million in a public float, much of it on the back of the lucrative 1900 phone-sex lines.

With all this going on, it didn't take long for the then conservative Communications Minister, Richard Alston, (known as the 'global village idiot' among IT, media and adult companies) to work out what was happening. Neither had it escaped the attention of the wily old conservative Tasmanian Senator, Brian Harradine. He was in the enviable position of having the balance of power in the Senate, along with his independent sidekick, Senator Mal Colston. Their votes on two of the Howard government's most important bills—the GST and the sale of Telstra—would make or break them. Harradine issued the government with an ultimatum: 'Ban phone sex and I'll give you the GST; ban porn on the internet and I'll give you the sale of Telstra.'

Harradine's Catholic upbringing and his adherence to the ethics of his beloved shoppies union made him intractable in his demands. He relied on the alleged harms to women and children from sexual media and what he called the 'odium' of it all to buttress his horse-trading. For anyone who read newspapers, he was on shaky ground and his claims were being white-anted by the increasing numbers of sexual assaults on children by priests. Clergy were not phone-sex users and wouldn't know porn on the internet if it hit them in the face. And yet Harradine claimed that sexual assaults on children were being fanned by this new style of pornography.

Agreeing to his demands was easy for Howard. Alston drew up an amendment to the Telecommunications Act to effectively ban 1900 services. The ALP initially agreed to support the bill, but under intense lobbying from Eros and a couple of other groups, eventually changed their mind. There was one possible way that the bill could be defeated and that was if Mal Colston voted alongside the Greens, Democrats and the ALP. This would result in a tied vote and the bill would fail.

Dealing with Colston would not be easy. Back in 1988, Robbie had had a furious argument with him in the corridor outside his office after attempting to lobby him on X-rated films. Colston fell into a rage and followed him outside the office, screaming, 'Hey, you, with the hat on! Get yer arse back here!', whereupon he tore Robbie's lobbying documents into shreds, threw them in his face and then spat at him. They had then come close to a fistfight before Colston called Parliament House security and had Robbie evicted from the building. His behaviour didn't go unnoticed, with a liberal senator next door coming out to reassure Robbie that he wasn't the first to experience that sort of violent flare-up.

Among his former Labor colleagues, Colston was not held in high regard. Many called him 'the quisling Quasimodo from Queensland', a reference to the damage he had caused the party with his defection and the unfortunate configuration of his facial features in later life. It had been alleged that in the early 1960s he was a prime suspect in an arson case at a Queensland school. More recently, he had been charged with 28 counts of fraud relating to the near-record amounts of parliamentary travel that he claimed under parliamentary business.

Knowing all this, I called his office to see if there was a chance I might swing him to vote against the bill. I didn't hold out much hope, but it was worth a shot. I spoke to a male receptionist who said he would put my arguments to the senator but he probably wouldn't be interested.

A few days later, Robbie was approached by a man who claimed to have been instructed to act for Colston. He said that Colston might be persuaded to vote against the bill under the right circumstances. A meeting was scheduled, but it never eventuated. Two or three days out from the vote, Colston himself rang the Eros office to say he would vote against the bill in exchange for an amount of $30,000, along with one other condition that might attract a defamation writ so I won't reveal it. Without waiting for a reply, he hung up.

I was gobsmacked. He sounded angry and slightly unhinged, so we quickly decided not to respond any further. This was going down a rabbit hole that had ferrets waiting at all the exits.

On 21 July 1999, debate began on the telecommunications bill late at night. The government had listed the phone-sex bill as the number-one item of business and the sale of Telstra, which was a more important piece of legislation, was listed at number two. But getting wind of the fact that Colston may have changed his vote, the government suddenly reversed the order of business an hour before the Senate sat and put the sale of Telstra first. They then kept the phone-sex bill off the agenda until the wee hours, and with fifteen minutes to go they did the unthinkable and brought it on with two other bills and gave them all about three minutes for debate. They brought down the guillotine and the President of the Senate called for a voice count on all three bills one after the other.

At this time, Colston was battling an aggressive cancer and was clearly drug-affected. His body language on the floor of the house showed him to be dazed and confused. Without going for a division, the President called that the 'Ayes' had it. The bill was said to have passed by one vote.

Later that night, however, some senators realised that they may have voted on the wrong bill. Uproar broke out with those opposed to it, saying their vote had not been counted. The ALP's Robert Ray claimed that standing orders had not been followed, and others implied that the government had purposefully misled the Senate. All to no avail. The government had given Harradine an iron-clad guarantee that they would ban phone sex in return for his vote on the sale of Telstra and nothing was going to get in the way of that.

The next morning Greens Senator Dee Margetts moved to suspend standing orders to revisit the vote. For whatever reason, Colston sat down with the Opposition, the Greens and the Democrats, and the vote was tied at 33 votes all. The motion to revisit the vote was one short of a majority and it failed. But it proved beyond doubt that had Colston voted the same way the night before, the government would have lost.

Following the vote, I commissioned a barrister's report on ways that the Senate could be forced to enact due process via a High Court action. The stakes were that great. But the report said it was unlikely that the High Court would want to try to tell the Senate how to handle its own procedures.

* * * *

When the tsunami crashed into the Indonesian province of Aceh in 2004, many felt the pain of those thousands of people killed, injured or left homeless by the tragedy. People rallied from all walks of life to make a donation or help the recovery effort.

I was very affected by the images and would tear up at the news each night. I had many sex workers and others from the adult industry feeling the same, and, like many other representative groups, Eros passed the hat around. In the space of a week, we collected around $20,000 from sex workers, adult-film producers, brothels, adult retailers and erotic entertainment companies. It was a donation that was not going to be made public and one that we thought the major overseas-aid groups would welcome.

I wanted to offer the funds to World Vision because it was well known and its then CEO, the Reverend Tim Costello, had once been offered a seat in parliament by the Democrats. He looked like an independent thinker with a broad social conscience. I called the main phone number for World Vision and told them who we were and how much money we had raised and asked about the protocol for donating a large amount like that. The person taking the call was enthusiastic and said that someone would get back to me. Later in the day, a man called and thanked me for offering the money, but then said that because it was from the sex industry World Vision could not accept it.

I was stunned.

'Why not?' I asked.

'I'm not sure,' he said. 'It's not my decision, but we can't take it.'

I asked him if Tim Costello was aware of this. He said he wasn't sure about that, either. I asked him if he would at least do me the courtesy of referring it to Reverend Costello because this snub was very hurtful to the many people who had made their donation out of genuine feeling for others. He agreed to do that.

The next day, the same man called back and said that Costello had said it was tainted money and was not acceptable to a Christian charity like World Vision. My blood boiled. It was an incredibly unchristian thing to do. I asked him if the child who had just lost their parents in the tsunami would mind where the money came from or the man who had lost both legs and couldn't work anymore.

He didn't answer, and said he was sorry but they had standards and had to live by them. When I asked him about the standards that had seen hundreds of children sexually abused by clergy, he said he had to go and hung up.

Later in the day I rang Doctors Without Borders who were more than happy to accept the donation, although they later called back to say they wouldn't accept another one.

The concept of 'tainted money' is completely anti-intellectual and defies any rational economic theory. How does World Vision know where all the money that goes into the church plate on a Sunday morning comes from? It's impossible to know. What about the sex worker who is turning tricks to keep her mother supplied with cancer treatment medications? Would all her income be immoral or only a percentage of it?

I'm no Bible scholar, but the story of Jesus's relationship with the former sex worker, Mary Magdalene, seems to persist despite repeated attempts by some to lessen the importance of it. The Bible tells us that she engaged in intimate behaviour with Jesus, washing his feet with her tears, wiping them with her hair and kissing them. It's clear that Jesus didn't give a rat's arse about Mary's former life as a sex worker, and in fact her love for him was all that mattered. The former sex worker was the first person at the cross after Jesus had been crucified, long before any of his male disciples.

So why does a clergyman like Tim Costello cast sex workers into the same boat as terrorists and murderers when it comes to their money? His hypocrisy was compounded a week later when World Vision sent a personal form letter to me asking for an individual donation. I have no idea how they got my address, but when I called them about it, they had the nerve to say that my own money was different to industry money. Who did they think paid my wages?

As a very sad final postscript to the matter, a few years later Tim Costello was in the national media admonishing Australians for not giving enough to overseas disaster relief.

20

HYPOCRITES

The modern sex industry exists almost exclusively as a counterpoint to organised religion. It's the only industry that is wholly based on the principle of 'forbidden fruit'. With no vice, scandal, guilt, shame or prohibition attached to sex, nobody would want to bite into the apple anymore. If organised religion had placed a prohibition on ankles or elbows years ago, ordered that they never be exposed in public and deemed them as inherently sinful parts of the body, guess what most porn magazines and websites would be offering? You got it. Elbow porn. Crinkly ones, smooth ones, young ones, hairy ones, even deformed ones. Penises and vaginas would be treated like ears and fingers.

People in the sex industry have long understood this phenomenon, and although anti porn campaigners can damage the personal lives of people in the sex industry, their efforts at prohibition mostly advertise what's on offer. It's something religious campaigners don't like to acknowledge because it's a no-win situation. They're damned if they do protest and damned if they don't.

Religion provides the high-octane fuel that powers the sex industry's growth. This was classically illustrated in Australia during the late 1970s when the 8mm sex-film business started to morph into the new X-rated video business. 'Stag' movies, as the name implied, had been secret men's business for twenty years and had limited appeal as far as sexual entertainment went. Women just did not want to go to football clubs for the obligatory drunken prawn and porn night. Neither did a lot of men, for that matter.

In the mid- to late-1980s, however, when Australia's churches started to campaign strongly against the new portable 'couple's porn' being produced on video cassette, all they did was to alert women to the fact that they could now watch porn in the privacy of their own homes with their partner. And they did. Not since The Beatles visited Australia in the mid-1960s, when we saw thousands of sexually mature girls and women wet their pants and have multiple orgasms over the sexy quartet, had there been such a mass outbreak of female lewdness. Of the over one million regular buyers of X-rated videos in the 1990s, Eros surveys showed that 70 per cent were being purchased by couples.

* * * *

The Welsh philosopher Bertrand Russell once said of Church clergy: 'Any average selection of mankind, set apart and told that it excels the rest in virtue, must tend to sink below the average.' For the victims of paedophile priests in Australia, Russell's words could not have been more apposite. For people working in the sex industry from the 1980s, they also struck a nerve. Although not victims of actual physical abuse, sex industry employers and employees nonetheless suffered constant emotional abuse and character assassination from church lobbyists. When religious investigators and government inquiries look to the causes of the abuse epidemic, they still fail to see the relevance of the sex industry in the debate.

David Marr's Quarterly Essay on George Pell, 'The Prince', from 2013, was probably the first belated acknowledgement of the role that Australia's sex industry played in bringing religious abuse into the public eye. The real story behind that 'outing' was never told but is integral to any proper understanding of how and why the churches conspired to cover up their abuse and their motivation in carrying it out.

As isolated sexual assaults by clergy started to appear in the media in the mid-1980s, church leaders became worried and quietly began work on a strategy to deal with the fallout. They needed to find a large corporate or institutional scapegoat. The emerging X-rated video industry, with its associated sexual goods and services, was the perfect choice.

Between 1984 and 1987, the mainstream churches simply looked on as Fred Nile and the Festival of Light misled the media debate about how adult pornography was leading to an increase in child sexual assault. Although Nile had a different motivation from the churches, his rhetoric was perfect for them. He was concerned that permissive parents would allow their children access to porn, but his favourite chorus line was: 'It's damaging to children' and 'We've had reports already of them hanging themselves. Murders and violence are increasing.'

Really? Kids hanging themselves because they saw a porn magazine under their parents' bed? This invocation of death and suicide would prove to be a constant theme in Nile's religious lobbying of state premiers and they all fell for it, never questioning his sources or his reliability. Even as late as November 2017, Nile was still lying when he told the NSW Parliament that voluntary assisted dying laws had been responsible for doctors asking family members to hold people down while they were injected with lethal drugs against their will. On this occasion however, he was forced to recant, instead blaming his God for 'prompting me' to say such bullshit.

In late 1987, the Catholic bishops joined Nile's bandwagon and pressured the Catholic attorney-general, Lionel Bowen, to ban X-rated videos across the nation. Given that Bowen's predecessor, Gareth Evans, had only just legalised them in 1983, this was always going to be a hard call, but the campaign waged by the Catholic Church received plenty of media. At this point, the church's PR machine went into overdrive and began an almost daily condemnation of porn, adult shops, brothels, gay and lesbian sex, and all other manner of adult entertainment. Mainstream film releases, like *Hail Mary* and *The Last Temptation of Christ*, allowed the church to further obfuscate on the issue of child sexual abuse.

Apart from the established churches, the campaign was also championed by half-a-dozen old-style moral campaigners. Chief among them was the lay Baptist preacher and federal ALP Member for Capricornia, Keith Wright. His campaign went under one of two names, depending on who he was trying to influence: The Porn Free Zone Campaign or Save the Children. He was backed up by a US evangelist and former McDonald's manager, Jack Sonneman, who led the Australian Federation for the Family. The Logos Foundation chief, Howard Carter, was in the mix as well, as was Family Association chief, Bill Muehlenberg. Two other politicians felt the need to use their offices to defend a moral position on porn—the ACT's Dennis Stevenson and, of course, the king of morality campaigners, the old independent from Tasmania, Senator Brian Harradine.

In 1995, and as a direct response to the formation of the Eros Foundation by Australia's sex industry, John Gagliardi, the leader of a large Pentecostal church in Brisbane, along with two Baptist ministers in the mould of Fred Nile, formed the Australian Christian Coalition. They based themselves within a stone's throw of the Eros office in Canberra. Their immediate purpose was to provide a foil to the dialogue on public morality that Eros had started a couple of years before and to continue the lie that the sex industry was harming children. Later, in 2001, they adopted the more political title of the Australian Christian Lobby (ACL), which still functions today.

However much the ACL, the Catholic Bishops Conference and the phalanx of individual moral campaigners issued pubic edicts on porn and forced religious positions on abortion and the growing LGBTIQ movement, they could not control the growing number of paedophile priests starting to appear before the courts. In 1990, the emphasis had shifted from unknown priests to high-profile campaigners. After moving its ministry to Toowoomba in the early 1980s, the strident anti-porn, anti-abortion and anti-gay Logos Foundation was gathering considerable support. Then its charismatic leader, the Reverend Howard Carter, became embroiled in a series of adulterous affairs that destroyed the group's integrity. He was also found to have led an extravagant lifestyle, squandering church funds. Logos fell apart soon after, but many of those who left ended up finding a new home with the emerging Family First Party and the ACL.

Then, in 1993, Keith Wright, was jailed for raping an underage girl in his parliamentary office and at the girl's home. The anti-porn movement's favourite son was also found guilty of sexually assaulting another underage girl. Wright, born and bred in the morality campaign's 'breeder' town of Toowoomba in Queensland, had come within a few thousand votes of becoming Queensland premier in the 1983 state election.

Soon after becoming the federal member for Capricornia, his proclivities quickly became known among his Labor colleagues, who gave him the nickname of 'Elmer Gantry'—the main character in a Sinclair Lewis novel about a hypocritical evangelist in the US during the 1920s. Appallingly, many Labor members turned a blind eye to Wright's behaviour. He refused to admit guilt over the rapes and indecent assaults and was sentenced to nine years in jail. The damage to the morality campaign was palpable in the community, but for the remaining religious lobby groups it was business as usual. They offered no explanation as to how or why their colleague had managed to fall so far. After all, there was never any suggestion he viewed pornography. He was only ever an assiduous Bible reader—even in jail.

By the late 1990s, the number of charges against church clergy had reached the 100 mark. If there had been the same number of used-car salesmen or plumbers up on sexual assault charges, there would have been an immediate inquiry. But still the political establishment fell in behind the churches. They ignored the public humiliation of Keith Wright and Howard Carter, as well as the overseas fallen angels like the Reverend Jimmy Swaggart and the Reverend Jim Bakker.

In 1997, I issued a media release saying court records now showed that the conviction of priests for child sexual abuse was running at four to one against all other occupations. This meant that the church and religious orders in Australia could be producing up to approximately one-third of the nation's paedophiles.

In 1999, Robbie and I looked at the evidence that was staring everyone in the face and decided to publish a list of all paedophile priests who had been charged over the past decade. It was a huge task and took over a year to complete. It meant employing a researcher and spending nearly $50,000 to publish and distribute 30,000 copies of a full-colour book called *Hypocrites* to every church, media outlet and politician in the country.

As the book was being prepared, I approached the ABC's *Four Corners* with a view to exposing the contents on national television. Our book claimed that up until 2000, there had been 640 charges of child sexual assault laid at the feet of paedophile priests. When ABC researchers looked at the evidence, Chris Masters pushed the 'go' button on a program that promised an 'unprecedented and dirty war between the sex industry and the church'. It even featured a debate between Archbishop George Pell and Robbie.

In the face of all the evidence our book supplied, Pell later claimed that Eros had published *Hypocrites* in an effort to sell more pornography. It was about as far-fetched and ludicrous a response as he could have concocted, and showed everyone that he was so detached from the issue of child sexual abuse that he should resign. The program also broadcast allegations that I was about to expose members of parliament who had double standards on censorship issues. Following the broadcast, the ABC ran an online poll asking viewers whose view they supported: Eros or that of Senator Harradine, who also appeared on the program. We received 96 per cent of the vote.

In the days following the program, I took hundreds of calls from people who claimed to have been childhood victims of clergy. We also received no less than six separate death threats, two of which were considered by the AFP to be serious enough to be investigated (one was ultimately found to have come from a Catholic priest in country New South Wales). Letters from prominent politicians flooded in. Many, like the one from the NSW Bible-bashing MP Bruce Baird (father of future premier Mike Baird) tried to trash our reputation as industry lobbyists. 'I can inform you that your publication has caused considerable damage to your cause amongst my parliamentary colleagues,' he wrote.

In publishing *Hypocrites*, I believe I was probably the first public advocate in Australia to officially call for a royal commission into child sexual abuse in religious institutions. This is what I wrote in the introduction:

> Nearly 450 individual child sexual assaults by church clergy are referenced in this publication as having been dealt with by Australian courts in the short space of 10 years. This shows that, as a profession, the priesthood has lost its direction and has become a real danger to the community. The scale of this travesty is so great that only the highest-level inquiry will get to the bottom of it.
>
> We ask for your help and support in encouraging the federal government to conduct a royal commission into child sexual abuse among church clergy and officials, immediately.

> We believe the terms of reference for such an inquiry should include the following:
>
> 1. An examination of the content and practice of training programs that church and clergy officials have undergone in the past and continue to do so in the present;
> 2. An examination of the effects, if any, that celibacy and sexual repression have upon child sexual abuse;
> 3. The nature and extent of the church's cover up of child sexual abuse within its ranks;
> 4. The need to reassess current government assistance to church-based education and training programs that deal with children, including taxation and other breaks, and;
> 5. The extent to which church leaders, who have presided over child sexual abuse cases in their jurisdiction, have affected current censorship regimes that deal with child sexuality and sexual violence in general.

Twelve years later, then Prime Minister Julia Gillard announced a royal commission into institutional responses into child sexual abuse, and although I felt some vindication and a degree of satisfaction, many of the issues that had led me to make that call have never been addressed in the inquiry. These still need to be investigated as they have major ramifications for the way in which establishment and 'trusted' groups in society can create elaborate and diversionary witch-hunts using the resources of the state.

* * * *

Having finalised the business end of the campaign, Robbie wanted to have some fun with the issue, too.

In 2001 we visited Archbishop Pell's St Mary's Cathedral in Sydney. Pell preached to his congregation here and so we thought we'd leave him a calling card next time he mounted the gothic sandstone staircase that wound its way up to the elevated pulpit. St Mary's is designed in every way to elevate the speaker to heavenly status with the pulpit's placement against the huge stained-glass display of saintly figures towards the end of the building. We reckoned that seeing a copy of *Hypocrites* (by now well known throughout most churches as the work of the devil) on the lectern next time Pell preached would send a nice personal message to him. Whether Pell ever saw the book we would never know, but it was nice to make the gesture. Robbie continued to leave books in other churches around the country.

With the genie well and truly out of the bottle, the figures in the book and the projections that it made were shocking. *Hypocrites* projected that 20 per cent of church clergy in Australia would eventually be identified as a perpetrator of some form of child sexual abuse. With the royal commission now identifying 7 per cent of all Catholic clergy in Australia as having been accused of raping young children, I wasn't far off the mark.

In 2009, while launching the Australian Sex Party, I became the first political leader to call for a royal commission into child sexual abuse in religious orders. I was laughed at and ridiculed for making such an outrageous demand. Only four years later, however, the Royal Commission into Institutional Responses to Child Sexual Abuse was established with many of those who had earlier scoffed at the idea now publicly supporting it. They were also hypocrites in their own right.

Hypocrites was a turning point in the debate over child sexual abuse in Australia. When it comes to adult sexual behaviour, repression is the regulatory model most often adopted by religious campaigners to deal with sex. For members of the adult goods and services industry, the regulatory model is more about expression. The figures coming out of the royal commission should be enough to persuade legislators about which model is best for the physical and moral health of the nation.

* * * *

Evidence of the increasing power of the religious right in Australia comes from two main areas. First, the number of registered Christian parties regularly contesting elections tends to fluctuate between four and six: the DLP, the Christian Democrats, Australian Christians, Rise Up Australia and now the Australian Conservatives. The overall number of registered parties regularly contesting federal elections is around twenty, meaning around a quarter of them are religious parties. Each of these parties might get around 2 per cent of the vote, which doesn't sound like much, but as a block it means they're in a position to approach both the Labor and Liberal parties at election time and offer them 6 to 8 per cent of the vote through preference deals in return for certain promises. Many seats and quite a few elections in Australia swing on far less than this percentage.

Of equal importance for secular Australians is the fact that 20 per cent of all Liberal and Labor MPs are equally committed to religion and religious morality as one of their basic reasons for being in politics. These players often have an undue influence on the rest of their party. Tony Abbott, Kevin Andrews, Scott Morrison,

Barnaby Joyce, Andrew Hastie, Eric Abetz and Craig Kelly all punched well above their weight on the marriage-equality debate. For Labor, the conservative Shop, Distributive and Allied Employees Union (SDA) has hung around its neck like a dead albatross for ages and was responsible for Julia Gillard's gut-wrenching statements against marriage equality while she was prime minister. This political situation is the fundamental reason why reform of issues like censorship, drugs, abortion, euthanasia, stem cell research, prostitution, sex education and gay marriage have all stalled over the past decade.

In 2010, when Robbie asked the Chair of the House of Representatives 'Billboard' Committee, Graham Perrett, for members on the committee to declare their religious affiliations before proceedings started, Perrett agreed to his great credit and 80 per cent of them came out unashamedly as having religious convictions. A week later, when Robbie fronted a Senate Committee on Censorship, his request for MPs on this particular committee to state their religiosity was slapped down by the religious right-wing chairman, Senator Guy Barnett. When Robbie protested that the public had a right to know whether committee members were basing censorship decisions on their religious values, Barnett told him to shut up and get on with it or risk being turfed out of the hearing. It was clear, however, that the same number of this committee was also comprised of many religious MPs.

* * * *

Jeff Sharlet's book *The Family* lays out clearly how the US religious right infiltrates governments using a range of strategies such as 'prayer breakfasts' and how these strategies have been imported into Australia over the past decade. These prayer breakfasts are now held in almost every parliament in Australia and most capital city mayors host them annually. They provide an opportunity for MPs to wheel out their religious credentials to church leaders and do some fund-raising with sympathetic business leaders.

Slowly and by stealth, Australians have been screwed by a group of flat-earthers who have skilfully infiltrated the major parties mostly by manipulating their preselection processes. Marriage equality has consistently drawn an average support rate of 65 and 70 per cent in public opinion polls and yet it took over a decade of intense lobbying, a one hundred million dollar plebiscite and any number of suicides to finally get over the line a formal relationship that is legal in 26 other countries. Legalisation of X-rated films in the Australian states has consistently drawn an average support of 72 per cent, while drug law reform polling shows a more distinct divide with country support running at around 35 per cent, while city support is around 80 per cent.

Prostitution, stem-cell research and abortion all draw majority support in the polls and yet there is no law reform. For generations of people who grew up on the 'make love, not war' philosophy with marijuana and ecstasy as their drugs of choice, abortion always an option as a last resort to an unwanted pregnancy and gay friends all around you, these poll results are what you would expect. Though the religious minorities who infiltrate Australian politics are almost exclusively Christian, most religions are as bad as each other when they get into politics, and the possibility of Islamic, Buddhist, Jewish or Hindu fundamentalists getting into parliament needs to be scrutinised just as much as Christians.

Hypocrites was a landmark publication. It brought the graphic nature and the true extent of church-based child sex abuse in

Australia before politicians and priests in a way that they had never seen before. The royal commission was another step forward in bringing this awful behaviour to the awareness of ordinary Australians. Now we need a process that explains *why* it happened. People still don't understand how or why thousands of people who were supposed to uphold the highest moral values of all, descended en masse into the depths of depravity.

21

TWO INTO ONE

After nearly eight years of bashing politicians over the head with sex and morality issues, I was starting to feel burned out. The exhaustive Non-Violent Erotica (NVE) campaign had not ended with a bang but a long whimper. Through the campaign with Andrew Robb we had saved porn from an outright ban, but we hadn't been able to get the new NVE classification over the line. Without renaming the X classification as something else we were always going to have a fight on our hands. In some ways, Senator Harradine had outsmarted us, though it still felt like we had gone twenty rounds only to land knockout blows on each other in the last round.

A reprieve of sorts arrived when a young woman called Sharon Austen knocked on my door in early 2000. She had just launched Australia's second adult company on the Australian Stock Exchange and wanted to join Eros. Sharon had been a well-known and well-liked brothel madam in Sydney and together with her stockbroker boyfriend had designed a public float for a new adult company with great ideas but not a lot else. They had raised $6 million, however, and were ready to go.

Before they began to trade, they travelled to Europe to check the progress of the German adult company, Beate Uhse AG, following its launch on the Frankfurt Stock Exchange in 1999. The woman who founded that company, Beate Uhse, had been one of the youngest stunt pilots in Germany before joining the Luftwaffe at the beginning of the Second World War. After the war, she started a mail-order business in condoms and sex education books that quickly grew into a large company. In 1962, she opened the world's first retail sex shop and despite repeated raids by German police for corrupting public morals, the Beate Uhse brand spread quickly throughout the country.

Sharon wanted to bring that same mainstream approach to adult retailing in Australia—and from there to the rest of world. Beate Uhse AG's chain of adult stores, initially based on the high streets of Germany, were starting to perform well online. Sharon had big ideas for online retailing in Australia and signed a memorandum of understanding with the German outfit about selling their products here.

When I saw the deal she had struck, I reckoned that the Germans had definitely got the better end of it. In return for their 30 per cent interest in Sharon Austen Ltd, they advised Sharon about what products were selling well around the world and they also gave her the rights to their German film library. There were many things wrong with this arrangement, but this was about selling sex on the internet in 2000—how could anything go wrong? Around the world, other websites were already beginning to charge millions of customers a

$30-a-month fee to access galleries of thumbnailed porn and the odd vibrator or cock ring.

Within weeks of her return from Germany, Sharon offered me the job as her Chief Operations Officer. It was a big decision and would involve leaving Canberra (and Eros) to live in Sydney. I talked it over with Robbie, who was supportive, and after a couple of days I decided to jump. It would mean finding a new CEO for Eros, a position Robbie did not want. During the phone-sex debates in the Senate, I had got to know one of then-Democrats leader Senator Meg Lees' advisors, John Davey. He had shown interest in the job if it ever became available. He was an openly gay man with a keen political nose and he was a rakish barrister by trade. When he jumped at the opportunity, I packed up a few things and moved to Sydney.

* * * *

Robbie was not coming with me. Our relationship was maturing well and I knew we would be on the phone every day, so there was no separation anxiety from either of us. We both worked for causes, not for money or an overly comfortable lifestyle, and if that meant we lived apart for a while, that was just part of the plan.

From the beginning, we had had an agreement about how we would deal with other sexual relationships. Not ending ours was the first rule. I felt like I had to formalise something with him after he had told me about a disastrous previous relationship. With two young children, his primary relationship had hopelessly broken down and he had then entered into a clandestine relationship with his partner's younger sister. It ended rather tragically when she was killed in a car accident and was later the subject of a novel called *Soaring* by

Ross Fitzgerald. I was angry with him when I heard about it, even though it happened years before we had met. I wanted us to be clear about what the protocols were if and when either of us felt sexually attracted to other people.

So within the first few years of our relationship we had agreed that as long as we were open and honest about our relationships there would be no room for jealousy, envy, emotional hurt or other bad stuff to happen. I wouldn't call it an 'open marriage' because we had no intention of marrying anyone, least of all each other, but it was an 'open relationship' in that we never closed the doors to anything or anyone. It's a funny thing, but when you trust someone enough to go off and have sex with other people something happens within that arrangement that takes the relationship to a different level.

I've often advised it to friends having relationship problems. Polyamorous couples reject the notion that exclusivity is the key to ongoing and abiding love. Our polyamorous relationship has, over the years, seen us occasionally tumbling into bed with other women in threesomes (once with a good lesbian friend of mine). It has allowed me to occasionally spend the night out with other men and arrive home at 4 a.m. to snuggle back into bed with Robbie and it has allowed him to see a couple of girlfriends from time to time—even one he had been in a relationship with before he met me. As long as everyone was aware of the situation, it worked well enough, and much better than if we had tried to schlep around the boundaries of a conventional relationship.

* * * *

In Sydney's Darlinghurst I found a beautiful, small art deco unit at the top of Liverpool Street in a building called 'Mont Clair'. The unit had original parquetry floors and a fish head spout in the bath. Later, I discovered a brilliant rooftop terrace where I could watch the nightly exodus of large fruit bats heading out from Centennial Park to the Botanical Gardens. The building was on a company title and the board had to approve new tenants. This involved an interview with the chairperson and a detailed application form. It was all very old-fashioned, and since I did not see my background in the adult industry as being an asset I started rebuilding my past and finding friends as referees who would say the right things. Unfortunately, when I discovered the identity of the chair, I assumed this wasn't going to wash. He worked in the NSW attorney-general's department and we had been trading volleys over the failure of NSW classifications laws for a couple of years. We had never met, but his letters were generally pretty stuffy and mostly dismissive of my views. In the end he was kinder than I thought he would be—we got on just fine. And I got the apartment.

The offices of Sharon Austen Ltd were only ten minutes' walk from my unit, in a converted terrace house in Stanley Street. To get there, I would go past at least half-a-dozen street workers each morning at the top end of Palmer Street. Further down that street was a building that was once Tilly Devine's famous brothel and would feature on Channel 9's crime series *Underbelly: Razor* a decade later. I was feeling right at home. I had spent a lot of time in the area in my Eros job, where Friday lunches on Riley Street outside the large adult wholesale company Calvista had become an institution.

As COO, my job was to ensure the company's compliance with state, federal and international legislation. This included providing advice on planning issues for future adult retail outlets and the preparation of government submissions and applications. It was also my job to oversee the establishment of the website and the selection and sourcing of products.

A new personal relationship was the furthest thing from my mind, and yet amid this dynamic workload it happened.

* * * *

Back in the early 1980s, I couldn't get enough of Elvis Costello. I just loved his crazy fusion of rock, punk and country and I still do. When he announced that his 1982 Australian tour would include a gig at the ANU bar, I was there. I was also keen on Sydney and Newcastle pub bands as many of them made it down to Canberra. My favourite was Pel Mel. Their first single in 1981, 'No Word From China', was played everywhere and they even performed it on *Countdown*. When it was announced that they would be the backing band for Elvis Costello's 1982 tour, I was over the moon.

Twenty years on and a few weeks into my new job at SharonAusten.com, I noticed a tall, good-looking man with greying wavy hair standing at the bottom of the office stairs staring up at me. We made a couple of jokes and he then introduced himself as Sharon's brother, Graeme Dunne. He had been Pel Mel's lead guitarist and vocalist. He certainly didn't recognise the skinny banshee from the fourth row of that Canberra concert, and, likewise, I didn't recognise him. But, as corny as it sounds, there was an immediate spark. Not a sexual one, though. I wasn't looking for that. I had just got back from a two week buying trip to the US where I had had a short relationship with a Broadway musical composer. Robbie was okay with it and although the relationship was nothing special, the composer and I were still corresponding. Back home, I was casually seeing a couple of other people, including a Sydney muso, so my sexual dance card was full.

Graeme worked for Sharon's stockbroking partner and had dropped in after work for a few drinks. We started to see a bit of each other via the after-work drinks ritual on the terrace and ended up going out for dinner a few times. Then, by a strange twist of fate, we just happened to travel overseas on the same flight, although I was in business class and off to meet his sister in New York, while he was off to Chicago to try and reignite an old dalliance. We met at Sydney airport and then again in Bangkok where we drank champagne together.

When we both got back to Australia we hung out a bit and started having very casual and very drunken sex. I went back to New York to work for a while which meant we didn't see much of each other, but arriving back in Australia in September of 2001, I found myself at the Penthouse Pet awards party at the Pure Platinum nightclub one night. It just happened to be the 11th. All of a sudden the glamour of the night started receding as the images of the Twin Towers on the little telly in the corner of the bar slowly overwhelmed the party. I tried to call my new friends in New York but couldn't get through to anyone. I felt like I needed to be with someone in a quiet space to digest what was happening. Robbie was watching it in Canberra with his eldest daughter and Graeme felt like the right person to call so I went over to his place to watch it all unfold.

That was the beginning. I guess you would say it was a relationship that was hatched while 9/11 played out. Graeme liked many of the things I liked: the beach, socialising, partying, shopping. I liked his friends, and although I could see that underneath his avuncular exterior he could be very dark and moody, I gradually fell in love with him.

* * * *

Graeme had a small unit in an older-style building in Darling Point in Sydney's east. It had a great garden and a pool where we had lots of parties. A two-bedroom apartment came up for rent not long after that and we decided to move in together.

Robbie came and stayed on a semi-regular basis, but would often bring a girlfriend when he came and the four of us would go out to dinner. We would retire to adjacent bedrooms for the night but we never had sex as a group. I think I was happier to be with Graeme on my own at this time. Graeme and I had a few moments, but generally it was a happy time there, with occasional camping holidays and trips to Samoa and Nicaragua. During that period, Sharon Austen Ltd merged with another adult company, Gallery Global Networks, whose owners I knew well. I took on a new role and Graeme became less and less interested in stockbroking. Towards the end of 2002, the lack of 'cause' in the corporate world was starting to mess with my head. Robbie was running Eros again in Canberra after John Davey's term as CEO had expired. But because I still wanted to live in Sydney, I started consulting to Eros through our Body Politics company.

At the same time, copyright and porn piracy was starting to become a big issue in the industry. Referring to porn as 'intellectual property' was a bit of an oxymoron for many people. For those that paid up to $5000 for the rights to duplicate a porn film in Australia, on the other hand, it was no small matter when they saw up to 30 of their new titles appearing in a rival catalogue. The Greek 'Mafia' were the main offenders, even though most of them lived on the canals up on the Gold Coast, and many were part of extended families with brothers, cousins and parents listed as company executives.

While most smaller X-rated retailers thought it was just something they would have to live with, the major wholesalers and retailers like Adultshop.com, Calvista and Gallery Global Networks (previously SharonAusten.com) decided to fight back by setting up their own copyright protection agency, the Adult Industry Copyright Organisation (AICO). Graeme left stockbroking to take on the job of running the new organisation and I went on to the board.

Over the next few years, AICO prosecuted a range of illegal operators in the civil courts and won over a million dollars in damages. But it was a losing game with the police unable to keep up with the movements of the pirates.

Meanwhile, a couple of years into the relationship, Graeme came down with a bad case of pancreatitis and had to be hospitalised for six weeks. We were both beginning to get on each other's nerves. Living and working together was becoming just too intense and I was feeling like I didn't really want to be in a relationship with anyone. So before he came out of hospital I packed up my things and fled to an apartment on my own in Woolloomooloo. It wasn't officially a break-up, but in my own apartment I was the gatekeeper again and I issued keys to both Graeme and Robbie. This way I was nobody's baby, but it did mean that I now had two men in my bed.

Initially, I had reservations about how it would work, but they quickly faded as we just got on with it. If we all went to a party, Graeme and I would tend to stay all night while Robbie would quietly slip out the back door after an hour or two and we'd all meet up at home later. Robbie and Graeme were not attracted to each other but were nonetheless at home with each other's nudity around me. There was never any jealousy or sexual lobbying, and every encounter together was like the first time. Sometimes Robbie or Graeme just wanted their own space and I would sleep with one or the other in separate rooms, but just as often we would all pile into the one bed.

None of my friends had lived as a threesome so there were no guides out there to chat about the dynamics of it all, and it was hardly the sort of thing you'd ask your parents about. Strangely enough, though, both Robbie's parents and mine were fine with it. We would often arrive together for family BBQs and birthdays, and even though cousins and friends knew we were living as three nobody treated us any differently. We probably lived this way for another few years on and off but in the end, Graeme moved back to his hometown of Newcastle when his mother died and ended up marrying and having his own family. We are all still good friends.

Because Robbie's and my relationship had never stopped, there was never a feeling of having to get used to being a 'couple' again, even though we were still living in different cities. The only difference being that my bed felt like it was my own again. I would recommend a dose of polyamory to anyone who is curious about it.

22

MEETING PETA CREDLIN

Not many people saw it coming, but a major Australian reality TV show inadvertently launched one of our most important censorship debates. It was the mid-2000s and Channel 10's *Big Brother* program took television cameras inside the bedroom of a group house and left them on all night.

More importantly, they streamed selected parts of the show over the internet in a first for Australian TV. Discarded underwear and pyjamas were scattered around the rooms and contestants snuggled up to each other, mingling farts with pillow talk in this highly charged albeit artificial environment. Channel 10 took one liberty after another in their quest to out-rate their rivals and prove that reality TV had finally come of age. When they tossed sexual practices like 'tea-bagging' and 'turkey slapping' into the living rooms of middle Australia, they landed like live grenades. When one exploded while Prime Minister John Howard was watching, things got messy.

In the Patten School of political philosophy, tea-bagging is a derivative of turkey-slapping and clearly has its origins in the US Tea Party. Tea Baggers are, in effect, unreconstructed Carpet Baggers: conservative types who like to pass themselves off as upholding people's civil liberties while they line their pockets with the proceeds of said liberties. The practice of tea-bagging typically sees a man 'dunking' his scrotum in his partner's mouth, often while she is asleep. Recent developments have seen this extend to wiping 'the bag' across a girl's face and occasionally dipping it in her eye sockets. I've often wondered about the sexual pleasure that men get from it.

The Turkey Slap is a Republican invention, and Donald Trump's description of his now famous 'pussy grab' comes from the same part of the body politic. The turkey slap sees a bloke slapping his soft or semi-erect penis on the side of a girl's face, although the ears and eyes are said to be a target as well. The practice came of age on *Big Brother* when two males were ejected from the house for performing it on a fellow housemate. Quite rightly they were ejected for being dickheads, although I did not consider the turkey slap as an assault with a dick-head, as some feminists have tried to argue. These days, turkey-slapping has now taken on a much wider meaning: to turkey slap a business colleague or rival is to thoroughly castigate someone in the close proximity of others.

For me, the turkey slap and Peta Credlin are intimately connected. Not only did she turkey slap most of Abbott's Cabinet, but she slapped me during the public debate that took off following the infamous *Big Brother* broadcast.

Back in April 1996, the Howard government had announced plans to further outlaw porn on the internet by drawing up legislation to allow for the prosecution of anyone who posted, transmitted, advertised or granted access to the retrieval of 'offensive material'. The definition of offensive material was unclear. The previous Communications Minister, Richard Alston, had already made it an offence to host adult content from an Australian internet service provider. The net effect of these laws was to send approximately $5 million a year in hosting fees to US companies, which up until then had stayed with Australian ISPs while doing nothing to stop Australian companies from getting their stuff online. This new announcement was going to fix that.

Helen Coonan was John Howard's Minister for Communications at the time and Peta Credlin was her chief-of-staff. Not long after the turkey slap event hit the tabloids, Howard asked Coonan to draw up legislation that would forever ban images like those on *Big Brother* from screens big and small around the country. Within weeks of a first draft of the Content Services Bill 2007 being circulated to a select group, I was handed a copy. The bill prescribed fines of $200,000 and two years' jail for those who dared to publish content online that would be X-rated or Refused Classification. It even handed out similar sentences for publishing R-rated material online without childproof locks on websites. The killer clause read that even if the content was hosted off-shore, the most tenuous link to an 'Australian connection' would be enough for the plods to proceed to a prosecution. Anyone who contributed in the slightest way to the making and hosting of the said X-rated content could also be caught by the new laws.

It was tantamount to a complete ban on adult material in or from Australia. My members were facing a very hard time if they could not use the developing online environment to promote and display services and products. Especially as the rest of the world was moving towards various forms of self-regulation on the internet.

* * * *

In the middle of all this my Mum's health nose-dived. Like me, she was rarely ill and when she was she just got on with it. She had made a quick and full recovery from breast cancer in 1996, going straight for the surgical option, but in 2005 she developed a cold which went to her lungs and soon she was diagnosed with pneumonia. She spent a few months in hospital and when she came out her lungs were scarred and weakened. Mum and Dad put their Bega Valley idyll on the market and in 2007 it sold—but not before Mum insisted on going to the 2006 Commonwealth Games, walking to almost all the venues without a wheelchair.

Moving back to Canberra, she was really starting to struggle and was now on oxygen for most of the day. In one of my visits she complained of pain in her hips and legs. The cancer had come back, this time in her bones. Doctors at Canberra Hospital wanted to give her radiation therapy to help with the pain but they were also trying to stop the spread of the cancer. For some reason no radiologists were available in Canberra so they put her on a plane to Wagga Wagga Base Hospital. Dad and I got in the car and drove down, but when we got there the plane hadn't landed. We booked a motel room for the night and went back to the hospital. The plane was late because she had fallen off the gurney onto the tarmac and when we finally got to see her she was acting very oddly. She seemed to be hallucinating and was unaware of where she was. The gruff radiologist who examined her was furious and asked why she was at his hospital in the first place. She was far too sick to travel, he said, and there was nothing he could do. It wasn't exactly what we wanted to hear. But we made her comfortable and said we'd be back early in the morning.

Dad and I had a very strange dinner that night, knowing that the situation was not good but still talking over various treatment options. We both went to bed about 11 p.m. Then Dad was awoken at midnight with a call from the hospital. Mum had just died. She was 66. We raced over hoping a miracle might happen but no—we were just faced with the nurses telling us something about kidney failure and salts. I wasn't really listening.

The drive back to the hotel that night with Dad was the most painful and lonely experience I had ever had. There was just nothing to say. Mum had gone like a soap bubble that had been listing badly in the air for a while and then had just popped. Dad's pain was palpable.

I went back to Yarralumla to organise the funeral and to be with Robbie. I think it took a couple of weeks for me to deal with what had happened but knowing Mum, she would have wanted all the family to have a drink and just get on with our lives.

* * * *

So that's what I did. I called my members to see how many individual email addresses we could muster to send a political message regarding censorship of the internet at the forthcoming federal election. To my delight, James Packer's PBL Media had just spent $300,000 putting their adult titles online, many of which were Category 1 Restricted. Once online, however, they became X- or R-rated because they were classified using film ratings rather than publications guidelines; something that completely defied logic and the experience of reading a book over that of looking at a screen. But, then, logic had never been a major factor in Australian censorship law.

PBL Media was pissed off that this new legislation would not only sink their recent investment but might also land Executive Chairman James Alexander in jail. I had also noticed that many of the nation's major publishers were reprinting classic literature that, if submitted for classification, would certainly have been banned.

If the laws on child porn had been followed to the letter of the law, some of these books, such as Anaïs Nin's *Delta of Venus* would have been banned and Penguin Australia's head honcho at the time, Bob Sessions, could also have been jailed or fined. Online, these books would become lightning rods for pro-censorship groups. Especially as now the conservative NSW Labor Attorney-General, John Hatzistergos, had just withdrawn the defence of 'artistic merit' around child porn—an action that left artists of all kinds incredibly exposed. So I called the Australian Publishers' Association with the news that some of their members were at great risk of prosecution under Coonan's proposed bill. They were suitably alarmed.

Armed with two new allies and their extensive email lists, I could now count on sending a powerful electoral message on censorship to some millions of people. As I had done in the past with Liberal Party Director Andrew Robb, I thought a similar lobbying tactic with the Liberal Party Secretariat might just work again. Clearly the parliamentary wing of the party was not in a mood to parlay. Brian Loughnane was the new party director, and so one cold and windy afternoon in September 2007, armed with proof of my millions of email addresses, I made the journey to Robert Menzies House in Barton to see him.

As I walked under the Tuscan order porte-cochere of the Liberal Party's national HQ, it reminded me of the old South African embassy. Inside, I was ushered into a beige and brown chamber lined with oil paintings of past leaders.

I showed Brian my stuff and told him that the draft legislation had pissed off some heavy hitters in the media as well as the porn industry.

'If you go ahead with this, I will knock on a million doors with the message that you are banning their favourite entertainment and not to vote for you.'

He heard me out and said he would think it over, promising to call me within a week. True to his word, he did. He told me to call the minister's office again and ask to speak to her chief-of-staff, Peta Credlin, who would have carriage of the issue. I rang and made the appointment without knowing that Ms Credlin was also Loughnane's wife. Brian hadn't told me that either, but because he was a straight shooter, I felt that he wanted the arguments to rise and fall on their merits rather than on the personalities of those involved.

A week later, I arrived at Senator Coonan's Sydney office and was ushered into a meeting room with half-a-dozen other people present. Two of her advisors were among them. I had recently lobbied these guys on the issue and sent them a written submission. I had also lobbied them over the Internet Corporation for Assigned Names and Numbers' (ICANN's) decision to create a new .XXX domain for porn sites and we had all been in agreement that this was a bad idea. With this in mind, I was hopeful of a warm response to my submission.

Peta Credlin entered the room from behind me. She walked halfway around the table without looking at anyone and took the seat directly opposite me. She was impeccably dressed and sported a hairstyle not unlike that of the perfectly coiffured ladies in the David Jones' makeup section. She sorted her papers for a couple of seconds, shot a furtive glance around the table, and then motioned to one of the advisors. He spoke for a minute about the intent of the bill and finished by saying, 'And we've decided to remove the words *an Australian connection*.'

It took a couple of seconds for me to register that with those few words the government was effectively backing away from criminalising porn on the internet for Australian traders. My campaign had worked. I started an internal brawl with the corners of my mouth which, against their master's better judgement, were beginning to move into an inappropriate smile. Just as I was about to lose the battle, help came from an unexpected quarter. Without warning, Credlin stood bolt upright in her seat and arse-bumped her chair back half a metre. She placed her splayed hands flat on the table, leaned forwards and fixed me with a withering gaze.

'If you breathe one fucking word of this to the media, the deal's off! If the Nats ever get wind of this, there'll be hell to pay.'

I wasn't 100 per cent sure what she meant here, but when this woman was talking about 'hell' it wasn't good. And, with that, she scooped up her papers into the crook of her arm and like a bad bout of palindromic arthritis, she went back out the same way she had come in.

A slightly embarrassed but respectful silence broke out in the room and stayed until her footfall had ceased in the hallway. Then everyone looked at each other like they'd suddenly realised they hadn't eaten in days, and with a 'no further questions' from one of the advisors, we all filed out of the room. It felt like a night at the Hellfire Club. I was a bit bruised, but inwardly I was glowing.

23

CONROY'S GAP

Driving from Canberra to Melbourne on the Hume Freeway is an easy trip these days. The road bypasses all the major towns and there's plenty of open space where you can just let your mind free-range as the kilometres go by. Between Yass and the dozy little town of Bookham, the road rises up into what appears to be a cleft in the mountain range. As you shift down a gear to get to the top of the rise, the road starts to widen at the same time as the grasslands above you appear to come together. It's a strange feeling. Large grey cement patches now line the walls on either side as you move into the centre of the mountain. It feels like being in the cleft of a huge brain—and then a sign whizzes by on the left saying 'Conroy's Gap'.

In late 2007 and early 2008, the federal Labor government's new Minister for Communications, Stephen Conroy, announced to the world that he was preparing to introduce an internet filter to get rid of child porn, illicit sex, violence and terrorism. In the years preceding this announcement, phone sex on the 1900 platform had been banned. Australian adult websites had been banned from setting up and being hosted within Australia. John Howard had tried to ban and then further restrict what could be shown in an X-rated film. R-rated computer games had been banned. State governments and local councils were cracking down on sex wherever they saw it.

Now Conroy wanted to take censorship of the internet to a new level by introducing the forced filtering of internet service providers, a path that totalitarian states like China and Iran had recently trod. It was a big, grey monolithic policy that had the potential to be everything that George Orwell warned us about in *1984*. For me, it was Conroy's Gap: a policy framed by moral panic and bad polling that was being driven through a deep gouge in Labor logic. And, in that space, the Sex Party was born.

At this time I was back into my role as Eros CEO even if I was living in Sydney and outside the Eros office in Canberra. Robbie and I had approached the Police Credit Union again about extending our mortgage to build a large office at the back of the house to accommodate extra staff as Eros's work load increased. I think I subconsciously sensed that Eros was about to morph into something bigger again.

A couple of weeks after Conroy's announcement, the likely effects of a filter became apparent to my Eros members. Their future plans were toast if it materialised. We'd heard it all before: government bans and restrictions aimed at eliminating violence and terrorism, but, in the end, just banning sex. We needed to fight this like before, but we needed something new.

After the 2007 federal election, the Family First Party held the balance of power in the Australian Senate. Fred Nile still presided over a similar position in the NSW Parliament and in Queensland an ultra-conservative independent, Liz Cunningham, held the key to government. A high-Anglican morality campaigner and attorney-general from South Australia, Michael Atkinson, was holding the Standing Committee of State and Commonwealth Attorneys-General (SCAG) to ransom on R-rated computer games and other issues. In the ACT, two morality campaigners—a former Canberra Raider and a former policeman—had also held the balance of power for a number of years.

Many local councils were also now being driven by one or two religious councillors to enact ridiculous local laws on adult venues. Whenever an adult bookshop made an application to open in Australia, religious groups represented by these councillors immediately lodged complaints about the negative effects to the community. They presented no formal research, no scientific evidence and no facts to back their assertions. And yet time after time, local governments buckled to these fraudulent claims and either refused a development application or forced the applicants to disprove the assertions in costly legal proceedings.

I remember talking about it one night over dinner with Robbie on one of my regular visits back to Canberra. He was plating up his signature pineapple tofu dish. He had recently been featured as a minor celebrity in Susan Parson's cooking pages in the *Canberra Times*. The dish had been photographed in all its beige and yellow glory and he was keen to make it for me. I would have preferred a steak, but I wasn't complaining. He did the cooking and I did laundry and it worked fine.

I was busy in the dining room arranging the napkins and lighting the two little sterling silver candles that sat on the end of the long table.

These little dining rituals drove Robbie mad. He was a TV-dinner kinda guy. But it was in my genes to 'make the table', and although I was the first person to *dance* on the table as the night wore on, I liked to eat my meals in the tradition of my mother and grandmother.

'Why is it that only religious nutters hold these balance of power positions and never sex workers or strippers!' I shouted to him in the kitchen.

'Religious politicians have big congregations behind them,' he shouted back. 'It's almost like you have to form your own political party to fight them.'

I moved the mustard pot into the centre of the table, but the thought of forming a political party got stuck between the sterling silver salt and pepper shakers. I could sense he was going deeper on it as well when he came out from the kitchen.

'What . . . you mean, like, form our *own* party?'

'Well, yeah, maybe . . .'

'What, like, the Sex Party!?'

The was a moment of silence before we both laughed out loud.

'The Sex Party!' We both said it again. And again, like a mantra, taking it to different level. We both looked at each other and knew that it was very good.

* * * *

The next day we formed a small working party—Ken Hill from Club X and Sexpo, and the CEOs of the two public adult companies, Craig Ellis from Gallery Global Networks and Malcolm Day from Adultshop.com—to get the concept of a political party out to Eros members. Within a few weeks we organised a meeting with a broader group of members at Melbourne International Airport to ratify the approach.

Mal Day and a couple of other large distributors hated the party name. They thought we needed to move as far away from sex as possible. Ken Hill argued strongly for it, saying that anything less would be too bland for where we were coming from. Robbie argued that if we weren't comfortable in our own skin, no one else would be. In the end, sex won the day.

We drew up a constitution and prefaced it with a suitable quote from the great philosopher and psychologist Havelock Ellis: 'Sex lies at the root of life, and we can never learn to reverence life until we know how to understand sex.' That should leave the ACT incorporations office in no doubt as to where we were coming from, I thought. We cobbled together a suite of policies based loosely around censorship, gay rights, drug law reform and rolling back the nanny state. Then we began the search for 500 registered members. I could count about 100 from within our family and friends, but to get the bulk of the names we needed a large event where there would be plenty of like-minded people.

Melbourne's 2008 Sexpo in November was the ideal occasion and not just for the crowds. Sexpo organisers had just been told that this was their last gig at the Melbourne Exhibition Centre. The reason given was that overseas exhibitors from more prudish countries would not hire other parts of the building while Sexpo was on. So we had a barrow to push as well.

On 20 November, the first day of Sexpo, I proudly announced the launch of the Australian Sex Party to 100 exhibitors, guests and journalists. I said the party was a sign of the times and an acknowledgement of the importance and scope of sex and gender issues in ordinary people's lives.

'People want their House of Reps members to balance the budget, but increasingly they want their senators to look after their rights and freedoms,' I said. 'The Sex Party is the beginning of a new chapter in upper house politics.'

* * * *

The party's first priority was to alert Australians to Conroy's proposed internet filtering scheme and the fact that it even threatened the existence of the Sex Party online through over-zealous filtering.

'Community attitudes to sex and censorship have been shown over and over again in polls to be more relaxed than ever and yet, in politics, the opposite is the case. When was the last time you heard a politician say something positive about sex?' I asked the gathering at Sexpo.

The party would co-opt Australia's 1000 adult shops as individual branches of the party and the four million Australian adults identified in La Trobe University's Sex in Australia survey (2006), who regularly purchased X-rated films, vibrators, adult books and lingerie, would make up its initial audience.

Finally, I left them with the idea that discrimination against sex industry workers and companies was rife in the community and that the party would work to bring in laws that would outlaw job and occupational discrimination.

'The Victorian government and the Melbourne Exhibition Centre Board have thrown Sexpo out of the MEC next year because they don't want to offend overseas countries who are shy around sex and want to hire another part of the building,' I said. 'Why should 70,000 ordinary Victorians miss out on their favourite show because their government is being overly cautious and bending their knee to puritanical regimes from overseas'?

We signed up over 1000 new members that weekend. Back in Canberra the following week, we threw a dinner for half-a-dozen party members and friends who came in and helped us prepare the 500 membership forms with the constitution to send off to the Australian Electoral Commission.

But before the ink (and red wine my father had spilled) had dried on our application to register the party, a couple of public sex debates broke out that were ripe for political comment. A few years earlier, Pauline Hanson had come out about her affair with her then staffer, David Oldfield. Now two Murdoch papers, the *Sunday Mail* and Sydney's *Sunday Telegraph*, had run front-page photos of a naked young woman who they said was Pauline Hanson above a heading that screamed, 'Please Explain'.

While the photos certainly looked like her, the paper's reason for running the story was basically slut-shaming. It's probably the first and only time I will defend Hanson over anything, but running a front-page story that she had posed naked as a young woman in the week before she contested the seat of Beaudesert in the Queensland state election could not go unchallenged. It was also a 'hypocrite' alert for Murdoch papers, which were running increasingly voyeuristic articles about the sex industry but unlike their earlier attitudes, were now starting to refuse to run sex industry ads. Hanson had vehemently denied the photos were of her and to prove it she said she would show her belly button in court to show she had an 'innie'.

As CEO of Eros, I issued a media release saying there was no public interest whatsoever in publishing nude photos of a candidate during an election campaign just for the shock value of it. 'If this had happened to a sitting member, it would have been viewed as a contempt of parliament and dealt with accordingly,' I said. Ms Hanson should have been protected by the parliament that she was trying to gain election to.

Public interest, I said, could only legitimise the publishing of private sexual information or photos in cases where monumental hypocrisy or illegal behaviour such as in the case of the former member for Capricornia, Keith Wright. 'Ms Hanson has never espoused policies or agendas related to sexual behaviour which would have made the publishing of those photos in the public interest,' I concluded.

The day after my media release, Robbie found a series of photos of a young female model in an obscure adults-only magazine from the Netherlands called *Colour Climax*. They were the spitting image of both Pauline Hanson and the model on the front pages of the papers. The young woman's partner in the photographic essay was none other than the legendary Long Dong Silver, a small, modest-looking black man with the largest penis in the adult industry. The main photo showed his gargantuan organ extending all the way to his knee with the surprised doppelgänger holding a hand to her cheek in a classic, 'Oh dearie me, I'm about to faint' pose. I sent out another media release claiming that this was the 'fake' Pauline Hanson in the Murdoch papers and attached the photo. Fairfax ran with the head-and-shoulders version, but their photo department reserved their right to allow journalists access to the whole photo.

Two months later, *Four Corners* aired a report claiming group sex and rape were endemic in the National Rugby League. The program outlined details of several scandals over the previous years, including a group-sex session with former player and now footy commentator Matthew Johns and another five players. The woman at the centre of it also said that Cronulla captain, Paul Gallen, had been in the room. The most disturbing thing about the allegations were the large number of players who didn't participate in the sex but were said to have stood around the room masturbating like zombies. Could this be the result of being in too many scrums over the years, I wondered, or was it more closely connected to male drinking patterns? I called for more NRL sex education about the role of brothels and escort agencies and the need for teams to seek out and adopt their local brothel.

'Footballers who want to engage in group sex should be educated by their clubs about how to organise these liaisons as legal, commercial arrangements,' I said in a national media release. 'Most rugby league clubs have made brothels and escort agencies "no-go" areas for their players, thinking that they were enhancing the moral standing of their teams. In reality, these prudish bans on commercial sex have inadvertently led to an increase in group sex with groupies who try to access popular players. The NRL needs to set up a brothel liaison office and to conduct brothel information sessions with all players, including those who profess to be religious.' The last line was aimed at the large number of NRL players who had just come out as practising Christians. A Christian Footballers Group had been formed a couple of years earlier by none other than the former Canberra Raider and balance-of-power politician in the ACT Legislative Assembly, Paul Osborne.

As the AEC edged closer to registering the Sex Party, the Australian Communications and Media Authority (ACMA), who had a blacklist of banned sites, was hacked and had the list published by WikiLeaks. At around the same time, the Classification Board's website was hacked and had anti-censorship messages splashed on its homepage. While a lot of the ACMA list was child-porn related, the other half was all about legitimate, legal businesses, issues and information, and included religious groups, tour operators, animal carers and even a dentist. It was exactly as we had predicted a few months before. Conroy said it was a technical fault. For the fledgling Sex Party, it was our first public pat on the back, and in April 2009 I was invited on to SBS's *Insight* program to discuss the government's filter, with Stephen Conroy a fellow guest

To his credit, Conroy had met with me twice before the program. On both occasions, he had told me that the filter would not block any of my members' content. Then he stopped taking my calls. My ally in the SBS audience was Mark Newton, CIO and network engineer for the telco, Internode. In front of the cameras, I argued strongly to Conroy that the internet was a global medium and did not recognise Australia's narrow X-rated classification system. Therefore, unless he changed the incredibly narrow boundaries of the Refused Classification category, it would be as if X was banned anyway. It would also ban most of the images in legal Category 2 Restricted magazines and have a host of further unintended consequences. He didn't see it that way, threatening dissenters with guilt trips. 'If you don't support the filter, you support child pornography,' he tried to argue back, even though later he would admit that the filter would not stop child pornography.

At the end of the show, when all the participants moved over to the green room for tea and coffee, Conroy started yelling at me. 'One fucking phone call, Fiona, that's all it would have taken . . . Just one fucking call!'

I was slightly taken aback. 'But I did try and call you . . .'

More haranguing ensued. My protests made no difference. He'd lost a couple of critical arguments on national television and had been seen to spawn a new political party against him. He was upset. I got it.

* * * *

On 17 June 2009, the AEC placed an ad in national newspapers stating that they had received an application for the registration of the Australian Sex Party and that they were now open for any objections. They got them in spades. They ranged from just being 'inappropriate' to 'downright obscene'. A lovely husband and wife alleged that I was involved in 'degrading women' through an inferred association with paedophiles, drug dealing and sex slavery. The complaint that caused the most grief for the AEC, however, came from a well-known Catholic lobbyist in Canberra who claimed that our name would raise 'orgiastic notions' in the minds of voters who saw it on the ballot paper. It was classic moral panic. Did he really think people would start beating off in the polling booths or expose themselves after voting for the Sex Party?

Section 129(1)(b) of the *Commonwealth Electoral Act 1918* says that an application by a political party applying for registration will be refused where the name or abbreviation of the party name is, in the AEC's opinion, 'obscene'. This issue had never previously arisen before in Australia and it sent the AEC on a Monty Python-esque search for the real meaning of the word. It made me wonder how party names like Rise Up Australia, Love Australia or Leave, and Family First all managed to scoot through the obscenity test in previous years. Using defamation-type arguments, the imputations that arose from these names were incredibly obscene. And what about the Queensland-based party Country Minded? I mean, the name just said it all.

Another objection was to one of our credos: 'The Sex Party—where you come first.' It was obscene and related to male ejaculation, it was alleged. We argued that the objector was devoid of a sense of humour. We also claimed he was being chauvinistic in that he had failed to include the female orgasm in his complaint, although we were prepared to accept that he may not have ever heard of that. Regarding his assertions that we may use double entendre in political adverting, we pleaded guilty. To the suggestion that our name did not represent what we were really on about, we asked, 'Does the Liberal Party represent "liberals"?' 'Does the Labor Party represent "labourers". And does Family First really represent most families?'

In New South Wales, it had already been established that using the words 'dickheads rule' and 'we're screwed' on how to vote cards was obscene. As to the nature of our party name, however, the AEC's five-page report said it was unlikely to 'deprave and corrupt' voters and they dismissed the objections. They said that 'public interest and concepts of free speech' needed to be taken into account, and that when these concepts were balanced with the 'double entendre' it was difficult to reach a conclusion other than that the name is not obscene. The perception by any member of the public that the name was obscene was simply not enough to ban it. In a final media release,

I wrote that the AEC appeared to be able to interpret community opinion on obscenity far better than the major political parties could. And, with that, the Australian Sex Party was officially registered on 9 August 2009.

24

DEMAGOGUES

'Hello, Sex Party. Can I help you?'

'Ahh, yeah . . . I just wanted to know when the next party was on?'

'What do you mean?'

'Is this the sex party?'

'Yes.'

'Well, you know . . . Like, when's the next one?'

'Oh no. It's not that sort of party. It's a political party. We run in elections. We've got policies and candidates and all that . . . I'm the president, Fiona Patten.'

'Will you be at the party?'

'You're not getting this, are you? The Sex Party is a political party that has policies to legalise sex, but it's not a sex party.'

'Are sex parties illegal?'

'No. Well, maybe in some states . . . It all depends on how they charge, I think.'

'So there's no party, then?'

'No. Well, we do have parties, but there's no sex at them, if you see what I mean?'

'So, it's like a sex party without any sex?'

'That's it! Look, would you like me to send you a brochure?'

'Okay. Are there pictures?'

This was an actual call received at the Sex Party offices in November 2011.

* * * *

Only a few months after getting the Sex Party registered and carving out a few square metres in the Eros office to house the new arrival, the federal government announced two by-elections for December 2009. One was for the seat of Bradfield in NSW, which was being vacated by the former Liberal leader, Brendan Nelson, and one was for the seat of Higgins in Victoria being vacated by the former treasurer, Peter Costello.

Neither sitting member was in ill health or beset by family problems; the main reason they were bowing out was because neither had any future leadership prospects. On a tax payer-funded salary that most Australians could only ever dream of, they forced the public to shell out over $1.5 million to run these by-elections. It was scandalous. I thought they should have been made to serve their full term or lose their substantial superannuation, along with the other perks that they were entitled to.

Robbie had once taken a visiting US porn star to meet Peter Costello. In 1990, Costello was made Shadow Minister for Corporate Law Reform and Consumer Affairs. Robbie was trying to get his support for the new Non-Violent Erotica (NVE) rating and had arranged for the diminutive Jamie Summers (star of the X-rated series, 'The Brat') to meet him through one of his advisors.

Before going up to Costello's office, Robbie had taken Summers to the Parliament House gym for a workout, as he had an orange lobbyist's pass which entitled him to go most places in the building. Andrew Peacock had spotted them getting sweaty on the bikes and called the attendants. They were both ordered out of the building and the *Telegraph* ran a story the next day about the 'porn star in the pool'. But Robbie, who still held a press pass courtesy of his relationship with broadcaster Phillip Adams, had doubled back on his tracks on the way out and took the Brat up to the meditation room under the big flag pole. Then they slipped quietly down to Costello's office at the arranged time. Costello was busy in the front room, but he took one look at them and stepped into a back room and never returned. He just aborted the meeting with no apology, no explanation, leaving an embarrassed staffer trying to cover his tracks.

In the same year as the 2009 by-election, Costello had recorded a bizarre Australia Day video in support of the firebrand preacher, Danny Nalliah, and his extremist Catch the Fire Ministries. Nalliah had blamed the 2009 Victorian bushfire disaster on the state's new abortion laws. He had attacked gay and lesbian couples, claimed to have visions from God, attended meetings at the anti-Semitic League of Rights, and had been prosecuted for vilifying Muslims in 2005.

Costello's video was effusive in his praise of Pastor Danny and his combative Christian teachings. At times, the former treasurer even broke out into a beatific smile, as if he had been hit by some divine light and couldn't contain himself. It was unhinged and insulting to non-religious Australians. Surely, I thought, the people of Higgins will be appalled at this extreme religious posturing from a supposedly rational former treasurer and support for the Liberals will slump. With this in mind, I nominated for the by-election.

In the Bradfield by-election, the Sex Party nominated Zahra Stardust, a 26-year-old feminist writer and law graduate who had also been a finalist in the Miss Pole Dance Australia 2008 and had just won 'most unique entertainer' at Miss Nude NSW. In the future, she would run for Lord Mayor of Sydney against Clover Moore. Zahra had worked with the United Nations Population Fund in Eritrea, with UNIFEM Australia (now called UN Women) on gender, development and discrimination, and with the Kimberley Land Council in the area of Native Title. She also worked as a trapeze artist and sported a distinctive range of hair colours, from bright pink to emerald green. She campaigned on the fact that women in Bradfield seeking an abortion still had to tread an illegal path and that children in many local schools received inadequate sex education. With the electorate being a hub of religious activity in Sydney, she also echoed my calls for a royal commission into child sexual abuse in religious institutions. In the years ahead, the Hillsong Church that bordered the Bradfield electorate would be exposed in the royal commission for a range of abuses. Zahra also campaigned on gay marriage, removing the GST on tampons and internet filtering.

As campaigning for the by-elections intensified, I received phone calls from two anonymous public servants working in Stephen Conroy's department to say that they were being denied access to the Sex Party website in probable contravention of the federal Discrimination Act and the Electoral Act. A few days later, the ban had spread to other government departments but talking to someone who could explain why was like trying to talk to someone on the phone at Facebook. 'Put the complaint in writing and we'll look at it.' They didn't. But it proved that broad-level government filtering simply didn't work and ended up banning all sorts of sites. The ban was eventually lifted months later but the culprit was never identified.

As campaigning started in earnest, Pastor Danny jumped back into the spotlight. He claimed that Canberra witches' covens had been holding blood sacrifices on Mount Ainslie as a way of hexing the parliament and of promoting homosexuality and abortion in the minds of unwitting MPs. He announced that he would march up the mountain, leading hundreds of chanting supporters, and conduct an exorcism of the evil poofter pagan rituals. I issued a media release saying that the Sex Party would march in opposition to Pastor Danny and we would conduct our own blood sacrifice: a halal sausage and kofta ball sizzle.

While the theatre of the event was not lost on me, neither was the incredible support that these right-wing religious extremists were getting from some very senior members of parliament. When John Howard had welcomed the Exclusive Brethren sect into his prime ministerial office in 2004, they had subsequently donated hundreds of thousands of dollars to the re-election of the Coalition. A year after the Higgins and Bradford by-elections, they would donate another $67,000 to the Liberal Party. Meanwhile, rumours of sexual abuse of children in this shadowy and secret Anglican sect were rife and years later many victims would come forward, with one survey of sect members showing rates of sexual abuse as high as 27 per cent.

It wasn't just senior levels of the Liberal Party that supported fringe religious sects. Since Kevin Rudd had become prime minister, the number of members of the Parliamentary Christian Fellowship (PCF) had risen from 75 to 84, which represented almost 38 per cent of all federal MPs. Membership numbers in the 'Monday Night Group', a shadowy Coalition Christian group that Rudd had also joined, were hard to evaluate but there were many. Along with the Lyons Forum, the existence of so many religious enclaves within the federal parliament should have been a major concern for a secular country like Australia, where only 9 per cent of the public claimed to be committed weekly worshippers. Rudd even went so far as to say that being a member of the PCF would not do his Labor colleagues any harm in advancing their political careers. As if to really showcase his religious approach to politics, he then announced he would address the Australian Christian Lobby's forthcoming AGM.

I issued a media release:

> The Prime Minister's address to the Australian Christian Lobby's (ACL) National Conference tomorrow should address the issue of child-sex abuse in Australian religious institutions and the reasons for its existence. Over 600 cases of child-sex abuse by church clergy have been dealt with in Australian courts over the past 20 years. There are approximately 20,000 church clergy employed by Australia's churches giving this sector the highest rate of child-sex abuse of any profession in Australia. Rudd's address to the ACL will conveniently ignore child-sex abuse issues and push for greater religious intervention in the nation's legislatures.

I challenged Rudd to visit a gathering of those on the other end of the spectrum: 'I have extended an invitation to Mr Rudd to attend this year's Melbourne Sexpo and address the 70,000 people who will attend this event and I genuinely hope he will consider this.'

Of course, he didn't, but my point was well made. He was pandering to lunatic religious groups as much as the Liberals were; 2009 marked a particularly low point in secular thought in Australia.

* * * *

At the same time, the then independent Senator, Nick Xenophon, called for a federal parliamentary inquiry into the Church of Scientology, alleging all sorts of rorts and misbehaviour including one case of child sexual abuse. I felt that any inquiry into Scientology would be discriminatory and biased against new-age religions unless it was balanced by an investigation into abuse in mainstream religious institutions. Xenophon's calls for an inquiry into Scientology needed to be investigated, but the 600 court cases involving the mainstream churches were already there and no one had mentioned looking into them. It took Xenophon another three years to come out in support of a royal commission.

Meanwhile, the Mount Ainslie event built to epic proportions with local media reporting a 'clash of cultures' between the Sex Party and the Catch the Fire Ministries. AAP reported that I had called on George Brandis as head of the Parliamentary Privileges Committee to attend the rally to ensure that MPs would not in any way be threatened in the line of their duty. I argued that God-fearing members of parliament were sufficiently lacking in intellectual rigour that, if threatened with 'eternal damnation' for voting in favour of gay marriage, they would really believe they were going to hell. In 2007, Archbishop George Pell had threatened politicians with 'religious consequences' if they voted to expand stem-cell research, and although a few high-profile MPs told Pell to bugger off, there were an equal number who didn't and pulled on the hair shirt and prayed even harder that night. Nalliah's threat represented as much of a contempt of parliament as any other threat to an MP—and the more religious the MP, the greater the threat.

The day broke cloudy and balmy: perfect for a pagan parade. Pastor Danny lead hundreds of his people, Moses-like, up the steep incline of Mount Ainslie. Dressed in a white polyester Nehru suit and wearing black wrap-around Ray-Bans, he looked like Kamahl doing an Elvis impersonation. The latest mini crowd-hailer was blue-toothed into a black microphone and pinned neatly to his lapel just above the gold-plated Lamy ballpoint pen that sat proudly in his chest pocket. He was a man on a mission, and with friends like Peter Costello behind him how could he go wrong?

He waded into the crowds with the megaphone blazing, pausing occasionally to flatten his thumbs on some sinner's forehead and then rock their head back with a well-rehearsed flourish and an 'out Satan!' for their troubles. His followers unfurled huge Australian flags at the top of the mountain and an epic chariot race around the loop road turned into something like Fellini's *Satyricon* with lesbian bondage babes, Sex Party supporters, Satanists and drag queens all joining in. Pastor Danny then moved to the terraced viewing platforms that faced straight out over Parliament House.

This was the moment we had all been waiting for. The crowds hushed in anticipation, and although the clouds refused to part Danny let fly with a dressing down of the queer demons and impure imps that were hiding out in the Speaker's box and in the non-members' bar. He left no one in any doubt of his magical powers. And, as the icy spring winds blew through cracks in the Brindabella Ranges to the west, we all gobbled down the last of our halal blood sacrifice before the pious and the transgressor together descended the mountain.

* * * *

Back on the campaign trail in Melbourne, things started getting weird. The Greens had preselected a nanny-state supporter, academic Clive Hamilton. He was calling for mandatory internet filters, new laws governing department store catalogues, and he even weighed into the Bill Henson debate, calling for greater control of the arts. He had been a founder of the left-leaning think tank, the Australia Institute, which had been the architect of Conroy's internet filter. He had written extensively about porn on the internet, sometimes devoting half of his articles and editorials to explicit depictions of the sort of depravity that people could find online if they really tried.

When a debate was scheduled between Hamilton and the Liberal candidate, Kelly O'Dwyer, on Jon Faine's ABC 774 Melbourne morning program, O'Dwyer pulled out. I called in saying that I had an opposing point of view to Hamilton on a number of issues and would like to keep the debate alive by filling in. The program's producer refused, saying that the Sex Party wasn't going to receive any coverage from 774 at all. I was gobsmacked. So Hamilton had a cosy chat with Faine instead. When one of our supporters called in for talkback, he was told by the producer that if he mentioned the Sex Party he would be cut off. I lodged a formal complaint with the ABC, but they basically said the station was within its rights to do that. However, after that things changed a lot and Faine even later confided in me that his son was a Sex Party supporter.

* * * *

The discrimination continued. On by-election eve, my friend Rebecca and I were thrown out of a popular South Yarra pub for handing out how-to-vote cards, while the Liberal spruiker was allowed to keep distributing his. On the morning of the election, I borrowed a plain white van from one of the major adult wholesalers. Together with my trusted friend and media guru from Joy FM, Dean Beck, we loaded the van up with election bunting, attaching red and yellow balloons to the back and VOTE 1 SEX PARTY signs along both sides. Then we headed off to visit the polling booths with care packages of water, lollies and hats for our volunteers. We'd been in the car for no more than fifteen minutes when halfway down Toorak Road we heard a police siren behind us. Sure enough, two young officers pulled us over. After a cursory check of my licence, they started grilling me.

'Is there anyone in the back of the van?'

'No, just leaflets and relief packs. Is there a problem, officer?'

'We've had a complaint that you're operating a mobile brothel out of this van . . . The Sex Party van . . .'

'Look, I'm a candidate in today's by-election for the Sex Party and I'm visiting polling booths. Is there a problem with that, officer?'

They both looked at each other. It was clear they had no idea there was an election on and had never heard of the Sex Party.

'We'd like to take a look at those relief packs.'

'Yes, of course, but I'm on a tight deadline and have a TV interview in half an hour. Can we go after that?'

'We just need to see the van first.'

We both got out and watched while they rummaged around for a few minutes. Then they walked over to me and said, 'Wait here,' and got back in their police car, which still had its lights flashing and was blocking a lane of traffic. A small crowd started to build on the footpath with people pointing and clicking their tongues at the little mobile brothel that had dared to invade the home of Carla Zampatti and Zegna. The officers stayed in their car for almost half an hour and when they finally came back to our van, I demanded an explanation. Now their story had shifted to another complaint about our posters being obscene. I wanted to know who had lodged the complaints, but they wouldn't say. I suspected that the complaint came from some Toorak toff rather than a rival party but I would never find out for sure. However, I believe that this was the first time a political candidate had been detained by police on an election day.

Kelly O'Dwyer ended up winning Higgins and Paul Fletcher won Bradfield—two of the safest Liberal seats in the country. And both went on to become ministers in Coalition governments.

We had suffered from a lack of everything in this campaign—including sleep! The Sex Party had $10,000 committed for each by-election. The Liberals spent over $1,000,000,and although there was no figure for the Greens, they must have spent well over $200,000. These rival parties had over 100 supporters in each state out on the streets handing out material and in the campaign offices. We had three, including our candidates. In both elections, we missed out on getting public funding by just a few hundred votes. But getting almost 4 per cent of the vote in two of the most conservative seats in Australia, with votes of up to 7.7 per cent in some booths, created an excellent foundation on which to build my strong Senate campaign in 2010.

25

RATFUCKED

In US politics, being 'ratfucked' means being subjected to a particularly virulent act of sabotage or revenge from a political opponent. The Ratfuck, whether used as a verb or a noun, is well defined in the title song of AC/DC's third album: a 'dirty deed done dirt cheap'. It featured in the Carl Bernstein and Bob Woodward book, *All the President's Men*, which described the Watergate break-in and the downfall of President Richard Nixon.

As far as I know, Kevin Rudd is the only Australian politician to ever use the term. At the 2009 Copenhagen Climate Summit, he told the media that 'those Chinese fuckers are trying to ratfuck us'. For an overtly Christian politician fluent in Mandarin, he probably should have stuck to what he knew best, which was diplomacy. He was as good at channelling American slang as he was at holding his liquor in a strip club.

I first heard the term while watching the US version of *House of Cards*. Robbie and I had started watching the first series on Netflix a couple of months out from the 2013 federal election and finished the last episode a few days before finalising our formal preference deals. With more than 30 parties contesting the Senate election, our preference negotiator, Craig Ellis, was on the phone night and day, proposing, modifying and then concluding deals with most of them. For some reason, the term ratfucking had become part of the preference deal lexicon, probably as a lighthearted way of labelling those who might not honour their deals. Not for a moment did I think that I would actually end up being ratfucked!

* * * *

The party was expanding in Victoria faster than anywhere else in the country. Volunteers came forward at the rate of three to one to other states. Moving to Melbourne made a lot of sense, so in 2010 I packed up my Woolloomooloo apartment and moved into an old red brick house in North Carlton. As with most of my rentals and purchases I looked for a place that would be suitable for work as much as it would be a private living space. With no money to rent a flash campaign office on Brunswick or Exhibition Streets like the big boys, I turned the Eros office into an election campaign war room. Two hundred Rathdowne Street in the gentrified Melbourne suburb of Carlton was an old Federation-Italianate house that I liked to think was similar to the disused office space that Birgitte Nyborg took over to run her campaign in the Danish political TV series, *Borgen*. The original tiles were lifting on the front porch, the paintwork was chipped and peeling, and inside the old wooden floors had been sanded so many times that some sections were only held together by the varnish. Butcher's paper, electorate maps and Sex Party posters were stuck on every wall in between a mass of political humour and satire that came courtesy of Robbie's days at *Matilda* magazine. Volunteers slept on couches and there was always plenty of wine in the fridge and pot in the kitchen drawer. It was the sort of house my mother would have loved to organise.

The 2010 federal election was the first Australia-wide campaign for the Sex Party. It was also a baptism of fire as we quickly learned that the key to electoral success for a minor party such as ours was to leverage preferences via the group voting ticket (GVT).

Introduced by the Hawke government, the GVT was a voting method designed to address the huge number of informal votes for the Senate. In some states, with so many candidates, it was no wonder that people mucked up the numbers or just didn't even bother. The GVT system gave the voter an option to either keep numbering all candidates or to simply select their favoured party and mark it with a '1' above the line and allow that party to determine the flow of preferences. With the average voter just wanting to get in and out of the ballot booth as soon as possible, it's no surprise that over 96 per cent took up this option.

Unlike the House of Representatives, the Senate is elected through what is known as 'single transferable vote proportional representation'. Basically, this means that the makeup of the Senate should be reflective of the proportion of the total votes a party receives, which is why in the past parties like the Democrats and Greens have been able to win seats where they could never have won them in the House of Representatives.

Preference flows for the GVTs are determined weeks before polling day and lodged with the Australian Electoral Commission by each party. The strategy for a minor party is to work towards achieving as high a primary vote as possible to keep you ahead of the pack and then add to that a good flow of preferences from smaller parties. With enough deals in place, you could parlay your accumulated votes to the point of putting yourself in a winnable position.

As more and more voters started turning away from the major parties, this scenario meant that if the minor parties combined their votes they could then get close to a quota. In my opinion, as long as the parties consolidating their votes had similar values then this system was a good one—and, frankly, was the only way for a minor party to get across the line. This is why the major parties hated it, particularly the Liberals and the Greens, although this same system is what allowed the Greens and an independent like Nick Xenophon to get elected to the Senate in their early days.

The problem for me was that some parties we could just never agree to preference. This included the racist, religious and just plain nutty parties. Strangely enough, the feeling wasn't mutual. When I had gone to Adelaide to launch our 2010 South Australian campaign, Family First pursued me to put a preference deal in place. They even drove out to the airport to meet me!

I mentioned this as an off-the-cuff remark to an Adelaide *Advertiser* journalist and it made front page news. Initially, Family First claimed it was a set-up, but both Craig and myself had emails to prove their advances, so they finally had to retract their denials and fess up. Their preferences proved instrumental in the final count on that election because even though I was leading when Family First was eliminated, their vote dropped on to the conservative Democratic Labour Party, who leap-frogged me, resulting in the

DLP candidate, John Madigan winning the last seat in Victoria. It was close. Out of 21 parties who had run we came in sixth place securing 2.27 per cent of the Victorian Senate vote and missing out on winning a seat by a couple of thousand votes. We had received over 2 per cent of the national Senate vote and had come in at fifth place in a field of 26 parties.

We were confident that 2013 was going to be a different story. We had learned a lot about the importance of preferences and which parties you could trust to honour their deals. Personally, I felt a lot more confident in dealing with the movers and shakers in the major parties and in prosecuting my case for favours from them. Party volunteers also felt like they had increased their understanding of what worked in terms of promotion on the street. The Sex Party name wasn't quite as shocking as it had been.

* * * *

While moving to Melbourne had been the right thing to do for the party, leaving my Dad on his own in Canberra was difficult. Since Mum had died, he was not in a good place emotionally. Mum had been his lifelong tour director and truly his other half. He never forgave fate for taking her before him.

Then when his black Labrador cross, Jaz, died in 2011, I could see that he had lost most of his emotional connections. He had a few friends who dropped in from time to time, as well as a group of old naval officers called the ROMEOS (Really Old Men Eating Out), but his three kids lived in different states. Robbie did the odd lunch at the Southern Cross club with him, but in his heart I think Dad felt like his life was pretty much over.

While I was attending Brisbane Sexpo in August of 2012, I called him three times, with no answer. He had also missed a couple of appointments including dinner with his old friend, Derek, who had called me to see if Dad was still in town. So I called Robbie and asked him to go and check on things. Before he could get there, Derek had let himself in to Dad's unit and found him dead in the hallway from a massive heart attack. I got the news at Sexpo and immediately got a taxi to the airport. In between my sobbing I called my brother and sister and by the time we arrived, the taxi driver was also in tears.

Dad's funeral was unexpectedly well attended—to the point that some people had to stand outside. In the death notice we stipulated no flowers but instead, a bottle of chilled champagne. Nearly one hundred people came back to our Yarralumla house each with a bottle. It was a great send-off but when your second parent dies, there is a sense that your adult life has well and truly started.

Dad was the first member of the Sex Party to die.

* * * *

As in the 2010 federal election, I ran as the lead candidate on the Sex Party's Senate ticket in Victoria at the 2013 federal election. Robbie became the lead candidate for Tasmania simply because he thought he could have a bit of fun with it. He decided to run on a platform of turning the Apple Isle into the cannabis capital of Australia, growing legal dope for medicine, industry and recreation.

We decided to have a stronger online presence for this campaign. Our friends at the ad agency, Fnuky, offered to run a crowd-funded television and online campaign ad for us called 'We're Fucked'. Within the first week, we had raised $15,000 through crowd funding—the amount needed for production to start. The ad opens with me looking all prime ministerial in front of the Australian flag and, with the national anthem playing in the background, I tell the nation that 'there's too much fucking going on'. Then, one by one, a conga line of ordinary Australians tells us why we're fucked. Two gay guys with a baby in their arms say they're fucked because they can't get married. A pensioner with two cops escorting him away says he's fucked because of the bag of pot in his top pocket. An old lady on life-support in a hospital bed says she's fucked because she can't die with dignity, and a young school girl in a Catholic uniform outside St Brigid's in North Fitzroy says she's fucked because she wasn't taught how to fuck. The old Catholic headmaster next to her then let's out a very long, '*Farrrk*!' and I finish off by saying, 'As much as we like sex, we don't want to get fucked.'

The ad had over 300,000 views in its first week online and was watched around the world. It was tweeted by celebs like Stephen Fry and replayed on national TV shows like *Gruen Nation* and *The Last Leg*. It looked like we were off to a good start.

* * * *

One of our key strategies in 2013 was to try to get Labor to preference me ahead of the Greens. We calculated that so long as we were still in the count at a critical juncture on election night, we would receive their surplus and I'd be carried over the quota.

To get to this point, however, we needed a strong preference flow from a good number of minor parties. Craig had deals in place with most of the progressives so we were looking good. A block of other minors, the Liberal Democratic Party (LDP), the Outdoor Recreation Party, the Smokers' Rights Party and the Republican Party, were all controlled by David Leyonhjelm of the LDP. Craig was negotiating a preference swap with Leyonhjelm similar to the one we had done in 2010, as well as trying to tie up the other three.

Part of the deal we were offering Labor was to preference them ahead of the Greens in the seat of Richmond, which was going to be a cliff hanger and a seat where our preferences could easily have determined the outcome. The Greens had pre-selected a po-faced feminist fundamentalist, Kathleen Maltzahn, who had set up the nation's largest anti-sex work organisation, Project Respect. She was trying to take sex work back to the 1950s and criminalise it again. It was a path we didn't want to go down. The new Greens leader, Christine Milne, had previously announced that the Labor/Green alliance deal of previous elections was over, so I assumed there wouldn't be much of an issue. Even though Prime Minister Kevin Rudd was said to have had conniptions about preferencing a party with sex in its name, we felt that we had a chance of pulling off the deal.

On a Friday afternoon, the day before we had to lodge the GVTs with the AEC, we heard that all hell had broken loose. Noah Carroll, the Victorian Labor Secretary, a man I liked and admired, turned up on my doorstep to explain that when the Greens had heard Labor was considering going to us before them, they had spat the dummy and threatened to walk away from all other preference deals that they had in place with Labor around the country. I couldn't believe they would go to such extremes just to keep the Sex Party out of the Senate; I had always believed, to a degree, that they were fellow travellers. It was my first real lesson in understanding that your 'enemy' was often a lot closer to home, although I had no wish to make an enemy of anyone. The deal with Labor was over. I was devastated.

Campaigning for the minor parties in other parts of the country was getting weird. The Minor Parties Alliance (MPA) run by the 'preference whisperer', Glenn Druery, was meeting regularly to look at ways to best preference the minors over the majors. The Sex Party had one foot in this camp and one foot out. From the beginning, we had told Druery that we would preference right-wing religious parties at the bottom of our list. He was happy to work with that.

Meanwhile, Craig was making progress with his own preference negotiations, but each day brought a new challenge. A week out from the election, it seemed like we might only get two of Leyonhjelm's voting block on board. Two days before the lodgement deadline of the Group Voting Tickets, Craig called Leyonhjelm one more time in an effort to get all his parties in the deal. He walked over to me after getting off the phone.

'Well, that was easy,' he said, slightly mystified. 'Maybe too easy.'

After haggling with him for weeks, Leyonhjelm was suddenly telling Craig we could have all the parties. For the first time in the campaign, we felt like we were inhaling success.

In retrospect, it was just too easy, but at that point we had no reason to doubt the deal. Leyonhjelm was a lawyer; he would presumably honour what was essentially a verbal contract.

Two days later, the deadline for submitting the GVTs expired. Our ageing little grey Toshiba fax had managed to carry all our forms off to the electoral commission for every state without a hiccup. Then—disaster.

Two hours after the deadline, Leyonhjelm called Craig to tell him that he hadn't got his GVTs into the AEC on time because his fax machine had malfunctioned. It was a 'dog ate my homework' excuse.

After his initial string of expletives, Craig told him he would get our lawyer around there in half an hour to take a statement from him, and we called the AEC to tell them what had happened and that we needed an extension on the deadline. The AEC refused, stating the legislation did not allow for late submissions.

Later that day, our lawyer had managed to get hold of Leyonhjelm's fax log that showed that he had had no trouble sending all his GVTs in all other states. It also showed that he had attempted to send two pages to the Victorian office of the AEC but that the 'stop' button appeared to have been pressed both times and the transmissions aborted. The log also showed that his fax machine was still cranking out faxes later that day.

We were effectively dead in the water. Only twice in the history of federal elections had a party not submitted GVTs this way. Not only had Leyonhjelm scuppered our chances by denying us his preferences (we had fulfilled our end of the deal and given him ours), but he had also denied the members of all four of his block the chance to get elected. The *Australian Financial Review* and *Crikey* both covered the fiasco a week later. In a filmed interview with Leyonhjelm, the *AFR* showed his state-of-the-art, industrial-strength fax machine sitting right behind his head. It looked like it would outlast him.

* * * *

When the dust settled after election night, we still managed to get the fifth-highest Senate vote in Victoria, and came in third place for that last Senate seat. The numbers were clear. If Leyonhjelm had honoured his deal, I would have been elected to the Senate. In a

Senate Committee hearing into changing the voting system in 2014, Glenn Druery told the committee that:

> The Liberal Democrats were not there [in his client group] because they had front parties, and they were certainly not very honest with quite a few groups at this election. There is a suggestion from Robbie Swan that the Liberal Democrats went out of their way to derail the Sex Party in Victoria. Many people are of that view. In fact, if the Liberal Democrats had submitted a Group Voting Ticket in Victoria, along with their front groups, then Fiona Patten would be a senator-elect right now.

Why did he do it? Some commentators said he had a grand plan to win the balance of power in the Senate, and if the Sex Party had got in as another libertarian party we would not support his firearms agenda or his wish to sell off state-owned assets. Who knows what went on in his Machiavellian mind. While it was clear the day after the election that we had lost Victoria, Craig's preference deals in Tasmania showed Robbie hovering around third favourite to win the last seat there. A few days later, after more votes were counted, he hit the front.

Two weeks on, towards the end of the count and without ever having set foot in the state, Robbie was still being called by the ABC computers as the winner. Antony Green called him to say that he couldn't believe it was happening, but it appeared he would win. A few minutes after the AEC's computers factored in all the below the line votes, the result was known. Jacqui Lambie from the Palmer United Party had beaten Robbie by just 244 votes. While it wasn't a ratfuck, it was another ratshit result. In retrospect, we should have called our campaign ad 'We're Ratfucked'.

26

GETTING ELECTED

Robbie says that I have the sort of personality that is best described by Chumbawamba's irritating but lingering anthem to inner renewal, 'Tubthumping'. The refrain is an energetic chant to dusting yourself off and having another go.

Wikipedia describes a 'tubthumper' as 'someone, often a politician, seeming to "jump on the bandwagon" with a populist idea.' The Urban Dictionary also defines the term as 'a drink comprised of whisky, vodka, lager and cider' and then, disturbingly, as 'a turd so extraordinarily long that, when dropped, it thumps on the back of the toilet.' Motions unparliamentary aside, I will grudgingly concede that some parts of that beverage might sometimes have had a bearing on my moods, but I reject the notion that I am a politician who jumps on populist bandwagons, although I have been known to jump on a few *unpopulist* ones. But it is true: I do recover from adversity quickly.

John Howard once described the possibility that he might bounce back from being dumped as Liberal leader as like 'Lazarus with a triple bypass' and Paul Keating once famously quipped that Andrew Peacock couldn't make a political comeback because 'a soufflé only rises once'. After running for public office six times before being elected, I think it's fair to say that without that bounce-back gene I wouldn't have kept at it. David Leyonhjelm's electoral sting was tough enough. One minute I was standing there having a mature conversation, and then, out of nowhere—wham! I was staggering around the room with a giant headache and little chance of winning the election I'd worked so hard on. I think I had a quiet weep for a couple of minutes when I realised the consequences of his actions and then I was over it, determined not to have my political plans derailed by a conservative dressed in liberty's colours. Besides, I still felt like I could carry my logical libertarian agenda into any parliament in Australia and make it work.

The more I looked at the Victorian parliament in the weeks and months after that federal election, the more convinced I became that it was a better platform from which to initiate social change, especially for an independent. Conservative independents who had managed to snag the balance of power in other parliaments had just about taken over the country. Geoff Shaw, the conservative independent in the previous Victorian parliament, had caused enormous problems for the Napthine government. He had no mandate, no policies and no reason to be there as an independent, having resigned from the Liberal Party just before they expelled him. He was facing misuse of parliamentary funds charges that could well have caused an early election.

The former accountant and nightclub bouncer was part of a charismatic Christian church and had very conservative social views on abortion, homosexuality and porn. He had been charged with assault before becoming a parliamentarian, led away from his ex-wife's house by police, and was involved in a road-rage incident in his electorate that police also had attended. He had been part of a melee on the steps of the Victorian parliament in which another man had suffered facial wounds. If someone like that could get elected, surely a former sex worker could. So, with that in mind and the 2013 election now behind me, I started planning for the Victorian state election in November 2014.

Robbie, on the other hand, was over it. He wanted to move up to our mountain property on the edge of the Kosciuszko National Park, write a few books and take daily walks. Since 1981 Robbie had been transforming it into a 120-hectare wildlife and wilderness retreat, and he now managed it with my help. But as much as I liked time alone and a few days in the mountains, I loved living in Melbourne. As he turned 60, Robbie had entered a more meditative phase. He was thirteen years older than me. While we were in our thirties and forties, this age difference hadn't meant much, but now I wasn't so sure. I think we had a quiet moment or two at this point about how we would go forward as a couple.

We came to a tacit understanding that if I won, Robbie wouldn't have to do the job with me, as long as I could still feel his support and wordsmithing. He wasn't going to be employed on staff and wouldn't have to attend a lot of party meetings or events. He would move out of his little Canberra unit and split his time between living in the bush and my place in Melbourne. It seemed like a good compromise.

Having contested six elections and narrowly missing out on winning two, a few of my Eros members were also starting to wonder if all this political effort was worth it. The time I spent on political and basic industry association issues was being questioned a little more than usual. While most of the political campaigns had not been about getting elected but getting exposure, they had nonetheless taken away resources from everyday industry association work. Persuading Eros board members that this was a valid path was made easier by deconstructing the industry's major problems. When compared with European and US sex industry issues, Australia's always came down to the politics of the situation. Eros's lobbying over the years had been effective without nailing some of the big issues. Almost single-handedly, we had established a nationwide grey market around some of the benchmark products and services, like X-rated films and some aspects of sex work in some states, that still remained illegal. This meant that while most of the time police turned a blind eye, traders were still at a huge disadvantage in the marketplace where they were regularly refused banking services, access to job creation schemes and other business facilities that most businesses just took for granted. The only way to change these entrenched cultures was to get active in political circles in the same way that the Church had done in the years before.

I started to look at a campaign to win a Victorian upper house seat. I chose the Northern Metro region because this was where I was living, but I also thought the last Liberal seat in this electorate was marginal and if there was a swing, it could easily come down to me or Family First.

As soon as Robbie saw my conviction, he committed to one more go, and in typical style and without saying anything he started his own private campaign. He contacted a group of Indian pundits from his meditation days and arranged for them to do a special Vedic 'yagya' or ceremony based on my time and date of birth, and a few other personal parameters. He paid a fee for a specific yagya that was supposed to assist people to get elected to public office by neutralising opposition and maximising 'support of nature'. Being a student of Vedic and Western astrology over many years, he also consulted his old friend and mentor, the celebrity astrologer, Milton Black.

They were both adamant about the outcome. Jupiter, that great benefic in the sky, would come to a rare standstill on my Midheaven, or point of public recognition, on election day, and would stay there for four days while the votes were being counted. Apparently, I also had Pluto on my ascendant in something called my Solar Return, which happened less frequently than Halley's Comet.

'You can't lose,' Robbie said. 'They're once-in-a-lifetime transits. The odds on both of them occurring in the same cycle are like winning Lotto.'

I wasn't convinced. For a party that prided itself on being pragmatic and evidence-based, some of Robbie's spiritual ideas raised a few eyebrows among the rank and file. The campaign would be a hard slog because there would be more parties running in Northern Metro than ever before (eleven new ones) and I had no war chest to speak of. Rather than the outcome being determined by cosmic forces, my election would depend on hard work and some smart marketing. If elected, I could well be the first person from an industry association to be elected to a parliament in Australia. I would certainly be the first former sex worker. It wasn't a bad position to campaign from, and soon we had a fresh campaign slogan—Take a New Position!

From the very beginning, this election campaign felt easier than the rest. I had a plan to engage with other minor parties that shared our agenda. I caught up with Voluntary Euthanasia party founder, Philip Nitschke, and floated the idea of doing some combined promotional work. Within a few weeks, we had done a joint letterbox drop, and later in the campaign we had three advertising scooters running around Melbourne's CBD. We used the same artwork for our joint promotion card, which had an image of a corpse with a party going on in the background. The ticket on the big toe read, 'Have a Happy Ending.' Another one said, 'We give a fuck if you want to kick the bucket.'

* * * *

Kris Schroeder was the lead guitarist for the Melbourne rock band, the Basics. He had formed the band back in 2002 with Wally De Backer (better known as Gotye), but when Kevin Rudd repealed the carbon tax in June 2013, the band got angry and formed the Basics Rock'n'Roll Party to contest the federal election. Now they were running for the Victorian state election, but they were having trouble working out how to play the preference game and needed help. Strategically, the Sex Party needed to lift our primary vote by a percentage point or two early on in the count to get up and over some of the better known minor parties.

I sensed a mutual attraction and called Kris. Soon after, we agreed to join forces for the last six weeks of the campaign. They were very laidback and we enjoyed a few drinks together and a game of snooker or two. Together we hired a large, flat-bed truck, put the band on the back and covered it with promo banners that read, 'Vote Sex,

Drugs and Rock'n'Roll'. The entertainment site Scenestr.com.au called it 'a cheeky hat tip to AC/DC's famous "It's A Long Way to the Top" 1975 truck gig along Swanston Street'. I would jump up on the truck between songs and deliver a political message on behalf of both parties. The truck stopped at various shopping centres and we even did a gig outside the former Pentridge jail.

When it came time to submit the Group Voting Tickets at the Victorian Electoral Commission on Hoddle Street a week out from the election, Kris wandered up with his card to show me. Freak out! He'd put Family First at number two after Ashley Fenn, their candidate for Northern Metro had called him and asked to exchange second preferences. Kris thought Family First sounded like a friendly name and, without knowing anything about them, thought it was no big deal. When I told him what they stood for, he was horrified and immediately wrote out a new ticket with the Sex Party at the number-two spot. That change would prove to have been crucial in my election.

* * * *

Working with Voluntary Euthanasia and the Rockers was easy and enjoyable. I liked forming coalitions in a way that benefitted both of us to the detriment of the major parties. Of course, a Sex Party election campaign wouldn't be complete without a bit of outrageous humour and satire. We looked at the worst possible outcome in terms of moral crusaders getting elected to the upper house and decided to create a collectors' card set for the event. We called it the House of Horrors with the tag line, 'Don't Let Victoria Collect the Set'. We printed 30 packs and sent them to media. The deck included Pastor

Danny Nalliah from Rise Up Australia looking like a mythical being from Dante's 'Inferno'; Inga Peulich from the Liberal Party dressed as Dracula, and Kathleen Maltzahn from the Greens, as the harpy from hell. As soon as they were printed they were gobbled up and the Museum of Democracy is about the only place to see one now.

As the election drew near, a sex scandal hit the Liberal Party and drew some very interesting lines in the sand. They disendorsed their candidate for the seat of Thomastown, Nitin Gursahani, claiming he had links with Bollywood actress and porn star Sunny Leone, and that he was intending to host a number of events for her in the final week of the campaign. Leone, star of such epic features as *Alabama Jones and the Busty Crusade*, had pretty much traded her porn career in for Bollywood and was doing well. But the Libs were having none of it, saying Gursahani 'did not reflect the values that underpin our party' and had not been forthcoming about his business interests in the application process.

It was a prudish and unnecessary thing to do in the last week of a campaign that humiliated one of their own for the sake of some quaint notion of Victorian-era morality. It had a ring of no-confidence about it and I thought it made the Liberals look weak and intolerant. We had run porn stars in almost every campaign and the media just accepted it. In fact, only a few months before this, two Sex Party candidates, Zahra Stardust and Angela White, had entered the record books by becoming the first two registered political candidates to make an X-rated film together. No one cared. *People* magazine was the only media outlet interested enough to cover the occasion. Mind you, the DVD was popular. Another first for us was running an 'out' HIV-positive candidate, Joel Murray, as my number two-candidate. Joel was described by one media outlet as the only candidate in the field to sport a nose ring.

In the last couple of weeks, I started hitting the phones trying to lock in preference deals. We were sweet with fellow travellers like the Cyclists, the Rockers and the Voluntary Euthanasia Party, but when it came to larger parties like Palmer United Party (PUP), I had no idea where we stood. Family First had been telling minor parties that they could bring PUP's preferences to the table in a deal.

I'd had a couple of calls with their preference advisor, James McDonald, who personally wanted to do a deal but I could tell he was being constrained by other quarters. He denied that there was any deal with Family First. About two weeks out from the election, PUP announced they wouldn't be standing any lower house candidates, so I decided to go straight to the horse's mouth and call Clive Palmer about the upper house. He was rude and abrupt on the phone: after I introduced myself and asked a general question about their preference strategy, he simply said, 'We don't need that,' and hung up on me.

The Greens stayed well away from us. They knew we had enormous issues with their Richmond candidate, Kathleen Maltzahn. Not only was she opposed to sex work but she was a supporter of former Brian Harradine staffer and Collective Shout founder, Melinda Tankard Reist. Maltzahn claimed to base her objections to sex work on feminist principles, but the flawed logic in her rhetoric said otherwise. Her position was that all women who were sex workers were victims of men's uncontrolled lust and needed to be saved. She never applied that same logic to male sex workers, whether they were servicing men or women. She was touting that classic male chauvinist position that says women are weak and incapable of looking after themselves, but men are strong and so must be okay.

Her constant labelling of Australia's 10,000 female sex workers as 'victims' also added to the weight of stigmatisation that they already laboured under. Again, not a very feminist thing to do to your sisters. If she was elected, I believed that Maltzahn would have pushed the Greens towards criminalising sex work in Victoria, along with other aspects of the adult goods and services industry. If you believe that all sex work is abusive and demeaning, then people who perform in X-rated films are almost in the same category.

I had long suspected that she was not alone in the Greens about pushing this agenda, and that if she had been elected it would have emboldened many in that party to embrace wowserism more than they already did. As it was, the Greens in Victoria were not allowed to accept passes to go to the races or the footy, which in my opinion, was like being part of an Amish community. Admittedly, they'd like to ban horse racing altogether so they claim it's to stop corruption but how much can you corrupt someone with a free ticket to the footy?

Damien Mantach was the Liberal's preference organiser and he was keen to do business, but told me I was up against it because Family First were running candidates in every lower house seat. That meant they had a huge bargaining chip when it came to preferences in the upper house. When I looked at that more closely, I discovered they were running husbands and wives as separate candidates in seats that were hundreds of kilometres apart. They also had very few supporters on the ground to hand out how to vote cards in many of these electorates, which made their support look paper thin. We had increased our volunteer base significantly and had all seats covered.

Still smarting from the federal preference sting in 2013, I was hesitant to deal with the Liberal Democratic Party in Victoria but, in the end, pragmatism overrode principle. If I could agree on a deal and meet their representative as they walked into the Victorian Electoral Commission to lodge their GVT, I could check it and then adjust my ticket accordingly. No more Mr Nice Guy on the phone. But, unbelievably, the LDP's Les Hughes wanted to deal with Family First in my Northern Metro region. After a twenty-minute conversation during which I reminded him that Family First would try and scupper just about every LDP policy if they were elected, I managed to talk him down. I couldn't, however, get him over the line in the South East region, where he insisted on preferencing Danny Nalliah from Rise Up Australia. This, he figured, would stop the evil Greens from winning the seat.

As it turned out, that preference flow for Nalliah actually led to the Greens beating the Sex Party in that seat by 250 votes.

Labor wanted us to give them everything. Noah Carroll played hardball with me to get second preferences in Northern Metro. He knew that without their big dump of unused votes at the end of the count, it would be hard for us to win, but I wasn't going to give away the chance for Sex Party candidates in other seats to get elected just to maximise my own chances. After three very intense meetings, I had a deal in place that we would preference them above the Libs and the Greens in some lower house seats and they would preference us second in Northern Metro and high up in two other regions. That could potentially see three of us get elected as long as we got enough early preferences in the count. This also meant that the Labor/Greens nexus that caused so much trouble in the 2013 federal election was finally broken.

As usual the Greens were the meanest and hardest to deal with. They were incredibly prescriptive and handed me a list of acceptable minor parties (acceptable to them) that we could place before them in each electorate. We finally came to an agreement that varied greatly across seats.

While all this was going on, I wrote an editorial for *The Age* that put the case for legalising both medical and recreational cannabis. I knew it was a gamble of sorts because to do it effectively I would have to out myself as a regular recreational user—something that no Australian politician had so far been prepared to do. If I could convince a small percentage of the newspaper's readers to vote for me, then it would be worth it. A week out from the election, it was published.

My main point in the piece was that there were 450,000 regular users of cannabis in Victoria that purchased more than $1 billion worth of weed every year. My second point was that more than 5000 of us are prosecuted every year simply for possessing it, many young kids who would carry a criminal prosecution for the rest of their lives just because they wanted to smoke a joint. The figures, I wrote, meant that we prosecuted people for possessing weed far more vigorously than we prosecuted for cocaine, and that this was an unwinnable war for the government. If I was elected, I would put forward a private member's bill to legalise and tax cannabis at a rate of around 30 per cent and raise $250 million a year that could go to schools and hospitals, just as it had in Colorado.

A week out from the election on 29 November, I sensed that the Sex Party policies were finally being heard. Roy Morgan had shown that Family First's vote had remained constant on about 2 per cent in polls taken in September, October and early November. Those same polls had showed zero support for the Sex Party, but then suddenly we were starting to attract 3 per cent of the vote. Sportsbet's odds had us firming to win a seat from $6 to $1.87 in the final week. While it made me feel good I was pretty relaxed anyway by this point, confident that I had done about as much as I could to win. The Shooters Party were on $1.30 and Family First had blown out to $4 alongside Rise Up Australia. The DLP were on $6, while Vote 1 Local Jobs, Animal Justice and the Cyclists were all at $7, with the Rockers at $8. The Socialist Alliance were the rank outsiders at $51.

* * * *

On the morning of the election, I felt calm. I spent the day visiting polling booths and doing media. After the polls closed, Robbie, our volunteers and myself all descended on my favourite venue in Melbourne, the old-style gentlemen's club with the modern agenda, The Kelvin Club. The early results were all over the place, but I was in party mode and not taking too much notice. By 10 p.m., I had moved ahead in Northern Metro and we were within striking distance in South Metro and South Eastern Metro. As the count went on over the next few days, my position got better and better. So did that of Rachel Carling-Jenkins from the DLP in the Western Region. In an interview with Fairfax, she said she was already looking around for fellow travellers on the crossbench but ruled out any alliance with the Sex Party. That would become 'the battle of the blondes,' she said.

Well, she was right in one respect, but in fact my real battle would be with another, older blonde from the Liberal Party—Inga Peulich. A few days after the election, with 60 per cent of the votes counted,

News Limited reported that I was 'on track to secure an upper house seat in the Victorian Parliament'. They used a photo of me in a scarlet dress with black fishnet stockings sitting reverse on a wing-back kitchen chair, a la Christine Keeler in the 1960s. I thought to myself that I should get used to this and not try to dodge it or start trying to act like 'a politician'.

'If elected', the report stated, 'Ms Patten said her first act would be to refer a voluntary euthanasia bill to the law reform commission. She hopes Labor and the Liberals will allow a conscience vote on the issue. Next on the list is drug reform. "I'm not there to stymie the government, I'm there to broaden debate," she said.'

As the count went on over the next week, it became clear that barring a failure in the counting, I had won the last seat in Northern Metro. The formal declaration of the poll, however, would still need to be done by the VEC computers. Some of the seats were simply too tight to call and needed the computer breakdown to definitively award the seat. Our candidate for the South East Region, Martin Leahy, was still looking like he was ahead on most counting. Our Southern Metro candidate, Francesca Collins, was coming second, but well within striking distance.

At the push of the button, I was elected but Martin missed out by 250 votes. Francesca missed out by 1000. As disappointing as it was to not win three seats, I was over the moon with our result. Hardened party apparatchiks probably take it in their stride, but for little old me it was a life-changing moment. Robbie and I went home after the event and just sat on the couch looking at each other in disbelief. We had done it. Against all the odds and all the permutations of the preferencing system, against all the naysayers who said someone from the sex industry could never be elected to parliament—it had happened.

I resigned as CEO of Eros and started to look at a timetable for reform in the Victorian parliament. A good result at state level also renewed my faith in federal politics and the possibility of building the state result into a better one at the 2016 federal election.

27

A NIGHT IN THE MUSEUM

The joy of winning in Victoria was somewhat soured a few days later when an ALP relic from another era, Gary Gray, went public with a call to stop minor parties from winning Senate and upper house state seats by changing the voting system. He referred specifically to my win and said, 'The Victorian election results could see up to eight different political parties operating in the new Legislative Council . . . The rise of single-issue "pop-up" political parties is a frivolous abuse of our democratic systems.'

Well, 30 per cent of voters had deliberately chosen a minor party because they were sick of decades of Liberal or Labor rule, but because his party wasn't cutting the mustard anymore, he thought he'd just get rid of as much of the opposition as he could rather than try to make his party more relevant to voters.

To say that the Sex Party was a single-issue 'pop up' party really pissed me off. I'd worked my arse off for five years to get the party to where it was and to win my seat. So had many other small-party organisers. I'd visited more community groups in a year than Gray would have done in his entire lifetime. I'd written more media releases and more letters to the editor than he ever had, and I'd spent more hours door-knocking and waving banners on street corners than he could ever have done. He was one of those many dinosaurs who had hardly been out of the party fold and simply rose up through the ranks as a staffer and then into the national secretariat before doing a stint with a fossil fuel company and then gaining preselection. He would never know what it was like to be a battler and form his own party. To do all the hard work and then to get elected.

His rant continued. 'Political pop-up parties are nothing more than manipulations of voter intention and stunts diverting attention from the real choices. They damage the fabric of governance.' It was an argument for machine politics and nothing more. Because I wanted to introduce new abortion laws, voluntary euthanasia and drug laws, and because I was sick of his party's patronising approach to adult sexuality, technology and community opinion, he was alleging that I was damaging the fabric of governance.

The fact that the Greens fell over themselves to support his call showed that they were of a similar mindset and wanted to stop small parties like us biting into their vote. More than that, they could see that under an optional preferential voting regime, it was likely that Labor would always lose their third senator to the Greens and not to some other party. Maybe that was the reason Labor eventually backed away from Gray's plan. But a Liberal government full of old fossils, together with the Greens, eventually legislated the changes and suddenly small parties were almost permanently locked out of federal politics.

* * * *

The Liberal/Greens plan to cleanse the upper houses of the nation was being shown for what it was in Victoria. With a record eight parties now represented in the Legislative Council, there was a real buzz around the parliament during the initial days that the house of review would finally become just that: a place where a wide variety of views were heard. In fact, many of the staff of parliament were excited to see how the instruments of governance would be tested with so many parties. It would come to pass that there was a record number of private members' bills, a record number of amendments made to legislation and a record number of inquiries established into the bills and issues.

Following my election, after the clerks had shown me where my new room was (as well as the nearest toilet), I was then pretty much left to check out the rest of the building on my own. I'd had a couple of small exploratory visits, but with the place buzzing in anticipation of a new parliament, I didn't see much. It was probably one of the most exciting times of my life, with only one regret—that neither Mum nor Dad had lived to see it happen.

Not long before the first sitting, I had a late lunch in the city with my art director, Ilia Chidzey. I was keen to show her the layout and design of the parliament so she had a feeling for the style of my new workplace environment. We walked across Spring Street, through a side gate and turned left past a large fireplace that had been built on to the back of the building but never used. The MP's entrance was adjacent to the car park, but the building was all closed up. As we were about to leave, I thought I'd swipe my new MP's security card just in case and was amazed to see how the old wooden door flew open immediately. With some trepidation, we walked through the security area and into a large corridor lined with ancient stone blocks. The silence was like a cemetery and the majesty was palpable. With no one around to direct us, we just started walking down the first corridor.

Built during the gold rush era in 1856, when Melbourne was one of the richest cities in the world, the building's underground areas were a lavish set of catacombs. At the end of the first corridor, we had lost our bearings. We turned right into another corridor that was lined with 100-year-old copies of bound Hansard reports on dusty bookshelves. Then we came across another corridor filled with old 19th-century balloon chairs, followed by one filled with chaises lounge. This one had been an old tunnel used to store coal in an earlier era but was now fitted with cave-like offices. I felt like Ben Stiller in *Night at the Museum*, except that this time the dinosaurs were members of parliament! Old black-and-white photos of past presidents and speakers lined the walls and over there, the T-Rex of them all, Sir Henry Bolte!

There was unused furniture everywhere. I had never seen so many large hat racks and wash stands. In the past, every crusty old MP must have had one in his office. Then we came across an old steam engine that was part of the air-conditioning for the building at the turn of last century. Many of the original outdoor areas had been enclosed over time, with one even said to have been used as a pistol-shooting gallery. There were flights of stairs that simply went nowhere and tunnels in all directions. Could one of them have been the legendary tunnel between parliament and Madame Brussel's brothel on Lonsdale Street? There were certainly plenty of them headed in that direction. Historians had rather tended to debunk that legend, although they had been more inclined to believe the story that she had been the beneficiary of one of the earliest telephones in the CBD, courtesy of her parliamentary clients.

The design and colour of carpet in the corridors under the chambers changed depending on which side of the building you were on. Red if you were on the Council side and green if you were on the Assembly side. Both are an ugly oak-leaf design that would look much better in a club. Their significance in the parliament is that the *Magna Carta* was written under an oak tree and is the enduring symbol of democracy in the Western world. Sadly, I would later be told that they had bought kilometres of the stuff in the 1970s so it wasn't likely to be changed any time soon.

Finally, Ilia and I found a flight of stairs that took us up to a landing near the Legislative Council and from there I slowly figured my way back to the rear security door.

* * * *

In my first few years as a house guest in this amazing mansion, I've taken to touring as many people I meet who I believe can contribute to the welfare of Victoria. I love any opportunity to further explore the nooks and crannies of this building. I also tend to open any unlocked cupboards or drawers looking for something interesting. To date, I haven't found anything except a spiral staircase at the end of my office corridor that appears to have been bricked up a long time ago. Maybe it's where the bodies are buried.

I have taken senators, sex workers, children and plenty of international guests for a wander. Even an astrophysicist from NASA. Often I'll pull an old Hansard from the shelf and we will check if anything interesting happened on the guest's birthday.

The library, in my mind, is the jewel in the crown. The dome in the centre of the ceiling is meant to replicate the Capitol Building in Washington DC. It is now shrouded in offices that were built around it in the 1950s. There was meant to be a similar dome built at the front but the gold rush ended before construction was complete and so it was put on hold.

I've fallen in love with the building and am still excited to walk up the imposing bluestone steps, although the large wooden doors that allow pass-holders in still need my shoulder behind them to open. When I sit in my chamber, I never bore of the detailed opulence and the bare-bosomed cherubs that float around the ceiling. Politicians never talk about this fabulous building. They seem to take it for granted.

28

MY MAIDEN YEAR

My inauguration as a Member of the Legislative Council of Victoria took place a couple of weeks after the election result had been finalised in December 2014. Over Christmas, I set up a temporary electorate office in the Treasury Building, while the Parliamentary Services Department combed shopping centres around Brunswick for something permanent.

The office was located between the conservative Liberal member Gordon Rich-Phillips and the two Shooters. It was a three-by-three metre bolthole tucked up under the eaves of Parliament House with an old east-facing sash window, a 100-year-old leather chaise lounge and a couple of desks. Originally it would probably have been an attendant's office. I could see that with a couple of staff members, Robbie and maybe a guest or two, it would be hard to even move around, but I was happy with it.

Hiring staff was the next cab off the rank. In the major parties, all these systems are put in place for you from head office and new staff are generally party members. Nearly all Liberal, Labor and Greens MPs would have worked in the office of another MP at some time before. My campaign manager, Nevena Spirovska, had been with me for a few years and naturally fell to the role of office manager. Finding a chief-of-staff for a Sex Party MP was a bit harder.

That summer, I also wrote my maiden speech, to be delivered when the first parliament resumed in March 2015. The maiden speech is a weird rite of passage because you have to make it before you are allowed to participate in parliamentary debates of any kind. It's a bit like losing your virginity in public. After you've done it, you've lost your parliamentary innocence and become fair game for anyone in the chamber to pinch your political arse. That's what it felt like, anyway—although I was allowed one vote first and that was for a new President for the Legislative Council.

* * * *

Everyone had seen the effect of having a partisan Speaker/President when Tony Abbott installed Bronwyn Bishop as the Speaker of the House of Representatives. She ejected Labor members on no less than 393 times, but only seven times from her own side of politics. My first criteria was to support someone who was genuinely unbiased. The Liberals had nominated their old President from the previous parliament, Bruce Atkinson. He had proven to be bipartisan in his calls and although I liked Labor's nominee, Gail Tierney, I reasoned that the crossbench would be much better served with a progressive Opposition President. The Greens thought similarly, and so Atkinson won by a good margin. Many said that it did not bode well for the new government to lose the presidency of the upper house, but I was simply looking after myself and it had nothing to do with the way I would vote on future issues. I'd also known Bruce for a long time, even before he got into parliament. At that stage, he was running an industry magazine for retailers. I had lobbied him on Eros issues as far back as the 1990s and found him to be a true small-l liberal with a good sense of humour and a broad outlook on life. He was one of the very few politicians happy to accept my personal invites to visit Sexpo and to meet with traders and hear their gripes.

Over the years, I'd known many MPs who wanted to see what Sexpo was all about but just couldn't bring themselves to abandon their political correctness. But some did take the walk on the wild side. In 1996, a Victorian MP entered the amateur strip competition up on the main stage and ended up wearing nothing but his undies and a mask in front of 2000 patrons. From memory, he had to be stopped from taking his undies off . . . Another had attended wearing a broad-brimmed hat, sunglasses and an actual raincoat, as if that was the uniform for Sexpo.

Following the election of a Legislative Council President, a call went out for seven acting presidents to help out in running the daily business of the house. I nominated and got one of them, which meant that over the next few years I would sit in the president's chair during each sitting. The first bill I got to pass as acting president was one to repeal Section 19A of the Crimes Act. This law singled out the crime of intentional HIV transmission for more harsher penalties (up to 25 years' imprisonment) than the maximum penalty for manslaughter (twenty years). With new anti-viral drugs around these days not many people die from HIV infections and so the inequality in the laws was obvious. It was also part of reducing the stigma around HIV/AIDS.

Life for a new crossbencher isn't easy. Because I held one of a few balance-of-power positions in the upper house, every interest group in town wanted to meet with me. If you want to be engaged in the many debates that come before parliament, you must be prepared to read about them extensively. If you're a backbencher from a major party, your minister does all the research for you, and if you are the minister, you have a department full of staff to do the hack work and research. As a crossbencher you don't have any of these luxuries. If you want to be on a couple of parliamentary committees as well, you can just about kiss your weekends goodbye.

The rationale behind who gets on to a parliamentary committee is that, as far as possible, it should reflect the makeup of the parliament. The Greens refused to go on any joint house committees except the main financial one: the Public Accounts and Estimates Committee. My fellow crossbenchers weren't keen on going on any committees either (I think they felt like they didn't have time or they weren't their responsibility) which is why I ended up on four of them—more than any other MP. They were: the Legal and Social Issues Committee; the Law Reform Committee; the Road and Community Safety Committee; the Electoral Matters Committee; and, later on, the Public Accounts and Estimates Committee. I was also on the White Ribbon Working Group and the Parliamentary Friendship Group for LGBTIQ people.

I didn't enter politics for the free passes to the races and the footy. Being elected was an amazing opportunity to help change many of the outdated and conservative structures around me, and I had decided from day one that I was in this for all I was worth. The daily walk up the steps of parliament and into one of the most ornate

Victorian chambers in the country was an extra bonus that never ceased to amaze me. Soaked in red velvet with Italianate *putis*, angels and lavish gold-leaf decoration, everything about my new work environment thrilled my senses.

In the last two weeks of the campaign, one of our ACT organisers, Jorian Gardner, had come down from Canberra to help out with the campaign. He had previously been Director of the ACT Fringe Festival and before that a political journalist and radio announcer. His public image as an *enfant terrible* had recently been enhanced by his removal from the Fringe Festival for running a burlesque event that satirised Nazism. It had been widely misinterpreted by plebeian types in the ACT administration as a 'Nazi burlesque performance' and because the festival was sponsored by the ACT government someone's head had to roll. At a loose end, Jorian had travelled to Melbourne to help out in the campaign. Although I knew he could be a very naughty boy, he also had more front than Myers, which was what I needed as I tentatively felt my way around the parliament in that first year.

When after a few months all the crossbenchers began to feel the crush of the workload, we approached the government for an extra part-time staffer each. I needed legal help more than anything, and I found a smart young law graduate, Danielle Walt, who was across all my issues.

* * * *

Minutes after being officially elected by the Electoral Commission computers at Etihad Stadium in late December 2014, I had held an impromptu press conference and was asked by reporters what were my most important objectives. I had no hesitation in naming the widespread suffering experienced by many at the end of their life as my top priority. I foreshadowed an early referral of physician-assisted dying to the Victorian Law Reform Commission.

The media immediately door-stopped the new premier, Daniel Andrews, to see what he thought of the idea. He was adamant it would never happen under his watch. It wasn't really what I wanted to hear regarding the first item on my agenda. If I was even going to get a hearing from the government, let alone any action on the issue, I had a lot of hard work ahead of me.

I know voluntary assisted dying (VAD) wasn't what most people thought would be my first legislative move, but then they probably hadn't met Peter Short—the Tic Toc man. I had launched the Sex Party in 2009 with a policy to legalise assisted dying, but I can't say that I gave it much thought after the policy was written. Then, in the run up to the 2014 state election, I met Peter, who was dying of oesophageal cancer and was on a mission to change the options that were available to him as his own clock wound down. His passion to change the law became all-consuming and, I suspect, helped to keep him alive in his last year. It ignited something in me as well, to the extent that I made a promise to him that somehow I would get VAD legalised during my first term in parliament. I had never made a promise to a dying person before and it felt like a huge responsibility.

A few days after my inauguration, I got some unexpected support. I was standing on the steps of parliament, absorbed in watching the traditional Aboriginal smoking ceremony, when a voice from behind me said, 'I'm very disappointed in you.'

I spun around to see former Liberal premier, Jeff Kennett, smiling down at me.

'Why?' I asked.

'Well, when the Sex Party got elected, I thought we'd all be having a bit of fun. But all you're talking about is legalising death!'

We both laughed and enjoyed a bit more banter before he turned to leave. But as he did he spoke more earnestly.

'Don't get me wrong. I support assisted dying . . . Just don't forget to enjoy your time here and have some fun.'

It was good advice and he lifted my spirits. If I couldn't get the Labor premier onside, then a former Liberal one was still a pretty good start.

The first week of parliament brought another surprise. The Greens first legislative action was to table a motion to refer the issue of VAD to the Law Reform Commission in almost the exact words I had used in my media conference. Not only was I now battling the government for support, I was battling the Greens to keep them from swiping my social policy initiatives. To be fair, they had tried to bring the issue into the parliament years before without success, and while it was annoying that they had stolen my thunder, I immediately threw my support behind their motion.

But I was beginning to have second thoughts about referring the issue to an agency outside of the parliament. The emails opposing the Greens motion were repetitive and soaked in religious dogma, but they made a couple of interesting points. First, that an issue such as this should be considered by the parliament and not a third party, and second, that any move on assisted dying would be to the detriment of other end-of-life services, such as palliative care. (Two years on, these same groups would completely reverse their logic when it came to the same-sex marriage debate, where they preferred to use a plebiscite on the issue rather than let parliament deal with it.)

I started drafting a different motion that moved for a parliamentary committee to investigate all end-of-life choices and issues including assisted dying.

I had already met with Dr Rodney Syme and others from the Dying with Dignity Victoria movement and they completely supported this approach. Assisted dying was just one part of a bigger toolbox for dying with dignity. By now I was also convinced that the Greens motion was not the way to go, even though I still supported it. But when it was put to a conscience vote, their motion failed. My intuition told me that if I didn't do something immediately the issue would simply fade too far from the parliament to be pulled back and we would have to wait another four years to raise it again.

The following week, using the arguments that the social conservatives had put to me and incorporating the advice from the dying with dignity lobby, I listed a much wider motion couched in community health issues to set up an inquiry into end-of-life choices, which included consideration of advanced-care directives and planning, palliative care, legal decision-making, and physician-assisted dying. I also referred it to a joint house committee of the parliament—a committee that I wasn't on. That way the anti-euthanasia campaigners couldn't say I was directly involved.

Peter Short had sadly died during the summer months preceding parliament's return. With the Greens motion defeated, a disinterested crossbench, a premier adamant that there would be no changes and a conservative Opposition that were never going to initiate anything in this area, I was determined to jam my foot in the closing door in the hope that a miracle would surface and the debate might still open up.

It wasn't a miracle, but shortly after listing my motion an angel of sorts did appear in the form of Gavin Jennings, the leader of the government in the upper house. He took me aside and said that my chances of success would be vastly improved if I allowed the government to introduce a slightly amended version of my motion and to send the issue to the Upper House Committee on Legal and Social Issues, which I was on, instead of the Joint House Committee. Governments can refer matters to committees without having to vote on them, and I knew that the last thing they wanted was another debate around a motion following the Greens' defeat. I also knew that Gavin was a supporter of Dying with Dignity Victoria and that this wasn't an easy discussion for him given the premier's stance on the matter.

I quickly agreed to his plan and within a week the End of Life Choices Inquiry was underway without debate and without a vote.

****

Having the government take my motion and move it themselves was an unexpected bonus. Independents like myself get only two spots per year to lead debate in the House. This time can be used in a number of ways. You can raise a topic to be discussed, move a motion to start a committee inquiry, move a motion to debate how terrible the government is, or introduce a private member's bill. It's basically a 'please discuss' mechanism that can eventually lead to a bill becoming an Act of Parliament, or it can die without a trace.

When the government put my motion to refer voluntary euthanasia to a committee, it still left me with two spots in the year to introduce a debate. I saw this as my opportunity to introduce a private member's bill to stop protestors from harassing women outside abortion clinics.

Abortion had been a hot button issue in Victoria since 2000. In that year, an anti-abortion protestor stormed the East Melbourne abortion clinic intending to burn it to the ground—along with everyone in it. Instead he shot and killed a security guard before being overpowered by clinic patients. Protests by religious campaigners had been constant outside parliament and the abortion clinic on busy Wellington Parade in East Melbourne, intensifying in the lead up to the 2014 election.

After my own experience of having an abortion over 30 years ago and having to run the gauntlet of these people, I was fired up. On many Saturday mornings, you would see me out the front of the abortion clinic with a bevy of committed Sex Party volunteers demonstrating against the anti-abortion group, Helpers of God's Precious Infants.

The group had been founded by a Catholic priest and was supported by prominent Catholics, including the Archbishop of Melbourne, Denis Hart. As the election drew closer, insults had been traded across the road outside the clinic. Helpers of God's Precious Infants would often bring in a large plaster statue of the Virgin Mary holding a baby Jesus on top of a wooden stretcher, and every year they held a special protest called the March for the Babies, led and organised by Liberal Victorian upper house member, Bernie Finn.

* * * *

Campaigning for this bill among my parliamentary colleagues quickly became 'not-so-secret women's business'. A small cross-party group of women emerged to lead support for the bill, including Mary

Wooldridge (shadow health spokesperson and leader), Jaala Pulford (Minister for Agriculture), Colleen Hartland (the Greens' health spokesperson), Georgie Crozier (shadow for children's health), Jaclyn Symes (government whip) and myself. It was my first taste of cross-party collaboration and it was a wonderful feeling to be united around an issue with a group of women that all had vastly different political affiliations. Since it was all about women's health, I suspect that it would have been a different process had men been involved.

Conscious that another woman, the DLP's Rachel Carling-Jenkins, would try to reopen the abortion debate at some point during her term, the group pulled in tightly with private meetings held in Jaala's office to discuss strategies. Following the first reading of the bill, various organisations, including women's health groups and family-planning groups, started to rally and I was fortunate to connect with the people who had drafted similar legislation in Tasmania.

The East Melbourne clinic, with the support of the Human Rights Law Centre, had just taken unsuccessful action against Melbourne City Council for not protecting them from the protestors. This in turn had ramped up the intensity of the religious demonstrators. Helpers of God's Precious Infants were pushing out ever more graphic and punishing leaflets and increasing the level of abuse towards women presenting at the clinic. They were joined by the Right to Life association and my crossbench colleague, Rachel Carling-Jenkins, to form a loose coalition to lobby against my bill. Maybe this was 'the battle of the blondes' that she had referred to when she was first elected. They lobbied, threatened and sent bulk emails, but the list of supporters in support of the bill far outweighed their numbers, evidence and public support.

It was difficult for the government to decide what to do. The bill was popular in the community and it wouldn't look good for the government to oppose it outright. Apart from a couple of right-faction members, most of them were supportive. But governments just don't generally allow private members' bills to proceed to a vote.

As the debate neared, I was still uncertain how the government was going to deal with it. The Liberals had agreed to a conscience vote and I was busy lobbying them individually, as well as holding party briefings using many of the skills that I learned as an Eros lobbyist. Others in the group were also writing and meeting with key people to ensure the success of the bill.

A few days before the debate was due to start, I met with the Health Minister, Jill Hennessy. She committed the government to introducing a similar bill within a few months if I would abandon mine. They used the excuse that it was technically flawed. It wasn't. But, as an excuse for not supporting the bill, it was plausible.

It was a hard decision to make. How would I face the staff at the East Melbourne clinic if I agreed to the government's plan and they then just let it lapse? On the other hand, allowing the government to take it over at this stage and introduce their own bill, assured it of success.

Sensing my reservations, Jill called me again to say that as an act of good faith she would stand on the steps of parliament with me and announce to the media the government's intention to introduce their own bill. She would acknowledge the fact that I had brought the issue before the parliament and that they would continue to work with me on developing their own bill.

At that point, I just jumped, and a couple of months later I stood with her on the steps to announce the new bill. And only a few months after that, true to her word, the minister introduced the safe access zone bill and it was not to be a conscience vote for the party, either.

The Australian Christian Lobby called the bill an attack on free speech. In reply, I said I was an advocate for free speech but not an advocate of a free audience. The Right to Lifers campaigned hard. They stood at the rear entrance to parliament as they did on most sitting days and waived appalling signs at the passing parade. One day, I went and stood alongside them with a couple of drag queens and a few Sex Party volunteers holding signs saying things like 'Wrong message, right place' and 'Honk if you support choice'. The old stagers didn't know where to look.

* * * *

The final sitting before the vote was one of the longest the parliament had seen since the state's new abortion laws had been passed in 2008. Everyone wanted a say. Opponents filibustered the proposed legislation for more than twelve hours on the first night, with the chamber calling it quits at 3.30 a.m. On the second day of debate, there were hours of ridiculous questions. Bernie Finn kept calling the clinics 'abortuaries' and then there was a debate over whether that was an actual word. Liberal MP Inga Peulich asked whether an aircraft flying at 149 metres over a clinic with a sign attached would run afoul of the legislation. She asked it eight times in various ways. What about a dinner party in a house that was less than 150 metres from a clinic where a conversation on abortion was taking place? The questions just got sillier and tempers started to fray. Finally, the vote was called at 4 a.m. and passed the upper house by 31 votes to eight.

29

DRUGS

When people ask how I got into politics, I often just say, 'Drugs.'

In my twenties, I had volunteered to work on the Health Department-funded needle exchange van in Canberra as part of the fight against HIV/AIDS. It was fun, but it also gave me my first experience of governments actually doing something sensible about illicit drugs.

Whether it was on the bus, in the AIDS Council or with my old sex worker group WISE, no one judged people for injecting drugs. There was one simple objective: to make their use safer and, in return, make the community safer. But while clean needles did reduce the spread of HIV and other blood-borne viruses, they didn't stop my friends from dying of overdoses. The illegality of the drug was causing that.

Some of my friends who had a very unhealthy relationship with heroin and other drugs would spend most of their waking hours working out how to purchase more. Sometimes the schemes were impressive and complicated, involving many transactions that would lead to the final score. I often thought they could be running amazing businesses instead of small-time Ponzi schemes that inevitably ripped off friends and family.

Alcohol, on the other hand, which almost always operated in a free market, was society's most problematic drug, yet more people die on the streets from heroin which was one of our most criminalised drugs. These are the two ends of the regulatory spectrum, but there is a sweet spot in the middle that governments miss when looking at illicit drugs. Tobacco almost hits that spot in that it is heavily regulated through taxes, restrictions on point of sale, and its harms are extolled in widespread educational campaigns. Maybe this is the reason that tobacco use is pretty much the only drug, legal or illegal, whose use is declining these days.

At the same time as I was setting up the Sex Party, the new psychoactive substances, or 'legal highs' as the media called them, came on to the Australian market. It was only natural that they found their home in age-restricted adult stores because the prohibitionist laws that Australia embraced could not deal with these emerging substances, especially the new synthetic cannabinoids that were different from anything we had seen before. They were ripe for regulation, but governments simply put their head in the sand and went down that well-worn but futile path of trying to ban each substance as they discovered them in the marketplace.

In the end, this led to a war of attrition between governments and the producers who would simply put out a new product every time one was banned. There was no limit to the number they could make.

One dealer told me that these young scientists could make a synthetic drug from just about every herb and flower in the garden.

The result of six years of this insane war was over 300 different synthetic compounds in the underground marketplace where before there had been none. As the former CEO of the adult industry's national association, I had presided over an industry scheme to try and regulate these new drugs via a scientific-testing regime, a holographic sticker scheme, and a centralised-reporting scheme on hospitalisations and adverse effects. It was a noble attempt, but this was really the domain of the Health Minister.

For a short time, New Zealand went down a different path and showed the world how it should be done. Their new laws ensured that anyone who wanted to sell or produce a new psychoactive substance (NPS) had to be licensed and have their product registered. They had to supply samples to the Health Department, have information about the substances listed on a public website, pay tax, and provide educational material and health contacts.

The new legal drug industry in NZ was led by Eros's sister group, The Star Trust. They showed their willingness to sell drugs responsibly by setting up health and welfare consultants to interview regular customers to ensure their drug use was not interfering with work and family, and that they were not on-selling any products, especially to children. It was the first time in the world that we saw the rise of ethical drug dealers, but, sadly, it didn't last long. The conservative media soon got to work on the scheme, accusing the government of legalising deadly drugs and destroying the fabric of New Zealand society, and the government abandoned the scheme within its first year.

It did, however, give us another model to consider. In the short time the regulatory regime was in place, there was a documented reduction in crime, fewer hospital admissions, and the number of outlets selling NPS fell by a massive 90 per cent as the compliant and ethical sellers gained a greater market share.

* * * *

In 2012, while still the CEO of Eros, I had attended a sex conference in London. Hungover and with a burned handbag from a night of decadent partying, I flew to Portugal the next day to meet Nuno Capez, the world's most charming man who ran the Lisbon Drug Dissuasion Commission.

Portugal had decriminalised the use and possession of drugs in 2001. This meant that anyone found with a small quantity of any drug was given a civil sanction rather than a criminal one. Part of that civil sanction was a meeting with the commission. At this meeting, you were interviewed by a psychologist and then a panel. If your drug use was out of control, you were given access to treatment straight away. If things weren't that bad, other options were offered.

After the mandatory espresso and Portuguese tart, plus some unsolicited fashion advice from Nuno ('Your shoes are stupid—stilettos should not be worn in a city made of cobblestones'), he invited me to sit in on a meeting where a waiter had just been picked up with some cocaine. The young man explained to the commission members that he didn't use it that often and when he wasn't out drinking he didn't give it a second thought. When asked about his drinking, he said that he probably drank more than his mates. He was offered a session to discuss tools to reduce his alcohol use rather than his cocaine use, and he took them up on it.

After lunch, Nuno took me to meet João Castel-Branco Goulão, a physician and senior Health Department bureaucrat who was the architect of the Portuguese model. Like Nuno, he was extremely charming. We met on the top floor of an ugly 1960s office block with brilliant views out over the city and were served more obligatory espresso coffee and tarts. The window ledges of his office were filled with mementos from dozens of countries, including various photos of João with dignitaries including the Queen of Spain and Richard Branson.

As we sat drinking espressos and smoking at the top of the Health Department building, he told me about how this world-first legislation came to be. Their decriminalisation process had the support of all sides of politics (support that still stands today). They had the support of the community, too, who saw drug use as a major issue and it was well known that the prime minister's brother was struggling with a heroin addiction—something that had influenced his position on how drug users should be treated. The laws haven't changed in the eighteen years, nor has the community support.

In the 1980s, when Australia was still a leader in drug policy, it was a tearful Prime Minister Bob Hawke who announced that his youngest daughter was a heroin addict. It was no surprise that our drug strategy at that time focused on harm reduction and on putting the addict first. Those brave policies had the support of the public, too. Sadly, the futile law-and-order prohibitionist approach had once again risen to the fore in Australia.

* * * *

Over the following days, I saw the fruits of Goulão's work. The treatment service was set in a sprawling old mental hospital, and focused on reintegrating addicts with families and work. The approach was tougher than in Australia in that the expectations of recovery and reintegration were stronger, but they got there through a kinder system. One that put the user first. The result was that less young people used drugs, very few people died from drugs and most people with an addiction got help.

The one unexpected result was that drug tourism had increased, but not in the way you might expect. People like me seeking answers to the drug problem were flocking to Portugal. Nuno Capez still hosts international groups every week. João Goulão's office has translated information about their scheme into over fifteen languages. Sadly, only a few countries have gone on to put what they learned into practice, but many European countries have adopted similar approaches to drug use, with Norway being the most recent.

Portugal is a wonderful people place and I loved it there. I had random conversations with many people, including a bunch of Swedish men about the (supposed) health benefits of snus, a tobacco product that you put under your lip. My Airbnb host was an academic also called Nuno. He had lived in Melbourne and was a sexual health academic who had written extensively about online sex. His boyfriend had lived in Sydney and was a tour guide. I also ended up spending an evening with a group of female winemakers celebrating the launch of their new wines. It was this trip and another one to the US that framed our party's policies around drugs in the early years.

* * * *

After the finalising of safe access zones around abortion clinics, I was keen to get a major focus on drug law reform into the parliament.

Our feeling in the office was that we only had three-and-half years before the next election to make a difference and there were no guarantees that I would be re-elected. I had been asking a lot of questions about drugs and was lobbying the government to deliver on its promise to introduce medicinal cannabis laws, but I wanted a broad drugs inquiry to investigate a different approach to the failed law-and-order one in Victoria.

I worked with the government and, in particular, the then chief-of-staff to the Minister for Police, Bob Stensholt, around developing the terms of reference for such an inquiry. On reflection, the breadth of the reference was too optimistic, but it had the support of the government and enough crossbenchers to get it up. The Opposition disputed it and not surprisingly it upset Inga Peulich, who in a speech to parliament gave me a great backhanded compliment by saying, 'I can certainly see that Ms Patten, who is in a powerful position as one of the independents, has used this opportunity to load up the terms of reference of this inquiry in a way that she can expect to deliver on her platform and that of her party. She has made it clear what that is.'

Well, of course it was. That was why I was bloody well there!

The terms of reference for the inquiry were finessed by the committee so that we touched on all aspects of the original reference but focused on the effectiveness of current laws in minimising drug-related health, social and economic harm, and how other positive reforms could be adopted into Victorian law.

* * * *

With my first year of parliament under my belt I was invited to Los Angeles to speak at the annual sex-tech conference, XBiz, and I used the opportunity to start my international investigations on end-of-life choices and more on drug policy. My dear friend Kat Sunlove had been a lobbyist for the adult industry in California for many years and sorted out a range of meetings for me with politicians and drug-reform organisations.

Their state legislature was also considering a bill to legally mandate the use of masks, dental dams and condoms in adult-film production. Californians love their porn so the issue was on the front page of the newspapers.

Even though the full legalisation of cannabis hadn't yet happened, the approach to cannabis was already very relaxed. Possession and use had effectively been decriminalised and the state was going to vote on legalising cannabis later that year. The ballot initiative was called the Adult Use of Marijuana Act and was looking positive. People smoked openly and an Uber driver even offered me some from his vape pen. At one of the conference parties at an upmarket hotel in Hollywood, there were more people smoking or vaping cannabis than tobacco. There also seemed to be less alcohol consumption. Again, there was an interesting cross-over between the adult industry and the cannabis industry. The new cannabis-industry journals were also run by former adult-industry writers and I met a number of business operators that were using their adult-retail experience to expand into the fledgling cannabis business.

Heading to Sacramento as an MP was a novel experience. Kat had organised some great meetings and the legislature itself was incredibly well disposed to overseas politicians. I was welcomed on to the floor of both houses of the legislature where they had put up an Australian flag and delighted in saying I was from the

Australian Sex Party. I met with many senators who were dealing with the taxation of medicinal cannabis and prescription monitoring of opioids. I could not have had better training for my year ahead, which would see the end-of-life choices inquiry report, the legalising of medicinal cannabis and the beginning of the broadest drugs inquiry that the Victorian government had ever allowed.

****

The new parliamentary year started up with the more draconian amendments to our drug laws. While on the one hand the government was starting to say, 'We can't arrest our way out of the drug problem,' on the other hand they continued to try doing just that.

Medicinal cannabis finally made its way into the parliament and it was a far cry from the recommendations that the Law Reform Commission had made. It was only to be available to children with certain forms of epilepsy. It was so depressing that after all the good work the commission had done and the overwhelming public acceptance of medicinal cannabis we would still not allow it for adults in palliative care, with nausea from cancer, with MS or even with epilepsy!

I put forward an amendment to have these other patient cohorts included. The Greens, Liberals and the government all opposed it. They said that it was a temporary problem of supply. I told them I could make a couple of phone calls and probably help them out with most of that, but they didn't take it seriously.

I knew that thousands of Victorians were accessing medicinal cannabis every day by illegally growing it themselves or buying from someone who was illegally growing. It's a basic supply-and-demand issue. If you don't open up the demand, you will never get the supply. If you only allow a small number of children to access the product, how can you expect an industry to grow from that? A year later nothing had changed.

Over the years, I'd met many wonderful people who had been making medicinal cannabis and distributing it (often free of charge) to people who were in real need. I recently saw thousands of original comments from medicinal-cannabis users written on the bottom of their order sheets and collated into huge clipboard files. Page after page of comments like, 'My cancer appears to have shrunk,' 'The fibromyalgia is so much better,' 'I can sleep for the first time in years without waking up and feeling like a zombie,' and 'My little boy's epileptic fits have stopped.' Yet now into my second year in parliament, it was still illegal in Victoria, with no real law reform on the horizon. Like many, I felt angry and frustrated with the lack of progress. Even Queen Victoria was known to use cannabis for her period pain and her doctor had declared it to be 'one of the most valuable medicines we possess'.

* * * *

As well as working with the Rock'n'Roll Party, the Sex Party has also teamed up with the HEMP Party for campaigning and running joint tickets. Although the temptation was always there to form a super Sex, Drugs and Rock'n'Roll party, it never happened. Over the years, I'd become good friends with HEMP's technical expert, Andrew Kavasilas, and the head 'head' at the HEMP embassy in Nimbin, Michael Balderstone. They'd invited me to the annual Mardi Grass festival on a number of times as a guest speaker and as a participant in the Hemp Olympics. I wasn't much good at bong-throwing, but I was on pole position for the champion Hemp Tug of War team that overpowered the local Nimbin police team in 2014!

On another occasion I was part of a small group of policy makers and cannabis growers who met in the Nimbin Town Hall to discuss a way forward for medicinal cannabis. Greens leader, Richard Di Natale, made an impassioned speech about not trying to get recreational cannabis legalised as it would interfere with medicinal cannabis. He even berated those in the group, like myself, who objected to his position and I asked him to consider the many people who were languishing in jail for growing pot. But he was determined that it was the sensible road to be travelling on. How things have changed for him since then.

Meanwhile, the drugs inquiry was going well, and by mid-2017 we had received hundreds of submissions and held numerous public hearings with every expert in the field. They all advocated for fundamental change. The inquiry asked the right questions: what should we be doing and who is dealing with drugs better than us?

* * * *

The itinerary for the committee's overseas study tour was the envy of every drug-reform advocate. Geneva, Lisbon, London, Denver, Vancouver and Sacramento were all on it. Five of the seven committee members came on the trip and for the first time in Victorian parliamentary history, we were accompanied by an assistant police commissioner.

I am never sure about the Swiss, but when I visited Geneva they surprised me with their kindness. I had wanted to swim in Lake

Geneva and found a huge swimming centre on the shore that had a fabulous 50-metre pool. Before I jumped in, someone had asked me my name and how far I intended to swim. I wasn't really paying attention, but it turned out they were timing me for a one-kilometre swim and for my good time I was presented with a little pewter medal!

The Swiss have been dealing with drugs in a compassionate and pragmatic way since the 1980s. Over two-thirds of young Swiss festival-goers get their drugs tested or databased prior to taking them. The Swiss opened one of the world's first injecting centres and have been providing heroin to people who need it for decades. They encourage people to snort or smoke their drugs because it is just safer than taking it intravenously. There are cafes at their injecting centre where users can learn skills and get a cheap meal. When arriving at the Heroin Assisted Treatment program, there are dog kennels out the front as many of the clients have dogs and it would be unkind to leave them outside during winter. They drug-check their patients and publish the information in real time. My overall impression was that the Swiss combined a compassionate approach to drugs along with a pragmatic attitude towards what worked and what didn't.

* * * *

Travelling back to Portugal, we met the head of the Portuguese police. Their headquarters were in a 16th-century convent at the top of a hill. In fact, we spent time with police wherever we went on the trip. On our visit to the UK Secret Garden music festival, the police had proudly taken us around in a golf buggy and we were introduced to some of the performers. They were having a wonderful time and were supportive of the onsite pill testing that was going on.

In Vancouver, the police took us on a tour of downtown Eastside, which had been hit hard by an escalating opioid crisis since 2013. While we were there in July 2017, four people a day were dying from overdoses. They proudly showed us around the pop-up injecting centres and the heroin clinic. The chief of police said that if he had his way he would give heroin to everyone who needed it. 'Wouldn't you rather they got it from me than the bikies?' he asked. I don't think any of us found that question particularly radical by that stage of the tour.

We visited cannabis plantations, cannabis-cookie bakeries, cannabis shops and parliaments. People hang shit on politicians for travelling overseas on these fact-finding tours, and no doubt part of it is a junket for some, but for us it was important that we saw how things could be done better. The recommendations that Victorian Assistant Police Commissioner Rick Nugent would have taken back to Victoria Police, along with those the committee made to the government, would not have happened without that trip.

* * * *

Back home, the stupidity of the current prohibition around drugs had been brought home to me a few years earlier when Robbie and I had visited a Daylesford antique dealer. It was a modern-day Steptoe and Son outfit with the back half of the shop piled high with junk that had not been touched in years. On a heavy oak table littered with anvils and augers, we spied it—an old, green linen-and-leather bound ledger.

I picked it up and blew away the dust, reading the heavy, hand-written capitals in ink. *Skewes Pharmacy, Camberwell.* I was instantly transported back to suburban Melbourne in the late 1930s around the time of the popular soapie, *The Sullivans*. Turning the first page, I came across the heading 'Heroin' and a list of the people that had come to the pharmacy to pick up a prescription. On the next page was 'Cocaine'. Then 'Indian Hemp', then one for 'Opium' and another for 'Morphine'. There was even a note at the beginning of the book to say that ergot was available. Ergot is a precursor to LSD, but I had never heard of anyone in Australia in the 1930s selling LSD through pharmacies.

Underneath each heading, written with a nib pen in a neat, cursive style, was the patient's name, their address, how much of each drug they had bought, the date, and a signature from the pharmacist and a stamp from the Chief Inspector of Poisons. There were hundreds of people listed. Many of them were coming back at weekly intervals. Mrs Sheils from Railway Parade came back regularly for her opium liniment, whereas Mr Brown came in for heroin fourteen times and then stopped coming. I suspect he had died from his cancer or whatever condition it was that he needed the drug for. The book was a reminder that so-called drugs of addiction were once legal in Victoria (and in other states) from the local chemist. The state didn't grind to a halt—in fact, we were just about to enter the most important nation-building era in Australian history.

Australia prospered when drugs were legal. During those years, people didn't lock their doors if they went down to the local corner store or visited a neighbour. Shops were not barricaded up like jails with people walking suburban streets at night with fear of being mugged. With access to these drugs, people weren't desperate to treat their psychological or physical pain by stealing or robbing to feed their habit. We've forgotten this. It's never taught in schools.

Most people have no idea that cocaine and cannabis were once legal in Australia.

Using the information from this old book I printed a brochure with the title, 'When Drugs Were Legal in Victoria', and sent a copy with my Christmas card to all MPs at the end of 2017. It was well received.

* * * *

As a moderate recreational cannabis user for most of my adult life, I've had enough experience to sift through the bullshit and the hype that surrounds it. As such, I'm comfortable in proclaiming cannabis the safest social tonic that we have. I think that if members of parliament across Australia were to swap half their alcohol consumption for cannabis Australia would be a much better functioning and compassionate country. Better still, if the 30 per cent of MPs in Australia who have used or currently use cannabis would stand next to me as 'out' users, sensible law reform would happen much faster. No other politician seems to have the spine to do this and it represents a terrible indictment of hypocrisy, fear and self-loathing in our parliaments that MPs can't be honest about their drug use.

30

MY MOVING STORY

My political interest hasn't always been in sex and drugs.

At the beginning of 2016, it was obvious that ride-sharing in Victoria was becoming popular, but the company behind it, Uber, was still operating in an unregulated environment. That meant that issues of insurance, fares and the safety of people using the system were not guaranteed by law. Uber was now part of the new sharing economy and they weren't going away. There had been endless discussion between the government and Uber but nothing had happened, which only meant more uncertainty for the industry. It needed a circuit-breaker, so in February 2016 I drafted a private member's bill to legalise ride-sharing.

Taxis had been my preferred form of transport for many years. The government appeared to be caught between wanting to do something about Uber but not upsetting the state's 8000 cab owners. Perhaps it was because regulating Uber was not like regulating another taxi service. Uber was a technological platform with drivers, cars and passengers incorporated into its app. No one had ever tried to write a bill before that put forward a code of responsibility for a technological platform. I worked long and hard with the parliamentary staff; it wasn't easy as there were no precedents to work from. No other state in Australia had tried to regulate ride-sharing in this way.

It took a while, but when I finally showed the bill to the government they refused to support it. The Opposition, however, via their Transport spokesperson in the Legislative Assembly, David Hoggett, decided to get behind it. I pushed forward. On the day that the bill was to be debated in the upper house, I had the Opposition's support and ostensibly the Greens'. So I had the numbers. If it passed the upper house, the government would be left with the option of agreeing to it or knocking it off in the lower house. This would not be a good look for the many people using Uber and for the increasingly angry taxi owners who feared that their monopoly was about to end and their businesses would take a substantial hit.

They were right to be fearful of these things. But these businesses also had to realise that like many industries, the internet was forcing many to make major changes to the way they operated. At this point, I started to cop some pretty yucky and intimidating comments on social media. One woman, who was the wife of a taxi owner, called me a slut and a whore. Others called me a 'filthy dirty excuse of a woman'. To my surprise, they were using the same language as morality campaigners!

But like a good politician, I did meet with many and asked them for a solution to the problem of an unregulated ride-sharing service like Uber operating among them. They couldn't come up with anything except ridiculous suggestions like 'turn off the internet'. Or pay all taxi-licence holders a million dollars per licence to compensate them for losses. When I asked them to provide some evidence to back up these figures, they went quiet. I suspect that this was because they worked in a cash economy and didn't declare all their income.

Halfway through the debate, it looked like I had the numbers, but before it could go for a vote, Jacinta Allan, the Minister for Transport, called to ask if I would adjourn the debate with the promise of the government introducing their own bill. She was in a tough spot. Before I could reply, she offered the same deal as they had done with the abortion safe-access zones bill. She would stand on the steps of parliament with me, credit me for introducing the debate, and give the public a guarantee that they would introduce their own bill to regulate ride-sharing within a certain timeframe. Once again it was a win for everyone, even though it hadn't been part of the government's agenda for the year.

What they didn't know is that I didn't actually have the numbers. The Greens had pulled their support for the bill at the last minute, citing a lack of amenity for the disabled. My bill, however, was to establish a legal framework for ride-sharing, while other issues like fares, taxes and concessions all had to be worked out later on by the government because they were budgetary items that only the government could control.

When they finally did introduce the legislation, on 11 August 2017, it was clear that they had used a lot of the work we had done in defining the responsible parts of ride-sharing technology. I also successfully negotiated major amendments to their bill that were supported by both the Opposition and the Greens around the levies that were to be paid on each Uber fare to compensate taxi drivers. It was a tough negotiation. The government proposed a $2 levy on all Uber rides that was open-ended. It allowed them to make millions from Uber passengers well after the taxi operators had been compensated. My proposal that eventually got up was for a capped $1 fee.

The taxi industry was pretty pissed off. Not long after the bill had passed I caught a taxi home with an owner-driver who recognised me. He got emotional on the drive and halfway through began using some threatening language. He called me a slut and insinuated that I needed to be slapped down. I got him to drop me off way before my house so he wouldn't find out where I lived. I was a bit concerned about catching cabs after that and only used Uber. It probably earned me as much agro from taxi drivers as the abortion debate generated with anti-abortionists.

31

VOLUNTARY ASSISTED DYING

In 2016, assisted dying had broad acceptance in the community. The committee that I had initiated had released its final report in June. It was now up to the government to respond.

Getting the issue to this stage felt like nothing short of a miracle. The committee staff for the End of Life Choices Inquiry had drawn up an extensive schedule of public hearings and consultations, starting with medical experts and academics. With five of the eight members of the committee also new politicians, I reasoned that this was also a great opportunity to learn more about each other, as well as the issues.

It had all started smoothly the year before, in 2015. We were methodical in working through the terms of reference, and while the majority of the 1000 submissions we received related to voluntary assisted dying, we looked at all of the issues equally. We spoke to a vast array of people: rabbis and priests; mothers and fathers; sons and daughters; doctors, nurses, volunteers and carers; and police, coroners, lawyers; and, even, other politicians.

In August 2015, the committee travelled to Shepparton and stayed overnight in a local motel. After dining with everyone at a restaurant in town, I went back to my room to read over my notes to prepare for the next day. I decided to have a small joint to help with that and lit up in the car park outside my room, walking off around the back of the motel to find a discreet place to smoke.

On my way, I stumbled upon my fellow committee member, the ultra conservative Liberal Inga Peulich. She was standing outside her room with a couple of glasses of Baileys and a cigarette. There was no way past so I stood and talked to her for a couple of minutes. She offered me one of her Baileys. I said no thanks and offered her a toke of my joint. She passed, but mumbled something about 'we've all had those moments at university'. We stayed chatting for a few minutes more and then I bid her goodnight. It was an odd but vaguely charming interlude. Here we were, the seasoned old reactionary warrior and the libertarian ingénue, getting to know each other via the social tonics of our generation. Was there the possibility that we could be friends after all?

Not likely. Soon it became clear that some members of the committee were more interested in the issues than others, and some were easier to get on with than others. These attitudes were on show for everyone to see in the public hearings. Some committee members sat there texting and paying no attention to the sometimes nervous or emotional witnesses as they told harrowing stories of loved ones dying in agony or in great distress. At other times, some members would ask inane questions of witnesses that showed they hadn't even read the submission. Sometimes they were just downright rude.

The regional hearings in Traralgon that September had me feeling raw. My friend Candida Royalle, the feminist pornographer from New York, had just died the day before. She had been comfortable at home with her friends around her, and since it had been expected she probably had a 'good death'. But, as always, it's an emotional time for friends and family. The committee had been hearing from local doctors, nurses and palliative care providers, and a few locals who wanted to speak personally. Unbelievably, Inga started referring to people dying under medical care in hospital as having been 'popped off'.

It was offensive to the doctors in the room, and particularly distressing to a couple sitting there whose 21-year-old daughter died in terrible circumstances from a brain tumour only months earlier. I looked up and saw the horror and the pain on their faces. I came so close to calling Inga out, but instead I excused myself from the hearing and spent 30 minutes pulling myself together outside. How could she be so insensitive? Is it the role of politicians to offend people in hearings just because they don't happen to align with their personal views? In my mind, it was a bridge too far, and the beginning of a bitter enmity between Inga and myself that continues to grow to this day.

Soon after this episode, Inga and some other members of the committee opposed to assisted dying simply stopped attending hearings if they knew that the witnesses were supportive of it. When the committee went to Europe in Easter of 2016 to see how VAD laws worked in other countries, this attitude was largely responsible for three of the members not joining the trip. (Committee travel is not compulsory but it is encouraged and learning as much as you can about an inquiry is considered the responsible thing to do.)

It was an intense experience lasting eight days with visits to six cities in four countries. We met with the governing bodies, doctors, nurses, academics, politicians and even opponents of the VAD schemes. We saw that the laws in other jurisdictions were compassionate and they made conversations about death easier.

I took every opportunity I could to speak to locals about VAD. In Amsterdam, I asked the people working in bars and hotels what they thought. Generally, the young ones were unaware of the scheme, while older people would speak about those they knew who had accessed it.

In Zurich, I spoke to a museum tour guide who was also a minister in her local church. I explained why I was there and she told me she had just signed her parents up to Exit International, which is the assisted-dying program in Switzerland. In Switzerland, it's not illegal to help someone commit suicide if there's no financial gain in it. This followed a court case in the early 1900s where a business man had gone broke, losing everything. He asked a soldier if he could borrow his gun to kill himself and the court found that it was legal for the soldier to lend him a gun to perform his own suicide. Since that time suicide has never been a crime in Switzerland and indeed helping someone to suicide can under some circumstances be seen as inspired by honourable intention.

Returning to Australia, I had the feeling that the stars were beginning to align.

* * * *

Going into this inquiry, my views had been firm. I wanted laws around physician-assisted dying to be as broad as possible. But the more evidence I heard, the more my views narrowed. I had thought that death should be as personal as possible and that government should not play a role at all. But the trip overseas taught me that the best outcomes for patients come about when there is a tight regulatory role model with review and accountability built in.

The Coroner's Prevention Unit had done extensive work on the issue to assist our inquiry. They found a disturbing trend in Victoria of older, terminally ill people suiciding once or twice a week—sometimes in the most violent ways. When they interviewed the families, the most common response was that they wished that their loved one hadn't died alone.

The most publicised of these incidents was a tragic case of a terminally ill man trying to kill himself with a nail gun. His son had woken up to hear a compressor going in the garage. When he went to investigate, he found his father had tried to shoot himself in the heart with the gun, and when that hadn't worked he had tried to shoot a nail into his temple. He died soon after, but his suffering had been greatly, and unnecessarily, compounded.

The story that has stayed with me most, however, was that of an elderly woman who had slashed her wrists. She did it over the toilet so as not to make a mess for the people in the nursing home when they found her. This lovely and considerate woman had been forced to die cramped over a toilet in a cold tiled bathroom because there was no legal and humane way for her to end the pain that had overtaken her at her end of life.

The committee's report ended up with 49 recommendations, the final one being 'that the Victorian government introduce a legal framework providing for assisted dying'.

As a response to the committee's End of Life Choices report, and following on from his very successful podcast series Better Off Dead, Andrew Denton roared into gear and quickly pulled together the campaign called Go Gentle.

I had first met Andrew at a weekend away at the home of the former Australian Democrats' leader, Don Chipp, in the early 2000s. Andrew and his partner, Jennifer Byrne, had also been invited and Don used to take much pleasure in getting each guest to speak off the cuff for five minutes on a particular subject that was hidden on a card under a plate on the table. Over the years, I had also lobbied Andrew about including my deeply satirical Sex Party ads on his *Gruen Nation* show on ABC TV at election times. Politely he had told me 'if they are good enough, Fiona, they'll get on. If not, they won't'. At least I knew where I stood with him.

As with many, Andrew's interest in the voluntary assisted dying was initiated by his father's difficult death some nineteen years earlier. He was determined to ensure that the recommendations made in the committee's report were adopted and that the laws were changed. He had some major-leaguers in with him as well, like the former Secretary of the Attorney-General's department Roger Wilkins AO and Dr John Collee, a retired GP who had gone on to write movie scripts like *Happy Feet* and *Master and Commander*. It was a campaign that Denton had funded by himself along with a small group of benefactors and he had also completed a similar tour under his own steam, making the wonderful podcast out of his many meetings and conversations. The public was listening to him, as were politicians.

The government had six months to respond, and in December 2016 they announced that they would support the inquiry's recommendations and initiate a ministerial expert panel with the aim of introducing voluntary assisted dying legislation the following year. Previously, I had been told that the premier would have great difficulty talking about any of it because his father was gravely ill. Sadly, he died in April 2017 of that year after what had been described as a brave and painful battle with cancer. Many people believed that it had a major effect on Daniel Andrews' outlook. It does for most people who sit with a dying relative or friend who is enduring pain and suffering.

Even though I knew the announcement was coming, I found it surreal to sit at the press conference listening to the premier, health minister and attorney-general. All the work we had done now meant that the wheels were starting to turn.

The process that got the bill to the parliament was meticulous. The expert panel was established and that brought everyone back to the table to go over the same ground that the inquiry had covered but in far more detail. The panel reported in July 2017 and the result was a detailed model for voluntary assisted dying legislation with broad regulations around it for Victoria. The campaigning to get the parliament to agree to the model could now begin in earnest.

One thing I have pondered since this time is what would have happened if the marriage equality postal survey and the campaigns 'for' and 'against' same sex marriage had not been waged? Would the Australian Christian Lobby and other religious groups have spent more time and money trying to stop the assisted dying bill? They did pull together a B team led by the ACL's affable Victorian director, Dan Flynn. His strategy was to bring in six or seven religious leaders from multicultural backgrounds to relate the 'horror' stories from their congregations and explain why assisted dying legislation should never be introduced. For the most part, it sounded like they didn't trust their congregations not to try and knock off bothersome relatives.

The executive director of the ACL, Lyle Shelton, was obsessed with marriage equality. While we were dealing with legislation that would act as a model for the rest of the country to legalise assisted dying, Lyle was out raising millions of dollars to 'fight' against marriage equality. I am on the ACL mailing list and not once did I see a call to arms or even an update on assisted dying. They focused entirely on marriage. If this was a strategic decision, one has to wonder how they feel about it now. They still have millions in their war chest, but have lost both battles. Of course, Lyle Shelton has now put his hand up to enter politics as Federal Director of Communications for the Australian Conservatives so maybe he plans to use those funds to get himself elected at some point. And speculating on that, does the passing of the Victorian VAD laws give him yet another campaign platform?

In the end, the bill was comfortably passed in the lower house by 47 to 37 and proceeded to the upper house with no one quite sure of how it would end up.

* * * *

Each time I vote in parliament, I must thoroughly research the issue to determine the direction of that vote. With the help of my office, I write my own speeches and get myself down into the chamber at the appropriate time. For Liberal, National, Greens or Labor MPs, this generally doesn't happen because you are instructed by your whip how you will vote, and if you are going to speak on a bill you are even provided with speaking notes that have been researched by a party official.

Because this was a conscience vote, however, none of those things happened; MPs from all parties had to do it all on their own. It made a huge difference to what was recorded in the Hansard. Many MPs gave the best speeches of their careers. Almost all of them were heartfelt, and whether for or against all were generous on personal experience and opinions rather than along party lines. This was particularly the case in the lower house. Death is a very personal subject and the contributions reflected a lot of compassion and eloquence.

By the time the bill reached the Legislative Council in November 2017, politics was beginning to rear its ugly head and some Opposition members were saying privately that their preselection was being threatened if they voted in favour of the bill. I am not sure whether this caused the tone of the debate to decline or whether some had simply not read the bill, but concerns about children being euthanased and greedy relatives waiting to kill off older family members started to be heard.

Inga Peulich accused me of not paying any attention to the bill, as if she had somehow forgotten that I had initiated it. She suggested amending the bill to insert a clause that made Labor's Gavin Jennings the first person to use the VAD program. She didn't say it on record; she just hissed it across the floor so it didn't make it into the Hansard. But we all heard her, and Gavin invited her to repeat it for the record or formally move her wishes as an amendment to the bill. Instead she spat the dummy, scooped up her large black handbag and raged out of the chamber.

Once all the speeches had finished (Daniel Young from the Shooters was the only member to not make a contribution), the process called

Committee of the Whole began, which meant that it could be dissected line by line. This process allows anyone to ask the minister (Gavin Jennings) questions about the bill and is designed to clarify the wording and the meaning of certain clauses. In this case, however, it was used as a filibuster by certain Liberals hoping to stall proceedings to the point that the bill would fall off the agenda. The same questions were asked in different ways by numerous people. There must have been a roster circulating among the bill's opponents; there was definitely a book being circulated among the filibusterers with suggested inane and repetitious questions.

After nearly ten hours of debate on the first clause of the bill, the government moved that a vote be taken in order to move on to the second clause. This was howled down by the Opposition's appointed spokespeople, Bernie Finn and Inga Peulich, who had now resumed her seat. They both almost turned purple and accused the government of trampling their rights with jackboots and using Nazi tactics to cut through the bill.

By my reckoning, if we had kept debating at that pace, it would have taken three months of parliamentary sittings to get through the whole bill. Everyone was prepared for an all-nighter. Some had sofas moved into their offices and some even had camp beds brought in. Kilos of unhealthy snacks were everywhere, although when the house sits all night the restaurant and library must also stay open, and the kitchen staff worked hard to provide healthy alternatives. At around midnight, $200 worth of potato cakes and hot chips arrived at the government whip's office courtesy of the Minister for Health. The house filled with cooking oil and vinegar and people from all sides descended on the food like seagulls!

Just before dawn, a short break was called. It was a surreal experience to stand on the steps of parliament in the same stillness and silence as the early morning after an all-night trip. As the first rays of the sun came up over the Treasury Building, the only movement up and down Bourke and Spring Streets was zombie politicians sucking in the air and getting their legs going again.

After sitting all night, the government's plan was to keep going after a short breakfast break. But that wasn't to be when Daniel Mulino, one of the government's dissenters on the bill, had an episode of some sort and an ambulance was called. He was okay, but it put a stop to proceedings until the following Tuesday.

* * * *

The break allowed me to go to Sexpo and to do some campaigning for our candidate in the Northcote by-election, Laura Chipp. Laura was the daughter of the late Don Chipp, the founder of the Australian Democrats and one of the most honest and libertarian federal politicians we've ever had. He had been a great friend and mentor for many years and had encouraged Robbie and me in everything we did. I think he would have been very happy that we had started the Sex Party, although I'm not sure he would have approved of the name. One thing I do recall him saying was that the name of a party was important.

Robbie had known Don since 1977 when, as a taxi driver, he had picked him up off the Senate taxi rank only hours after Don had announced to the nation that he was leaving the Liberal Party. Robbie had driven him around for three hours while he did all his media engagements. Halfway through, he started having chest pains.

Robbie then arranged to teach him Transcendental Meditation. Don later claimed it had saved his life and stopped him from having a future heart attack. He and Robbie remained friends for the rest of his life.

* * * *

Back into the debate the following Tuesday, Bernie Finn led the circus by reading a long article into the Hansard about serial killers executing disabled children. It was not only totally irrelevant to VAD, but the author he cited was well known for her theories on how aliens hypnotise abductees, especially deaf people. The opponents of the bill were getting desperate.

Tempers frayed, and again Hitler and fascists were the go-to insults. As the leader of the debate, Gavin Jennings was extraordinary. He maintained his cool throughout the entire process, even though he had been on his feet for over 48 hours without sleep. He answered every question and batted away the insults with humour and good will. Bernie Finn became petulant and insisted that every clause in the bill be voted on. Every time a vote was called, the bells rang for three minutes. Had we divided on every clause, the bells would have rung for nearly six and a half hours. As it was they rang for at least five!

Almost as sleep-deprived as us were the stalwart lobbyists who sat in the public gallery through much of the debate: Andrew Denton, his campaign manager Paul Price and Nia Sims, a 43-year-old woman with a rare auto-immune condition called scleroderma which would almost certainly see her use the new laws at some stage if they were enacted. They had already sat through the debate and the committee process in the Legislative Assembly. Dan Flynn from the ACL and Margaret Tighe, the formidable anti-abortion campaigner from the Right to Life Association, were there intermittently, and I was pleased to see that she was present for the final vote in the Assembly.

Eventually the opposing forces ran out of steam and on the afternoon of 22 November 2017, a week after the bill had been introduced into the upper house, it finally passed. The chamber erupted in the same way the House of Representatives did when the marriage-equality laws passed. Although still stunned and sleepless, we all rallied for a few celebratory drinks at Strangers. Eventually everyone disappeared home, but I couldn't sleep and didn't really want the amazing emotions I was feeling to end. The lack of sleep added a certain 'sheen' to the final proceedings and everything became soft around the edges. It was like the end of an ecstasy all-nighter from the late 80s. I was incredibly happy and it still brings pleasure thinking about that day.

I rang Andrew Denton and he was feeling the same, so we met for a quiet and somewhat dreamy meal, going over the campaign and what we would do next. We both agreed that the Victorian laws, being the first in the country, would probably end up becoming the most conservative, as other states moved past some of the red tape to pass their own end-of-life choices legislation.

32

AN INJECTION OF SANITY

About ten years ago, I received a phone call from a friend telling me that my old boyfriend Neil had died of a heroin overdose. Weirdly, I didn't feel shocked. Just deep sorrow and grief. I had a similar reaction when I heard about other friends and acquaintances who had died this way. You've thought about it so many times that it becomes part of your internal dialogue, in the way you might wonder, 'What time is it?' or 'Have I locked the door?' Or 'I wonder if Neil is alive today?' You worry every time the phone rings. When you love someone whose life has been taken over by a drug, you hope for the best and expect the worst.

On the other hand, there are just as many people who have come through the experience and gone on to lead amazing lives. Even in my own family, I have witnessed the victim of a hopeless teenage heroin addiction transform themselves some fifteen years later into very senior management roles in major national institutions.

In heroin circles, there are many reports of addicts with decade-long habits who suddenly stop and completely turn their lives around. It's just a matter of keeping them alive until that day arrives.

* * * *

From the beginning of my parliamentary term, I had been working on ways to get a supervised injecting centre opened in Victoria. I had spoken alongside Australia's pre-eminent expert on drug harm reduction, Dr Alex Wodak, at a number of conferences and at the celebrated Nimbin Mardi Grass festival. We had become good friends and spoke regularly about the need to take the regulation of illicit-drug use out of criminal justice entirely and placed inside the health system instead. He is a pioneer in this field and his common-sense approach to policy is world-renowned.

In early 2015, just a couple of months after I was elected, I visited the Medically Supervised Injecting Centre (MSIC) in Sydney. It was about three blocks from where I had lived in Woolloomooloo a decade earlier. I had been a regular visitor to Kings Cross since the 1990s, visiting adult shops and meeting with traders; I knew the area well. Open drug use on the street was a common sight. I remember the weeks after the centre opened in 2001 and the immediate impact it had on the neighbourhood. Overnight, the streets emptied of people injecting drugs. The number of ambulance sirens blaring late at night dropped noticeably. It was a palpable change to the way Kings Cross had operated for two decades.

I was struck by how simple the centre's operation was. Led by its charismatic director, Marianne Jauncey, the staff cared about its clients. Instead of giving them a syringe, wishing them good luck and hoping that they didn't overdose in the laneway next door, addicts were now understanding that someone actually gave a fuck about whether they lived or died. More importantly, the staff did not judge them for their drug use.

After a person scored their drugs, they could now come into the centre and register. They were then taken to a room where they met a health professional and were provided with equipment and a space to inject. If anything happened to them, like if they overdosed or had a fit, there was someone there to attend to them straight away. Once they had used their drug, they went into the recovery room where they could talk to a social worker or not, and have tea or coffee. For many, it was a place where they could get a referral to another health service, an addiction specialist or homelessness support, along with the opportunity to have a chat.

* * * *

By the end of 2016, there had been a significant increase in the number of overdose deaths in Victoria, particularly in North Richmond, and the pressure was mounting for a supervised injecting centre. In a 300 square-metre area, 26 people had died of an overdose that year. Many more had overdosed but didn't die. There was open drug use in the streets and hundreds of used syringes were being picked up each day. The number of ambulance, police and paramedic callouts was increasing at an alarming rate. It was reaching epidemic proportions.

All this pushed the local residents, the local council and a wide variety of health agencies to the brink, and they started campaigning for the government to do something. Both major parties, however, could only see one solution and that was to throw even more law-and-order and emergency services at the problem. It was what we'd come to expect from both Liberal and Labor on drug strategy and it explained why the nation was being crippled by a multi-billion dollar illicit drug trade that lines the pockets of organised crime.

The campaign to have a supervised injecting centre was originally started in the late 1990s by the celebrated lawyer Robert Richter QC, Dr Alex Wodak, and public health champion David Stanley. Alex and I had already had numerous conversations about how to get the campaign up and running again and these men, along with the Yarra Drug Health Forum and the Drug and Alcohol Foundation, provided the initial support I needed to get going. No other MP appeared willing to take it on.

In the last sitting week of parliament in December 2016, I read my bill in the parliament for the first time. It was titled 'Drugs, Poisons and Controlled Substances Amendment (Pilot of Safe Consumption Room and Pill Testing) Bill 2016' and was 'a bill for an act to amend the *Drugs, Poisons and Controlled Substances Act 1981* to provide for the pilot of a safe consumption room at a specific location and for the pilot of the testing of specified substances by certain authorised health practitioners at public events and for other purposes.'

This was what was called a 'first reading'. The bill itself had not been written yet and I had optimistically added a pill-testing pilot program as well. 'First readings' simply gives everyone notice that you are planning to introduce a bill. Sometimes politicians just make up titles for bills but never go through developing them. But I thought it was worth a shot adding pill testing to an already ambitious bill. Even if it was just an attempt to shoot another hole in the major parties' continued 'tough on drugs' policies. After early discussions with my team, however, it became obvious that we could not do both in the same bill, which strangely made us all the more optimistic about the injecting centre pilot.

On 14 December 2016, I attended a coronial inquest into the death of 'Ms A.' She was found dead from a heroin overdose on the floor of a toilet in a Hungry Jack's outlet in Richmond with a needle hanging out of her leg. She was 34, lived with her mother and brother, and was the mother of two children. While the Coroners Court was primarily investigating the death, it was also looking more deeply into the issue through its prevention unit, which researches trends in death and explores ways to prevent them happening again.

Mapping Ms A's life through government agency records painted a very sad but not uncommon picture. A long history of drug use, violence, mental-health issues and family alienation. She was well known to health services and outreach workers in North Richmond where she had sought help to break her addiction numerous times. In the year Ms A died, 172 other people died in Victoria from an opioid overdose. When you read the coroner's report into her death, the utter helplessness that she must have felt in the last few years of her life is evident and heart-wrenching.

* * * *

The coroner's report on the death was due in January 2017 and I hoped it would be released prior to the debate on my bill in late February. This report would make recommendations to the government and, under the law, the government was required to respond.

In fact, there were two ways to get a supervised injecting centre trial up and going in Victoria. One was through legislation, while the other option was to open one with police support and the use of their considerable discretion powers, meaning that they could say that they would not use the existing laws to prosecute either the people using drugs or those helping them in a designated area. I knew Victoria Police could not express an opinion about establishing a trial, but they were aware of the Sydney centre and individual police officers had told me that they had heard positive reports from their NSW counterparts.

In January 2017, I met with the Chief Commissioner of Victoria Police, Graham Ashton, and asked him whether he would be supportive of a model where police could use their discretion. The response was a quick and emphatic 'no'. Only legislation, he said, would provide officers with the clarity they needed to act around this issue. Although he would not agree to turn a blind eye to an unlegislated centre, I left the meeting confident that the police would not oppose my legislation to set one up.

By the end of January, we had over 50 high-profile experts and organisations sign an open letter in the *Herald Sun* calling on the government to support a trial. These included the AMA, the Salvation Army, the Nursing and Midwifery Federation, the Ambulance Employees Association and the Pharmacy Guild of Australia. Former Liberal premier Jeff Kennett was also publicly supporting it at any chance he got.

Most importantly, the media was supportive, including the conservative *Herald Sun*. This was vital in convincing the government that they could be brave and would not be attacked on the law-and-order issue. There wasn't really anyone opposed to it now except the Police Association Victoria, the premier and the leader of the Opposition, Matthew Guy.

I had had a long relationship with the Police Association going back to the 1990s when I had received their support for a review of censorship laws in Victoria. It had been a good experience and had been important in educating police about what type of material was in modern adult shops—notwithstanding Victoria's outdated and prudish censorship laws. This had meant police did not waste their time prosecuting harmless porn when they were needed on the streets to stop violent crimes.

I had arranged a meeting with the Deputy Secretary Bruce McKenzie, the retiring Secretary, Ron Iddles and the new Secretary, Wayne Gatt. It was close to Ron's last day and he thought the association should support the trial, however Wayne wasn't convinced this was the first battle he wanted to have with the government; he had already raised it with his executive and they were not unanimous in their support. It was a lively and friendly conversation. Having the Police Association on side would send a powerful message to the government, but Wayne could not be swayed. Ron, on the other hand, committed to supporting it once he had retired, and true to his word he did.

On the first week back to parliament in early February 2017, I tabled my new bill, though without legislation for pill testing, and started campaigning with my colleagues. I had already had meetings with relevant ministers and privately no one opposed the trial. The premier, however, was still adamant that it would not go ahead. I had similar problems with the Opposition. I had Jeff Kennett making calls in the background to leader Matthew Guy, but even that was not enough to get him over the line. The Alcohol and Drug Foundation, the AMA and the Pharmacy Guild called on all MPs for action. The local residents were organising and campaigning. Even the traders on Victoria Street that had previously been opposed to the trial had now changed their minds and were providing guarded support.

I decided to run a public launch of our campaign called 'End the Needle Nightmare' where speakers included local residents, the Salvation Army, the local pharmacists, Robert Richter and an ambulance driver. Representatives from many organisations attended. A large media contingent turned up and filmed our portable billboard travelling up and down the streets.

We had started the launch in a car park just off Victoria Street in Richmond. While the media were packing up, police started attending to someone in the laneway and picking up a bunch of used needles. At the same time, another guy started openly dealing in the car park. The media crews couldn't believe what they were seeing. I thought it was a tragi-comic comment on just how bad the situation had become when a drug user would hit up only metres away from a media event promoting a safe injecting room.

* * * *

I had tried everything to get the major parties on side. When I first spoke to the government about a trial, I was told by Gavin Jennings, Martin Foley and their advisors that they couldn't support it without a major show of public support. I had since delivered on that and the local business and residents groups were extremely vocal. Then Labor had said it would need support from doctors, and I found a way to get the AMA to back it. Then their fear had been the media and the conservative *Herald Sun*, but I was able to show them a stream of positive articles. This really stopped them for a minute—until they came back with the retort that the media was so fickle that it would turn on the government once they agreed. I promised them that would not happen because they were all philosophically behind an injecting centre. Then one senior government MP even asked me if I could get that in writing from the *Herald Sun*. Fark!

In the week leading up to the parliamentary debate on the bill, I had done everything the government had asked for in terms of demonstrating public support, but it was clear they were still not going to support it. I felt like the hostage whose kidnappers had asked for ransom after ransom and were still going to throw me into the lake. I wanted to win this debate, but I knew it was bound to fail. With this in mind, I decided to put the issue in front of a parliamentary committee for a quick and specific inquiry just to keep the bill alive. The odds weren't good, but I was desperate. My drugs inquiry was by now up and running, and it was receiving numerous submissions calling for an injecting centre, but it was a different forum and no help in this debate.

Then came the breakthrough. The day before the bill was to be debated, the coroner published her report on Ms A's death with an emphatic recommendation for the urgent establishment of an injecting room. With this high-profile recommendation in the media, I asked the government if they would support a quick parliamentary inquiry. They agreed. My crossbench colleague, James Purcell, agreed to put up the amendment to refer the bill to a committee and we were still in business.

* * * *

The inquiry was agreed to by the Legislative Council in February 2017 and was undertaken by the Legal and Social Issues Committee which both myself and Liberal Inga Peulich were on. We received about

50 submissions and over 90 per cent of them supported the trial. The Australian Christian Lobby and Drug Free Australia were the only two groups to oppose it. The committee travelled to Sydney to see their supervised injecting centre. For me it was one of a few visits I had had earlier. We also visited North Richmond where some of us went on a tour of the area to see the hotspots. We witnessed open drug use, we listened to angry residents, we saw numerous syringes on the streets and many drug-affected people. We heard about how residents would hear users going into the back alleys behind their homes to hit up. If they didn't hear them leave, they would call an ambulance. The fear of finding someone dead in their front yard was all too real for many. With the constant ambulance sirens and the heightened state of alert, it was remarkable how compassionate the residents remained.

Afterwards, we held a roundtable discussion at the North Richmond Health Centre. Outreach workers told us about attending overdoses in the adjacent multi-floor car park, dealing with overdoses in the stairwells of public-housing estates, and the desperation of their clients. We heard about the drills that the local primary school holds to ensure that the children know what to do when they find a syringe in the playground—or, as once happened, a body. There were addiction specialists present, lawyers and local government representatives all giving up their time to meet with us.

Inga was in true form, ignoring everyone, texting on her phone and occasionally negating something an expert said. Following the meeting, I tried to engage with her as we walked up Victoria Street. Since she had not come on the neighbourhood tour or the trip to see the Sydney centre, I was trying to tell her what we had seen. She asked who had shown us around Richmond. I told her it was Greg Denham from Yarra Drug and Health Forum and Judy Ryan from the residents' group. She laughed and said that if *she* had taken us on a tour of the area we wouldn't have seen any needles. Then she moved on to a conspiracy-theory rant where she alleged that experts like Robert Richter QC and David Stanley had lied to the committee and that the Coroners Court had done something to cause an unfair stacking of the submissions before it. When she had made these accusations in the inquiry to the State Coroner, the judge had rejected them out of hand.

I took the bait and our discussion became heated. The rest of the group dropped away from us at this point as the argument developed. I pointed out that she hadn't listened to anyone at the roundtable as she was immersed in something on her phone. How very fucking dare I? She had been dealing with an urgent family health matter, she said.

'So why didn't you go outside and deal with it?' I asked, and as we arrived at our meeting with the traders, she let rip.

'Fuck you! Fuck off! Just go fuck yourself!'

It was one of those moments when you long for a classic one-liner to cut through, but nothing came. I thought that she might have been on the verge of having a go at me and if that had happened it would have been on for one and all. It was bad enough that two of my parliamentary colleagues were witnessing all this out of the corner of their eyes but, a full-on scrag fight on the main street of Richmond between two upper house members of parliament would have been a very ugly sight. That moment set the tone for the rest of the inquiry: if I said something was white, she would bark back that it was black.

* * * *

On a cold August morning in 2017, nearly 500 local residents and supporters marched down Victoria Street calling for the safe-injecting room trial under a banner that read 'You talk, we die'.

The rally was significant as communities like this are usually campaigning against the issue at play. Now, however, the residents of Richmond were pleading for the trial. It was supposed to be a non-political rally, but the Greens had brought their placards out in force and I was incredibly impressed with the way they coordinated themselves to ensure that their MPs and their signs were consistently in the background for the TV cameras.

Despite having been in the Victorian parliament for twelve years, the Greens had never done anything to progress the establishment of a supervised injecting centre. As it began to gather momentum, however, they were right on to it as if it was their own bill. Their media releases and signs said it all: 'The Greens call on the government to establish a centre' and 'The Greens will get this done.' It was really bloody annoying. They had done the same thing on safe access zones a couple of years earlier. I was beginning to learn that it was a regular tactic.

Meanwhile, I was madly lobbying the government as were the other interested organisations, residents and families of those who had lost loved ones to drugs. On 17 September, the Police Association announced that they would not oppose the trial. It was a pivotal moment in the debate. The next day I got the nod that the government was drafting their own bill to ensure the trial would go ahead.

* * * *

The debate in the house was without surprises. Inga Peulich slammed the bill and suggested I was 'latching on to an issue that she thinks she is going to get a little bit of media attention on and she runs with it'. She put forward her strong belief that there had 'never been a war on drugs'. Her contribution was nonsensical and rambling, and she ended it by expressing her disappointment at the AMA for getting on the 'bandwagon'.

Rachel Carling-Jenkins, now with Cory Bernardi's Australian Conservatives, was the only other speaker against the bill. She quoted extensively from the shadowy Dalgarno Institute, an abstinence-based religious organisation that was certain that all research around injecting centres was wrong.

On 30 October 2017, I stood at a press conference in North Richmond alongside the premier, the police minister, the planning minister and the mental health minister as the government announced that they would enact their own legislation to set up a pilot Medically Supervised Injecting Centre.

I felt like cheering madly and hugging the people around me, but it was a law and order issue and so we all had to maintain grave faces in case the Liberals would accuse us of being soft on crime. Saving lives is apparently a serious business. But deep down I did feel strangely quiet. Then a postscript to the day that no one could have foreseen. No sooner had Daniel Andrews finished speaking did a woman overdose less than 100 metres from the press conference. The ambulance staff who were nearby rushed over and managed to save her life, but it was an extraordinary epilogue to an extraordinary day.

33

SEEING REASON

Following the 2016 federal election result, it was clear that some of those who had previously voted for the Sex Party as a protest vote had started to look elsewhere. Our previous campaign videos 'Jerk Choices' and 'We're Fucked' had worked well in the larrikin style, but our 2016 campaign video, 'The Vati-Can-Can', was different. Set to the tune of 'The Candyman Can' from the film *Willy Wonker and the Chocolate Factory*, it had big production values, a very gay cast, and some clever wordsmithing from the Fnuky ad agency team.

It drew a formal complaint to the Tasmanian Anti-Discrimination Commissioner with the lyrics at the centre of it:

Who can bring the kids in?
Indoctrinate their views.
Bring them into churches with a sleazy priest or two.
The Vatican. The Vatican can.

Who controls the weddings?

So gays can't say I do.

Blame it on a book and a 2000-year-old Jew.

The Vatican. Oh the Vatican can.

Who makes all the dying

Suffer till their blue?

Read their rights and watch them choke on their own spew.

The Vatican. Oh the Vatican can.

Who's got all the money

With zero taxes due?

Hidden in these buildings with a bank that's kept from view.

The Vatican. Oh the Vatican can.

Committed Catholics everywhere were scandalised. It was exactly the response we were hoping for. However, we weren't expecting some of our own supporters to take us to task over not taking the piss out of Islam, too. It was a fair point: we should have included all religions. In some ways, the Church had been a shorthand way of addressing all religious organisations.

Attracting funds had also been difficult under the Sex Party name. Many businesses, organisations and individuals wanted to donate, but shied away at the last minute, saying that a transfer to the 'sex party' on their banking records just looked dodgy. It was time to expand our horizons and a new name was part of that.

Up until this point, only one new name had ever been suggested, and that came about on April Fools' Day in 2015 when I claimed that the Sex Party was joining with the Shooters, Fishers and Farmers Party (previously the Shooters Party) to create a new political grouping with balance of power in the upper house called the Sex Pistols. The new party was to have a wide range of policies including legislating for the mandatory wearing of BDSM gear for all duck hunters, making it compulsory for all clay-pigeon targets to be rainbow-coloured and allowing members to carry shotguns in parliament. I said that the Shooters MLC, Jeff Bourman, would take the role of the 'pistol whip', while the other Shooters MLC, Daniel Young, was reported as saying, 'Bullets and bongs are just natural bedfellows.'

The New Daily, *Crikey* and many other media outlets all rated it the best April Fools' joke for 2015. Incredibly, a few journalists emailed our media release back with comments about it being a bad idea and others asking to be removed from our mailing list. The office phones ran hot for a few days with some very confused people.

Getting Google and Facebook ads was also always complicated, and Sex Party candidates were being told to move on when setting up stalls at shopping centres alongside Labor and Liberal party tables, with posters occasionally ripped off walls. In one instance, two nuns from the Missionaries of Charity, set up by Mother Teresa, were photographed tearing down our Tax the Church posters from a pole in Collingwood. The *Sydney Morning Herald* quoted a church spokesman saying, 'No one should be at all surprised that sisters of the Missionaries of Charity [. . .] would be taking offence at the policies of the Sex Party.' I replied by saying that if the nuns would like to visit me and confess, that would be an end to it.

Our lead NSW Senate candidate in the 2016 federal election, Dr Ross Fitzgerald, had been a respected academic and author. As many people working in the public service know, a candidate must resign before declaring their candidacy in an election. They are nearly always reinstated after the election if they don't win. Ross had resigned from the NSW Civil and Administrative Tribunal (NCAT), of which he had been a valued member, but after the election, he wasn't re-appointed, with one of his seniors telling him that 'standing for the Sex Party had tainted the Tribunal'.

* * * *

On the brighter side, I wanted to keep things moving and my political opponents guessing. I had some heavyweight candidates just itching to get involved if only I would change the name of the party. President of the Rationalist Society of Australia, Meredith Doig, had run as our Victorian Senate candidate in 2016 and had been lobbying hard for a name change.

I canvassed Sex Party members about the idea, and when I was happy that there was a majority I asked the party director, Douglas Leitch, to formally put the idea of changing the name to members in January 2017. In August, we voted on 'Reason' as the new name. The *Herald Sun* quoted me as saying, 'We are closing the Sex Party and are starting a new organisation. This is not about rebadging. It is about a new movement. It is not Left or Right, it is running on what is pragmatic.'

We chose Reason because it is the single most important human faculty that is lacking in our parliaments at the moment.

One of the great failings of modern politics is the lack of forecasting by the major parties beyond the electoral cycle. There's no forward thinking. We know that the population is ageing. We know we will have significantly more elderly people soon and significantly less people in the workforce. By 2050 the number of people over 85 will have quadrupled. I don't see any forward planning for this.

I'm also stunned by the politicisation of parliamentary processes like Question Time, where government members ask government ministers to elaborate on how fantastically they are doing. The Opposition then asks them to elaborate on how badly they are doing and how well they were doing when they were in government. All they are after is a 'gotcha' moment.

We need a Ministry for Food to protect food safety from terrorists and big multinational companies that behave like terrorists. In Victoria, we need a Ministry for Fashion where that industry brings more money into the state than sport. We need rational thinking and radical change. Fact checks and not fat cheques.

And let's forget about running elections on law and order. Mental health underpins almost all law-and-order issues and yet we waste our time treating the symptoms of poor mental health with increased police budgets, increased surveillance and increased jail time. If people's mental health was improved, these other issues would disappear. We need some radical common sense to cut through these dense layers of ignorance that surround old-style politics. We need back bone not bullshit.

We need to defy the deniers and apply reason to the knee-jerked, poll-driven, gut reactions which drive policy from the major parties these days.

34

LAST RITES

When I was eighteen, I visited the Vatican. As I walked up to the main gate, I remember seeing beggars and people in obvious poverty sitting around the walls, selling trinkets. A few hours later, safely inside, I was confronted with the most overwhelming opulence. I remember thinking that just one of the gold candlesticks on any of the altars could have fed all those people for a year. It was a concept that has stuck with me ever since.

When I was living in Sydney in 2000, I would often walk past St Mary's Cathedral on the edge of the city. For a number of years, Cardinal Clancy had one of those fundraising thermometer signs installed on the premises calling on people to help raise $5 million. At first, I assumed that it was to feed the ever-growing population of homeless people that gathered in the parks around the enormous cathedral. But no. They were raising funds to build spires on top of an already opulent church building.

Armed with these early impressions along with my experience of religious orders over the years, I read a bill during the last sitting week of the Victorian parliament in December 2017 that would be the first of its kind in Australia. It was a bill to effectively allow for the taxation of religious institutions by amending the *Charities Act 1978* to exclude 'the advancement of religion' as a charitable purpose.

* * * *

Charitable purposes at law are those considered to be performed for the public benefit, thus saving the government from having to do them. Tax breaks are considered the most economical way of helping charities to perform more of this work.

Granting charitable status to religious organisations is an historical artefact that was redefined in England in 1891 when four charitable heads were identified by the government of the day: the relief of poverty, the advancement of religion, the advancement of education, and any other public benefit that did not fall under these three heads. Today these charitable heads reside within Section 7 of our own *Charities Act 2013*, which states that 'Certain purposes (are) presumed to be for the public benefit.' It goes on to say that in the absence of evidence to the contrary, a 'purpose' has presumed to satisfy the requirements of a public benefit if the purpose is 'the advancing of religion'.

In the past, the courts have ruled that a presumption of public benefit exists just because someone goes to church. Of course, this is totally unproven and without a shred of evidence, and runs contrary to much of the behaviour that we witness from the many religious nutters who make it into the newspapers these days. All the same, including religion as a charitable purpose dates back to a time when welfare as we know it today was not dispensed by the state but largely by the churches. The role of religion in life was vastly different from what it is today with social services dominated by the church. Now governments administer all manner of pensions and benefits, and even hand out funds to church schools and hospitals.

* * * *

The way in which organised religion relates to Australian society has undergone a major shift over the years. Using census data, only 0.4 per cent of Australians said they didn't believe in religion back in 1911. In 2006, that figure had grown to 19 per cent, and in 2011 it had climbed to 22 per cent. (Even then only 10 per cent of the believers said they were active participants in their religion.) The 2016 census saw the figure for those claiming no religion soar to 30.1 per cent and, for the first time ever, this group had more adherents than any religion. It's an atheistic exponential curve, and by the time the next census comes around in 2021 it's quite possible that 50 per cent of Australians will say they don't believe in any religion.

With this in mind, making the 'advancement of religion' a charitable purpose is not logical. There are plenty of good charities out there full of atheists and agnostics. Financial privileges that are handed out to charitable organisations represent lost revenue for Treasury and are clearly indirect subsidies to these organisations by the state and ultimately by the tax payer—including the third of the population that doesn't believe in religion.

So how do you measure whether the practice of religious belief confers tangible benefits on society? Well, first of all, the test has to be about public benefit and not beneficial intent. Public benefit can be proved by having a look at an organisation's tax return and seeing where they spent their money. Religious organisations don't have to submit returns so nobody really knows this. Beneficial intent is claimed by all religions, but it is as nebulous as the virgin birth or creation theory.

In Victoria, and in many other states, charities are exempted from land tax, payroll tax and stamp duty. At a federal level, they can be exempt from income tax, capital gains tax, GST and fringe benefits tax. Religious tax exemptions and handouts cost Australia $31 billion per annum according to an analysis by John Perkins of the Secular Party. That's about the same size as our entire defence budget. It's a huge amount of money that would eradicate poverty in Australia—certainly homelessness. It could change the face of education and makes the nation's roads the safest in the world.

Instead we hand this windfall over to an industry whose business is faith in a supernatural being. Of all the registered charities in Australia, 37 per cent report 'advancement of religion' as their charitable purpose. It's the largest category there is. But given the latest census and the rapid decline in religious belief, I'd suggest they're not doing a very good job at it.

Quite apart from the philosophical arguments about whether advancing religion is a good thing or not, many people have had a gut-full of religious cranks, sex abusers and jihadists. How can anyone claim that the Christian churches deserve a tax break? They have raised 2000 convicted paedophiles among their ranks, requiring a royal commission costing the taxpayer $372 million and a compensation fund that could well run into the hundreds of millions. How is this providing a public benefit? It's a public disgrace.

All major religions have significant blots on their character, ranging from state-sponsored terrorism to ethnic cleansing, and although my bill has nothing to do with freedom from or freedom of religion, it has everything to do with showing that religion in and of itself is as flawed as any company or individual and is no more deserving of a tax break or public funding than you or I are.

Max Wallace, author of *The Purple Economy*, puts it this way:

> Churches would pay their electricity, gas and other related expenses. But when they put their garbage out to be collected, when a church catches fire, or should there be vandalism, they expect garbage collection, fire trucks and police without paying for them. Similarly, they expect footpaths, roads and other infrastructure to be paid for by other rates and taxpayers while making little or no contribution themselves.

Most of Australia's major religious organisations run active investments through companies that engage in a range of businesses dealing with food, insurance, entertainment, superannuation, property development and much more. They also invest in a large range of 'out of sight' passive investments, like shares, bonds and interest-bearing deposits. To get a handle on the scale of these religious empires, the Catholic Church is the largest non-government inner city property owner in Melbourne.

I have no doubt that our Pentecostal Treasurer, Scott Morrison, and other religious members of all parliaments in Australia will be working in the wings to make sure that my bill doesn't succeed. No doubt there are enough religious campaigners within the two major parties in Victoria to make it hard for the bill to pass either house. In fact, it could even be that the bill affects the budget to such an extent that only the government can introduce it. But as with safe access zones around abortion clinics, legalising ride-sharing, setting up a wide-ranging drug law reform inquiry, electronic petitions in the parliament, legalising voluntary assisted dying and getting a medically supervised injecting centre open, you never know your luck until you try.

EPILOGUE

Someone asked me recently what I would do if I was PM for a day. I told them I'd try and do a Gough Whitlam and choose a very canny attorney-general to work with (probably Gareth Evans) and then just go for it!

The first thing I would do would be to create a national program to address the first thousand days of a child's life. I believe that many of Australia's problems could be overcome within a few decades if we recognised the importance of that first three or four years in a human being's life. If we supported families more during that time, I think we could close down half the nation's gaols, which are, at present, populated by people who had a shit start in life.

To do this we would need to shift our focus on a number of areas, but health is paramount. We need universal health care for children—no matter what. We have to shift our attention from major hospitals to community and primary health care, and put dental health into

Medicare while we're at it. (Why can you go to a doctor and be bulk billed for a headache but not a toothache?) Most Australians would much rather have a couple of good health care centres in their neighbourhood than an extra $10 in their pay packet through tax cuts.

In fact, I'd overhaul the whole tax system by implementing all of the recommendations of the 2008 Henry Tax Review and not just one of them, which is all that has happened. We need to re-evaluate how we raise and spend money. Maybe we need to hypothecate our taxes so that, for example, taxes on alcohol and tobacco just go to health. And no taxes on women's sanitary products!

At the other end of life, we need a whole-of-government ageing strategy. How will our society cope when there are more people retired than are working? What sort of infrastructure will we need to support all of these older people? How will we afford it? What about people who want to be able to live at home as they age, but still contribute to society? Do we have the policies in place that will allow this?

Following that, I would re-think the three tiers of government and try and combine state and local governments into a small number of regional governments or cantons as the Swiss do. There is so much duplication of government services in so many areas.

Obviously I'd try and legislate all the issues I've been actively involved in within Victoria. Legal voluntary assisted dying, decriminalisation of drugs, legalisation of cannabis and the replacement of cotton with hemp as our main fibre from the soil. I'd set up national taxation laws for religious bodies, change the laws on land tax to encourage affordable housing and generally change the way we think about owning property. I'd invest more in science and create a super ministry for food that started with soil and went all the way through to labelling in supermarkets. I'd advance Australian manufacturing and take a fresh look at the export of our natural resources, which currently come back as a finished product for us to buy at ten times the price of the raw ingredients. We grow trees, chop them down, send them off to China and then buy all our paper from them at inflated prices. And wherever a renewable source of energy could be applied, I'd be signing up for it.

* * * *

At time of writing, the shift to the right in the Victorian and Federal Liberal Parties makes me very uneasy. All the reforms that I've had a hand in enacting in Victoria over the last few years could easily go if the Liberals win the coming state election. Abortion, voluntary assisted dying, safe injecting rooms and even medicinal cannabis. At their last state council meeting, the Liberals voted to criminalise sex work again after more than 25 years of a legal and regulated scheme. In this they were helped greatly by the Greens and their Richmond candidate, Kathleen Maltzahn, who has for 25 years led Australia's largest anti-sex work campaign, Project Respect. The Green's leadership stayed silent on the issue the whole time. They gave tacit support for her reactionary views which were also supported by the Australian Christian Lobby. And the religious right in the Liberal Party used all of that to vote in a policy that will plunge sex work back into the hands of organised crime.

It's depressing because the Liberals in Victoria have traditionally been more progressive than in other states, but now they feel it necessary to shore up the conservative vote which has been splintering for quite a while between Cory Bernardi's Australian Conservatives, the

Shooters, One Nation and a few right wing religious parties. There are still a few actual small 'l' Liberals in parliament and it's been a pleasure to work with them on a number of my issues. Notwithstanding their need to try and soak up other conservative votes, I'm amazed that they seem to be ignoring the fact that the majority of the population is moving toward a more liberalised social agenda.

So why are they going in the opposite direction? Why are some Liberal branches in Victoria now stacked with Mormons and in NSW with Muslims? I think a lack of gender diversity has a lot to do with it. Too much testosterone in the room makes a party do dumb things like embracing hard core religious campaigners as candidates and staff. These people come from places where men are the head of the household and so it flows that when they get into parliament they think they have a god-given right to be head of the state or head of the country.

For much of the last few years I've seen Labor fighting with itself more than the opposition. Factional disputes are their Achilles heel. They too need to recognise that the community is becoming more socially progressive. All of my reforms—abortion laws, VAD, Uber, safe injecting rooms, drug law reform committees and taxing the church—were all initially met with a very strong 'no' by Labor and often from the premier himself. With the support of a few committed progressive members in the Labor Party, we managed to overcome that resistance, but make no mistake about it—Labor is not a naturally progressive party just yet.

For a party that has three members in the lower house and five members in the upper house, I'm surprised how little the Greens have done in introducing new legislation. Individually, they are genuine people and I support a lot of what they do. But I have heard Greens' officials argue that their mere presence in parliament has the effect of changing policy. In effect, they just have to turn up and the world is a better place.

* * * *

I fear the rise of an antipodean Donald Trump or Rodrigo Duterte. With both Shorten and Turnbull seen by many as weak leaders, I think it's only a matter of time before a 'strongman' emerges from within either of the major parties with a populist agenda to 'make Australia great again'. One of the ways to stifle the effects of a Trump-style leader is to always make sure there is a sizeable Senate or Upper House cross bench containing progressive small parties. As we have seen, this makes it very hard for these kinds of leaders to enact their agenda. The only problem with this strategy is that ever since the 2016 Senate voting reforms were passed by the Coalition, with the help of the Greens, minor parties can no longer win seats in the Senate on their own. Whatever made Greens leader Richard Di Natale think that championing voting reform proposed by Malcolm Turnbull, Eric Abetz, Tony Abbott, Mathias Cormann and Peter Dutton was a good thing for a fair and equitable Australia is hard to understand. Starting as a minor party themselves, the Greens clearly saw an opportunity to get rid of any competition from small parties and in so doing they committed themselves to the same brand of machine politics that the other two major parties are engaged in.

The only hope for minor parties to break into politics now is to do what ABC psephologist, Antony Green, has suggested. If minor parties can band together in the wake of the Liberal/Green voting rort, and bring their members and supporters together in three or four large coalitions, those new groupings could get elected. However, that's not an easy thing to do for say Animal Justice and the Pirate Party, and its virtually impossible for say the Reason party and Rise Up Australia to come together over anything except a good blood sacrifice.

* * * *

It's strange reading over this memoir now that I've finished it. I can see so many stories and people that I haven't included. Often you tell those stories that best define yourself and your own life rather than the stories of the important people in your life. It seems vaguely unfair but that's what the publishers want! It's definitely split-personality stuff, writing about your own life as if it was someone else's. It's as if there are two of you. Two of me! Perish the thought, Robbie says. But, you know, sometimes that could actually be quite useful.

Some people get to politics through wanting more for others, while some get there wanting more for themselves. From my observations of three and a half years on the red leather, it's about 50/50 in the Victorian parliament. At a party level, it's my view that all the major parties—Labor, Liberal and Greens—will choose politics over policy if it gives them a 'win'.

I never knew I would take this particular path in life, but then I have never been one to think much about what a path in life even looks like. I'm not in parliament because I set out to become a politician. I'm here because it was a necessary step in trying to change bad laws. If I am lucky enough to be re-elected at the next state election, I would not run for a third term. It would be time to let someone else with a fresh perspective have a go. But even then, I don't think I'd be too far from politics.

INDEX